SAVING LIEUTENANT
KENNEDY

BRETT MASON is Chair of the Council of the National Library of Australia, a member of the Council of Griffith University and Adjunct Professor in the School of Justice at the Queensland University of Technology. He was formerly a senator for Queensland, serving in the ministry, before being appointed Australia's Ambassador to The Hague and Permanent Representative to the Organisation for the Prohibition of Chemical Weapons. His previous book, *Wizards of Oz: How Oliphant and Florey helped win the war and shape the modern world*, was published by NewSouth in 2022.

'Brett's superb book is published in the middle of a period of intensifying relations between the United States and Australia. It reintroduces us to a critical time in the origins of that relationship. The story of Lieutenant John F Kennedy's rescue of his crew from his sunken torpedo boat PT-109 was a seminal narrative in his presidential run. As was the critical role played by an Australian coast watcher and his supporters in the Solomons in the completion of the rescue. Great coincidence is its arrival as JFK's daughter is US Ambassador to Australia. A great moment for a carefully accurate rendition of the story. A story written with great flair. A must read.'

The Hon. Kim Beazley AC, former Leader of the Opposition and Ambassador to the United States

'*Saving Lieutenant Kennedy* has it all – drama, courage, history and heroism. A masterful account of a critical juncture in history, Mason brings to life a legendary story that defined John F Kennedy as a war hero and a leader for Americans and millions of people around the world.'

The Hon. Joe Hockey, former Treasurer and Ambassador to the United States

'A story of war that warms the heart. American hero and future President rescued by laconic Australian. A rattling good yarn. Read it and be inspired.'

Professor Robin Prior, University of Adelaide, author of *Conquer We Must: A Military History of Britain, 1914–1945* and *Gallipoli: The End of the Myth*

'A rare mix of historically accurate writing, a tale worthy of a novel and a moment in time that played its part in future Australia–US relations, *Saving Lieutenant Kennedy* even includes a coconut with a rescue message carved into it by JFK! Once you start reading, you won't want to put it down until you've absorbed every last detail.'

Peter van Onselen, Professor, University of Western Australia, author (with Wayne Errington) of *Victory: The inside story of Labor's return to power* and (with Wayne Errington) *John Winston Howard: The Definitive Biography*

SAVING LIEUTENANT KENNEDY

THE HEROIC STORY OF THE AUSTRALIAN WHO HELPED RESCUE JFK

BRETT MASON

UNSW Press acknowledges the Bedegal people, the Traditional Owners of the unceded territory on which the Randwick and Kensington campuses of UNSW are situated, and recognises their continuing connection to Country and culture. We pay our respects to their Elders past and present.

A NewSouth book

Published by
NewSouth Publishing
University of New South Wales Press Ltd
University of New South Wales
Sydney NSW 2052
AUSTRALIA
https://unsw.press/

A catalogue record for this book is available from the National Library of Australia

ISBN: 9781742237879 (paperback)
        9781742238845 (ebook)
        9781742239781 (ePDF)

Design Josephine Pajor-Markus
Cover design Luke Causby, Blue Cork
Cover images (clockwise) Eroni (Aaron) Kumana and Biuku (Nebuchadnezzar) Gasa, Islander scouts who made the rescue possible, source unknown; USS PT-105 during exercises off the US East Coast, 1942, Wikimedia; JFK in the Solomons mid–1943, John F Kennedy Presidential Library and Museum; Lieutenant Reg Evans, c.1945, Australian War Memorial

In memory of Dad,
who first showed me the moon and the Americans

And in memory of Mum's uncle,
Lieutenant Frank Barrett DCM,
coast watcher of 'M' Special Unit,
killed in action in New Britain
on 24 October 1943, aged 32

CONTENTS

INTRODUCTION

For a few days in early December 1941, a convoy of nine American ships led by USS *Pensacola* warily circled mid-Pacific Ocean. The troops and equipment onboard had been dispatched to bolster US forces in the Philippines. But after the bombing of Pearl Harbor, the Philippines too were now under Japanese attack. 'Orphans of the storm', the officers and the men of the convoy were no longer sure of their destination. Would they be turned back to Hawaii or return to the US mainland?

Finally, on 12 December, they received new instructions, which were broadcast over the PA system: 'Attention all hands, this is the captain speaking. We have been ordered to proceed to Brisbayne, Os-tral-yah'. The crew were confused. 'Where did he say?' 'Brisbayne, where's that?' 'Are they on our side?'

The 'Yanks', as we would call them, didn't know much about us – and we didn't know much about them either. But they were now on their way, eventually a million of them. And, with Australia virtually defenceless against the Japanese onslaught, we were very pleased to welcome them to our shores.

Twenty months later, a young American naval officer leapt from an Islander canoe and waded through surf to a beach at Gomu (now called Makuti), a tiny speck of land in the Solomon Islands archipelago. There, a middle-aged Australian coast watcher was waiting for him. 'Man, am I glad to see you', beamed the relieved American. 'And I'm bloody glad to see you, too!' replied the Australian as they shook hands. The American was Lieutenant John Fitzgerald Kennedy, the future president of the United States, shipwrecked a few days earlier, after his patrol torpedo boat was rammed by a Japanese destroyer; the Australian, Arthur Reginald Evans, a lieutenant in the Royal Australian Naval Volunteer Reserve and an intelligence officer in central Solomons, now coordinating the rescue of Kennedy and his crew.

By August 1943, Australians and Americans knew a lot more about each other. But for the tragic and trying circumstances that brought the two peoples together, it had been by and large a happy encounter, though not without its share of drama and tension. And there was still occasional confusion. Kennedy, for one, thought that Evans was British or maybe a New Zealander. This was an easy enough mistake to make; Solomon Islands were, after all, a British protectorate at the time. More importantly, most Australians, from Prime Minister John Curtin, down to the average man and woman in the street, saw themselves as British. But the wartime encounter with Americans sparked questions about our national identity. As war changed America, so war – and America – would change Australia too.

*

For most of their histories, Australia and the United States had very little to do with each other. Suddenly, in late 1941, Americans discovered Australia, just as we, who had before only known silver screen gangsters and cowboys, discovered real, flesh-and-blood Americans.

From Brisbane residents looking on full of hope as the first American troops disembarked from USS *Pensacola* on 22 December 1941 to the unlikely friendship between Prime Minister John Curtin and General Douglas MacArthur, these early contacts and understandings laid the groundwork for the following eighty years. Out of a wartime coalition against Japan was born a friendship between the two nations, reflected not just in an ongoing security alliance but in strong economic, cultural, social and interpersonal links.

This is neither a comprehensive study nor a critical analysis of the US–Australia relationship. It is a story about how and why it started, about how we first got to know each other. It is a story of the beginnings – the birth, or perhaps rather a shotgun wedding – and the foundations of the bond between our two nations, however shaky, tenuous and wary they have sometimes been. Above all else, from Jack Kennedy and Reg Evans to millions of American servicemen and Australian soldiers and civilians, it's a people's history: a story of two nations from opposite sides of a great ocean, similar in some ways but very different in others, unexpectedly blown together by the winds of war, and what we made of each other – and how that has mattered ever since.

Late 1941 to mid-1943 was the most dangerous time in Australia's history. At war since 3 September 1939, most of our troops had been sent to fight Nazi Germany and its fascist allies in Greece, the Middle East and north Africa. Australia itself lay defenceless as Japan commenced its juggernaut through Asia and the Pacific. It was the hour of our greatest danger and our greatest need. With Britain fighting for its own survival, there was only one other country in the world that possessed the manpower and resources to come to our aid. When Reg Evans replied to Jack Kennedy on the beach at Gomu, 'And I'm bloody glad to see you, too!' he could have been speaking for his nation as a whole, one that over the previous year and a half had come to know the Americans as saviours of Australia and determined liberators of the south-west Pacific.

Two long and bloody years later the war was over, but its experiences and memories would continue to colour the post-war world. The story of Reg Evans and Jack Kennedy was not yet finished; it would have many postscripts. So would millions of other stories. Many of them would serve to bind Australia and America more closely, as indeed would Kennedy's. When he eventually found out that the coast watcher responsible for his rescue was an Australian and not British or a New Zealander, he joked with Prime Minister Robert Menzies that Australia was 'responsible in a way' for his administration. But his gratitude and affection for Australia was sincere. He was, as he said himself, 'all for Australia'.

And Australia, by and large, was all for Kennedy. Our relationship with America more broadly has been more equivocal, and certainly less romantic, but never less than consequential. If the wartime marriage was one of convenience, we are still together eighty years later. Our bonds are made strong not just by mutual affinities but also common challenges. If the handshake on the beach between Kennedy and Evans symbolised its beginning, the story is still being written today.

CHAPTER 1

'SEA-MINDED, SHIP-CRAZY'

Arthur Reginald Evans was born in Leichhardt, in Sydney's inner west, on 14 May 1905, the oldest of three children to parents Stuart, a public servant, and Edith, a home-maker. 'Arthur' being perhaps too stuffy and 'Reginald' too long for laconic Australians, Evans would go through life known to all simply as 'Reg'.

'Always sea-minded, ship-crazy', as he later described himself, Evans applied to enter the Royal Australian Naval College at Jervis Bay straight from high school. The college, established only in 1911 and with a limited intake, rejected young Reg. Undaunted, he joined the local military reserves as a cadet, eventually rising to officer rank.

In his early twenties, bright and resourceful, Reg cast about for opportunities and adventure. There was romance at the time about travel and work in the south Pacific, much of it cultivated by the large shipping and trading business created in 1881 by two Scotsmen, James Burns and Robert Philp.

Burns, Philp & Co first became influential in colonial Queensland, developing valuable early trade links with islands of the Pacific as well as a less savoury reputation for influence-peddling and a buccaneering spirit. The great

Australian poet and author of 'Waltzing Matilda', Banjo Paterson, thought Burns '[as] near to an Empire builder as we ever saw in these parts', noting that '[a]nywhere that there was a risk to be run and money to be made you would see the flag of James Burns. If he had been dealing in diamonds instead of copra and bananas, he might have been another Cecil Rhodes's understudy.'

In their first few years of operation, Burns, Philp were involved in 'blackbirding', or carrying Pacific Islanders to work on plantations, commonly in north Queensland, having coerced or deceived them to join the ship. The labourers were paid little, sometimes nothing at all. Some called it the labour trade, others the slave trade. Edward Docker, a historian of the practice, wrote that Burns, Philp were initially 'doing rather well out of its recruiting sideline', but with political and newspaper pressure mounting, the company left the ill-reputed trade by 1886.

By the time Evans joined Burns, Philp, the founding infamy was long past and forgotten by the perpetrators, if not the victims. It was a legitimate business, and business was good. From the late 1890s, steamers would run from Sydney and Brisbane to British New Guinea, German New Guinea, British Solomon Islands, and the Anglo-French New Hebrides, now Vanuatu. Subsidised first by the colonial governments of New South Wales and Queensland, and then by the new Australian Government in 1901, the trade between Australia and Pacific islands was a lucrative one for Burns, Philp, who enjoyed a virtual monopoly. The company 'became shippers, storekeepers, copra-buyers, bankers and insurance agents and ran copra plantations'. On this 'new frontier', the planter, miner, overseer and trader came to be regarded as romantic or even heroic figures. 'What a wonderful life these plantation chaps have,' enthused William C Groves, a noted Australian educator and anthropologist, 'I'd give the world to exchange places.' It was exactly the adventure and start in life young Reg itched for.

*

Worlds away from working-class inner Sydney, John Fitzgerald Kennedy, known to all as 'Jack', was born in Brookline, Massachusetts, just outside Boston, on 29 May 1917, the second of nine children to Joseph Sr and Rose Kennedy. Jack's father was a successful businessman with strong political connections in the Democratic Party, which would later see him appointed the chairman of the Securities and Exchange Commission and US ambassador to the United Kingdom. Rose shared her husband's strong political roots; her father, John 'Honey Fitz' Fitzgerald, was successively a state senator, US congressman and mayor of Boston.

Born just a month after the United States entered the First World War against the Central Powers, Jack Kennedy's life would be shadowed by war and the threat of war – both hot and cold. But his early years were, if not altogether idyllic, then at least safe and comfortable. He was brought up in a world of striving and success, though not without discrimination against an ambitious family of Irish Catholic roots. Increasingly wealthy and influential, the Kennedys sent their second son to schools in Boston, New York, and eventually Choate, the famed Connecticut preparatory boarding school, in 1931. Already brimming with personality, wit and irreverence, if not yet academic distinction, upon graduation in 1935 his classmates voted him 'most likely to succeed'.

In what exactly wasn't entirely clear to the eighteen-year-old Jack. His father's interests – a powerful inspiration and influence for a young man – ranged from Wall Street, albeit diminished in the Great Depression, through the glamour and celebrity of Hollywood movie-making, to politics and public service. With good looks, natural charisma, family connections and considerable promise, Jack would find many doors open to him, whatever path he ended up choosing. The next few years, at home and abroad, would surely concentrate his mind and put his options in focus.

As 'sea-minded' and 'ship-crazy' as Reg Evans, Jack's life-long fascination with the sea and sailing started with family holidays at Hyannis Port on Cape Cod in Massachusetts. History and geography made the Atlantic America's first ocean, the country's dominant eastern seaboard facing their 'Old World', not least the Kennedys' and the Fitzgeralds' ancestral island itself. The Pacific did not yet have the same cultural, economic and strategic importance, nor, consequently, the same hold on the national imagination. For young Jack, the west coast at most meant the sunny white beaches down the road from his father's Hollywood interests. But all that was soon to change, for Jack Kennedy, as well as for America.

*

In 1929 Reg journeyed by Burns, Philp steamer to New Hebrides to work as the assistant manager of a coconut plantation.

There was still a touch of the frontier about New Hebrides at the time of Reg's arrival. Since 1906, the islands were jointly administered by the British and the French in a so-called 'condominium', with dual systems of law, education, currency, prisons and police. The cynics thought this colonial duplication was better described as 'pandemonium', but it did make for variety, which extended even to capital punishment. The British carried out public hangings until 1925 and the French public guillotinings as late as 1931. There is no record, however, of Reg witnessing such a spectacle.

During the 19th century, British and French business-men set up cotton, coffee, cocoa and coconut plantations in the islands. For the few hundred Europeans living and working on plantations it was an isolated existence that required much self-possession, tenacity and inventiveness. Many other recruits did not succeed in this exotic yet challenging environment. Not so Reg. Adventurous and open, good with people, and with a sound head on his shoulders, he had found his place. In New Hebrides young Reg fell in love with the Pacific islands and their peoples. Here he learned the most important skill: how to earn the trust of and get along with Islanders. Recruiting a local Ni-Vanuatu for plantation work was difficult in a place where, as a 1927 colonial commission of inquiry observed, 'The necessities of life are supplied by his yam garden, which is usually worked by women', while extra income could be earned far more easily by farming cash crops on the side. The Islanders did not need or want the low-paid work. Bad memories of blackbirding also persisted, souring relations. Yet, for all that, Reg must have been good at what he did, for the skills he acquired in New Hebrides would later mean the difference between life and death in his secret wartime work in the Solomons.

But for now, clouds of another kind were gathering on the horizon. Filled with ads for insecticide, tobacco, and shipping timetables, the *Pacific Islands Monthly*, whose first volume was published in Sydney in 1930, gave its front page on 16 December of that year to 'Asiatic Menace in the Pacific' and 'the economic evil', including the 'very serious and rapidly growing problem' of the 'Tonkinese in the New Hebrides'. The Chinese, it was argued, were at least partly responsible for the 'cruel depression of the copra market' and time was now ripe for the 'exclusion of Asiatics' from Solomon Islands, as they had already been excluded from the Territory of New Guinea.

The global economic slump, which commenced the year before, only worsened racial tensions. With copra prices in a freefall, island trade declined, and Reg's first south Pacific venture finished quicker than he would have liked. He returned to Sydney. Jobs were now scarce, but Reg's personal qualities held him in good stead. Keen to get back to the islands, Reg eventually secured a job as a manager and accountant on Makambo Island, not far from the Solomon Islands' administrative centre at Tulagi. Back he went to the south Pacific, hoping for a longer stint this time.

Permanent European presence in the archipelago was only half a century old at the time. With the northern part initially annexed by the Germans and the south by the British, by 1900 Britain claimed a 'protectorate' over the whole. Its colonial presence, however, was limited. Solomon Islands were seen as a distant, wild and unpredictable place in the early 20th century. Arthur Mahaffy, a British colonial officer, was provided with twenty-five members of the local armed constabulary and tasked to 'discourage the headhunting that blighted the Western Solomons ... and stood in the way of developing commercial coconut plantations'. But economic activity remained marginal; conflict and violence frequent. Local inhabitants, who practised agriculture, fishing and trade, were not impressed by foreigners who introduced blackbirding, new diseases, and unpopular taxes. Christian missionaries would prove more influential than colonial enforcers. Arriving in the islands in the mid-19th century, first Anglicans and then other denominations established a strong Christian presence among the largely Melanesian population and provided basic education and medical care.

By the time Reg arrived on Makambo Island in November 1936, the copra trade had picked up again and tourists were starting to visit Solomon Islands, including Makambo itself. The local Burns, Philp manager even asked the Islanders to dance for the visitors on Burns, Philp ships. Modern tourism had been born. Reg, meanwhile, loved his work and was good at it. As in New Hebrides before, he liked the locals, and the locals liked him too. They would remember him.

Just prior to the outbreak of war in Europe, Reg left work on Makambo and went out to sea as a purser on the Burns, Philp inter-island cargo ship, the *Mamutu*. Having just rolled out of a Hong Kong shipyard, the 35-metre-long *Mamutu* was a fine vessel and Reg was now in charge of its finances and supplies. He was finally able to indulge his passion for sailing and he 'got to know the islands like an old friend'. This too would soon come in handy.

Now in his early thirties, Reg was in his prime. At 164 centimetres in height, and with a slight build, he was not physically imposing but was sure and steady. He was fair, though years in the Pacific tanned his skin and lined his face, which was long, almost angular, with friendly blue eyes. If his face was thin, his smile was broad and warm. It lingered. He was reserved, perhaps even unassuming, but with a ready wit and sense of fair play. People found him likeable and dependable; he had depth and quiet authority about him. Not the least of it, he had also managed to catch the eye of an interesting and creative young woman, Gertrude Slaney Poole, from a prominent Adelaide family. Things were looking up on all fronts.

*

In September 1935, Jack Kennedy travelled to Britain. It was his first major sea voyage. Having graduated from Choate, he was now hoping to study for a year under the prominent English socialist, Harold Laski, at the London School of Economics. Eighteen, charming and witty if somewhat footloose and undisciplined, Jack was excited by the opportunities, both intellectual and social, of going abroad. With the rise of vibrant and seemingly successful totalitarian and authoritarian regimes throughout Europe, democracy and its liberal institutions seemed exhausted, their future uncertain. Jack was keen to understand the tensions shaping the political landscape.

But he was, not for the first time in his life, beleaguered by a serious digestive complaint, forcing him to return to the United States after only a few weeks in London. He enrolled briefly at Princeton University before again succumbing to the illness and entering hospital, then convalescing at a ranch in the warm dry air of Arizona.

By the summer of 1936, he was ready to start again. He commenced at Harvard in the northern fall and, while not yet a serious scholar, was prominent in extra-curricular and social activities. Funny, bright and gregarious, he had friends aplenty on campus. Young men and women were drawn to him and sought out his company, a portent of the personal magnetism that would pave his way to political success. Jack was also competitive, this too a valuable political attribute, though for now channelled to excel in football, sailing and swimming. Little did he know that his strong swimming ability would one day prove vital to his survival.

His interest in foreign affairs was reignited during a European tour with his lifelong friend Lem Billings. Jack's father advised him to go 'before the shooting starts' and so, in the summer of 1937, they made their way into the wary calm before the storm. Echoing the Grand Tour tradition of the European elites of yesteryear, Jack and Lem took in the premier cultural sites, recording their sometimes acrid observations of European peoples and personalities. France was fun but disorganised and spent. Italy, they judged, was cleaner and better run. At first they had respect for Germany's accomplishments but became irritated by its nationalism and regimentation. In Munich, Jack recorded that 'Hitler seems popular here, as Mussolini was in Italy, although propaganda seems to be his strongest point'.

Later that year, President Roosevelt appointed Joe Kennedy as ambassador to the United Kingdom. Very soon, the Kennedy family became prominent in Britain and Jack's parents entered the elite of British society. It was a long way from the ethnic and religious discrimination against the Irish that Joe Sr had known as a child and young man. He had made it.

Jack travelled to London to join his parents at the end of his sophomore year in July 1938. He worked for the summer in the embassy, enjoying both his job and the social whirl. He was keen to better understand international relations and the emerging role of the United States. Back in Harvard, he quickly negotiated a return to Europe to research his senior year honours thesis on the origins of Britain's appeasement policy. He was again in Britain in the early spring of 1939 where he enjoyed tea with, among others, a young Princess Elizabeth.

Slowly, perhaps even reluctantly, Jack was starting to question the great constant of United States foreign policy, that of isolationism. In the disappointing aftermath of the Great War, Jack knew most Americans thought the sacrifice of blood and money had been in vain and did not want to get caught up in another European war. His father was among the most prominent voices against foreign interventions. Yet something was nagging at Jack. After the Great War, Britain too was sick of European conflicts and the public feared another war might destroy Britain and its empire. Yet it was Britain's very lack of preparedness that emboldened Hitler and his allies. Might America's isolation too assist Germany, and potentially Japan, and in the long run make the world less safe for the United States? Perhaps it was in America's interest to take a stand.

From Britain Jack toured the continent to research his dissertation. With Europe on the cusp of war, 22-year-old Jack Kennedy was fascinated by the rising ferment.

Whether in Fascist Italy or Germany, Communist Russia, or in the shaken and vulnerable European democracies like Czechoslovakia and Poland, Jack was captivated by the febrile political atmosphere. He returned to London just in time to see Prime Minister Neville Chamberlain and Winston Churchill, soon to be back in government as First Lord of the Admiralty, explain Britain's decision to finally confront Hitler. Churchill's oratory, classical if not overblown, was made for war. Its power to summon and move people was not lost on the young American.

Jack Kennedy, an ambassador's son listening to the war debate in the House of Commons in London, and Reg Evans, a ship's accounts man sailing between the islands of the Solomons archipelago, could not have known their paths would soon cross. The south-west Pacific was a long way from Europe and its troubles, and the United States was still a long way from war. And Australia and America, long separated by distance and indifference, were still, as late as 1939, strangers to each other.

CHAPTER 2

PERFECT STRANGERS

For most of their histories, Australians and Americans were kept apart by sheer distance. The Pacific Ocean, that vast and misnamed body of water, covers virtually an entire hemisphere of our planet. Today, it takes less than fourteen hours to fly over it, but before the age of globalisation the journey between Australia and the United States could take months. During the 19th century few had good reason to embark on such a long and arduous crossing.

In the seventy years between 1820 and 1890, only 16 000 Australians went to the United States, a majority of them for the California gold rush in 1848. These fortune-seekers proved unpopular ambassadors. Dubbed the 'Sydney Ducks', most were seen as 'thugs, scoundrels, thieves, aggressors, queue jumpers, and as "the most abandoned men and women"', not surprising for people who came from a colony where convict transports only ended in 1868. Brazen and lawless, the Australian arrivals set up dens of iniquity by the dozen near San Francisco Harbor. There, at the base of Telegraph Hill, the American patrons were as likely to be robbed as entertained. So infamous were the Ducks and their 'Sydney Town' redoubt that the Californian legislature even contemplated prohibiting the entry of convicted criminals to their state. It did not come to pass but, to the relief of their hosts, most of the Australians dispersed once the gold was exhausted. Eucalyptus trees, their one lasting gift to their hosts, to this day turn Californian forest fires into raging infernos.

Among those who returned to Australia, some, like prospector Edward Hargraves, were convinced gold could be found here too. Keen eyes scanned the countryside and soon spotted geological features familiar from California, hinting at the possibility of riches buried underneath. By May 1851, Hargraves and his collaborators, armed with techniques learned in America, struck gold around Bathurst.

The gold rush was to change the face of Australia. Within twenty years of Hargraves' discovery, Australia's population more than tripled to 1.7 million. About 18 000 came from the United States to try their luck. As the Stars and Stripes 'flew above stores and saloons at Ballarat and Bendigo', a few Americans made fortunes, if mostly from the miners rather than the mines.

These were men like Freeman Cobb, the founder of the Cobb & Co coach service, and George Francis Train, successful luxury goods importer at only twenty-four years of age. Ever a colourful personality, Train later claimed to be the inspiration for Jules Verne's novel *Around the World in Eighty Days* and even mounted a quixotic campaign for president of the United States. Most 'Yankees', as they were indiscriminately called by the locals, eventually returned home, but not before introducing Australians to rocking chairs, alarm clocks, iceboxes and kerosene, the last two of great importance on the goldfields. All in all, it was a less fraught legacy than eucalyptus trees.

Gold aside, neither Australia nor the United States possessed much to interest each other. With little trade or traffic between the two, a more sustained encounter had to await the turn of the 20th century and the coming of the contest for naval supremacy in the Pacific. Where commerce had previously failed, common security concerns would now increasingly bring the two nations closer together.

*

Large, resource-rich but population-poor, and, most importantly, distant from the seat of Empire, Australia tended to glance north with unease. When not anxious about mass immigration from an overcrowded and land-hungry China, Australian colonists lived in fear of an expansionist Russia. Coastal batteries were built to protect cities and ports and lookouts kept for the Czar's frigates. While it is easy to dismiss such scares as alarmist, as sometimes they were, the Russians did occasionally eye Australia as part of the 'Great Game' against Britain for imperial supremacy in Asia. But so long as Britannia, in the words of a patriotic song, ruled the waves, Australia remained safe from external threats.

Such a state of affairs, however, could not survive the emergence of new powers eager to assert their place in the Pacific sun. In 1895, Japan humbled China, replacing it as the dominant power in the Korean Peninsula and annexing the island of Formosa (now Taiwan). Ten years later, it was Russia's turn to be humiliated. The Czar's army was bested, his Far Eastern and Baltic fleets destroyed and sunk in the twenty months of Russo-Japanese war for control of Manchuria and Korea. The prospect of Japan supplanting Russia as the would-be overlord of Asia and the Pacific was met with alarm in Australia. 'The stupendous struggle in the East must awaken [us] to the fact that we have been living in a fool's paradise', Allan McLean, trade minister in the Reid government, observed of Russia's defeat in 1905. 'Japan has astonished the world ... We now find one of the great naval and military powers within a very short distance of our shores.' To make things worse, in 1906 Britain withdrew its last major warships from the Pacific to face the growing threat from the Kaiser's rapidly expanding navy. Australians felt exposed and defenceless.

At the other end of the ocean, the United States was also unsettled by the unexpected and unwelcome shift in power in north-west Asia. In 1898, America went to war with Spain over independence for Cuba, and in victory acquired Spanish imperial possessions in the Caribbean and in the Pacific, including, most importantly, the Philippines. Having also recently annexed the Hawaiian archipelago, its interest and influence now extended well into the central and western Pacific. From 1907 on, wrote American military historian Henry Gole, 'war with Japan was a concern, even an obsession, for the US Navy'.

Not coincidentally, that same year President Theodore Roosevelt dispatched the largest fleet ever to circumnavigate the globe, a signal to friend and potential foe alike that America too had arrived on the world stage as a power to be reckoned with. Made up of sixteen ships with a crew of 14 500, including junior officers such as William Halsey, Husband Kimmel, Raymond Spruance and John S McCain Sr, who would go on to become admirals and top commanders in the Pacific in the Second World War, the 'Great White Fleet' was second in size only to Britain's Royal

Navy. So christened on account of their stark white hulls, the American armada's primary mission was diplomatic, albeit of 'the gunboat variety'.

Such a show of Anglo-Saxon power suited Australia's prime minister, Alfred Deakin, and he jumped at the opportunity to host the fleet in August and September 1908. It was an audacious move, since Deakin had not consulted the Colonial Office in London, and it foreshadowed both Australia's greater independence from Britain and its turn to America. But while the British might have been unhappy, residents of Sydney, Melbourne and Albany were rapturous in their welcome of the Americans. In Sydney, at least half a million greeted the fleet, more than five out of six of the city's population. Elated crowds lined the shores and joyous functions were had, 'producing an orgy of pro-American and anti-Japanese sentiment'.

Deakin made much of the common heritage shared by Australians and Americans. After the visit he even proposed an expansion of the Monroe Doctrine to cover Australia's neighbourhood. First articulated in 1823, President James Monroe claimed the western hemisphere as the exclusive area of influence for the United States, barring all other powers. By including the western Pacific within the doctrine's ambit, Deakin hoped that Australia would be better protected by the United States' growing military might. The British government refused to support Deakin's proposal and it was never put to the Americans, who in any case would have been unlikely to accept. Still, these were all signs that the Pacific, once an impassable ocean, might soon 'become a lake'. And if the lake could not be a British one any more, it was better for it to be American than anyone else's.

As it transpired, fear of Japanese aggression proved to be off by three decades. When the First World War broke out six years after the Great White Fleet's visit, Australia and Japan found themselves unexpected allies, working in parallel, if independently of each other, to strip Germany of its colonial possessions across Asia and the Pacific. In the northern Pacific, the Japanese occupied the Mariana, Caroline, and Marshall islands; in the south, New Zealand took over Samoa, and Australia commenced its administration of New Guinea. The Japanese warship *Ibuki* even escorted the 1st Australian Imperial Force as the Diggers left Albany on 1 November 1914 and made their way across the Indian Ocean to the Middle East. But as the Japanese navy's budget grew during the war to double that of the army, so did its ambitions, the admirals developing a taste for overseas expansion.

In Europe, meanwhile, the war brought Australia and the United States together against the Central Powers, though only after years of complaints from the Diggers about the dithering Americans taking their time to enter the conflict. Once they did, the Sammies, as the Australians called them after 'Uncle Sam', were more than welcome. Most famously, at the Battle of Hamel in July 1918, American soldiers even fought under Australia's Lieutenant General John Monash. It was their second engagement of the war but the first time ever that American troops had served under a foreign commander. Despite initial objections from the commander of the American Expeditionary Forces, General John 'Black Jack' Pershing, and reservations from Monash's British superior, General Sir Henry Rawlinson, the result was a textbook triumph of coordinated armour, artillery, air force and infantry action that lasted ninety-three minutes – only three more than Monash originally planned.

Both the Diggers and the Sammies could be proud, Monash later writing that the American contingent 'acquitted themselves most gallantly and were ever after received by Australians as blood brothers'. One of their ranks, Corporal Thomas A Pope of Illinois, was awarded the highest US military decoration, the Medal of Honor, for single-handedly rushing a German machine gun nest at Hamel, bayonetting some of the crew and holding the rest at bay until they were killed or captured by his unit. For the same action, Pope also received the Distinguished Conduct Medal from King George V, on the recommendation of an Australian officer. Pope was the last surviving Medal of Honor winner from the Great War, dying in 1989 at age ninety-four.

American soldiers might have returned home after the war ended, but America would remain increasingly present overseas through its chief new exports: popular culture and consumer capitalism. Throughout the 1920s and 30s, Australians, like many others around the world, enthusiastically embraced a whole cornucopia of American imports, including jazz, Rotary clubs, magazines (such as the popular *Ladies Home Journal*), home appliances and cars. Californian bungalows even began to replace local Federation architecture. But it was silent movies, later enriched by sound and eventually Technicolor, that most commonly showcased America. To Australians, who flocked to cinemas on average twice a week, 'America really existed as the gangland, the western saga, the musical comedy hall, and the home of romance.' Meanwhile, Australia could only offer back Errol Flynn; not an insubstantial contribution, but the Australian artistic invasion of Hollywood would have to wait until later in the century.

Of the real America, Australians knew much less and what they did, they did not particularly like. Gotham-like urban jungles, with their big city bosses, Prohibition, speakeasies, and gangsters were all much of a muchness and nothing to compare with the wholesomeness of Dame Nellie Melba, Don Bradman and Phar Lap. 'Some of the attitudes are not necessarily based on sound information,' C Hartley Grattan, an American author who visited Australia frequently between 1927 and 1940, wrote in his book *Introducing Australia*. 'They are mostly prejudices, fortified by stray bits of fact and fiction picked up here and there in the press and the movies and welded into a picture of American life which is apt to be unfavorable.' It was the Sydney Ducks in reverse.

If Australians knew few things about America, they knew even fewer real-life Americans. A meagre 15 000 United States citizens visited Australia throughout the 1920s. In 1921, there were only 6404 US-born citizens living in Australia; a dozen years later there were 6066. Many had a reputation as 'loud' and 'excessively cordial'. But as an American journalist, Mack Matthews, reported, in private they would complain of 'Australia's obsolete business methods, obnoxious social customs, and general economic instability' – all the bad bits of Britain without the redeeming quality of 'Old World' glamour – before raising a popular toast: 'To Australia – the land where the flowers have no fragrance, the birds no melody, and women no virtue.' As for their compatriots back home, 'the American public was so disinterested in Australian affairs that it was not even aware that Australians disliked them'.

*

This lack of affinity might, at first, seem strange. To an outsider, the two continent-spanning nations appear quite alike. For one, they share, in Mark Twain's words, 'old ties of heredity'. Both, after all, began as British colonies peopled by principally British stock who dispossessed Indigenous inhabitants. Once fabled lands – Australia first imagined by Europeans as 'Terra Australis Incognita', America initially mistaken for 'the Indies' – in time they similarly came to represent in the contemporary imagination the promise and potential of 'New Worlds'.

The Australian and American founding stories are certainly symmetrical. The 'First Fleet' of eleven ships, six of them convict transports, left Portsmouth on 13 May 1787 to establish a penal colony at Botany Bay. The next day, in Philadelphia, delegates began assembling to draft the Constitution of the newly independent United States. By the time the fleet's commander Captain Arthur Phillip had founded a settlement on the shores of what would later be known as Sydney on 26 January 1788, the Constitution had been signed by delegates and ratified by five states. All thirteen did so by mid-1790, before the arrival of the Second Fleet in Sydney.

The timing of these events was no coincidence. The colonisation of Australia commenced when it did largely because Great Britain had lost its American colonies and with them the traditional dumping ground for its criminal class. But their different character already pointed to diverging futures. Convicts were never a significant proportion of the American population. From settlement, Britain's Atlantic colonies were overwhelmingly a magnet for political and religious dissenters as well as those simply looking for a better life in a new world, unencumbered by the hierarchies and habits of the old one.

As a consequence, the American temperament has always possessed a strong individualistic, libertarian and entrepreneurial streak. But also a spiritual, if sometimes messianic one. Travelling in the 1820s, French diplomat and historian Alexis de Tocqueville was struck by the 'religious atmosphere' of the United States. No visitor to Australia, distinguished or otherwise, has ever been so struck.

If America's first European settlers arrived with hope, promise and faith in God, Australia's arrived with chains, foreboding and faint hope in God's mercy. It was, historian Robert Hughes wrote, the 'largest forced exile of citizens at the behest of a European government in pre-modern history'. It took decades before free settlers started arriving in numbers, and when they did it was to an existence more precarious and therefore more dependent on the state's protection and patronage. Australia's frontier spawned mateship, unions, and a collectivist ethos. American colonists eventually rebelled; Australian colonists, a more egalitarian yet at the same time quite conservative bunch, grumbled (if often with larrikin humour) but almost always obeyed, most with loyal enthusiasm.

When nationhood eventually dawned, wrote author and speechwriter Don Watson, Australia, unlike the United States, 'was soldered together not in a fiery furnace but through a protracted series of lawyers' meetings'. Consequently,

Australia grew in temperament more like its safe and steady sister dominion of Canada rather than the revolutionary and radical United States of America. No wonder then that whenever Australians and Americans met, they might have spoken the same language, but they did not quite understand each other.

*

The end of the First World War saw Australia and the United States retreat again to their opposite shores of the Pacific. They also reverted to their historical form. Australia continued to look to Britain, now war-drained and diminished, for defence as well as political and diplomatic guidance, while America sank back into isolationism.

After intense effort to secure the Versailles Treaty, the US Senate failed to ratify it and refused to join the League of Nations. America's subsequent insistence that war debts be paid in full provoked much animosity around the world, including in Australia. Many believed that America's demands contributed to the onset of the global Great Depression in 1929. As haemorrhaging national economies skulked behind the walls of protection, what little trade there was between Australia and the United States now became the victim of tariffs. Australia naturally favoured British and empire goods, punishing other imports. Americans saw the 'Empire preference' as an 'unadulterated evil', though, hypocritically, they raised trade barriers of their own. In 1935, the minister for external affairs, Sir George Pearce, could state with confidence that Australian–American relations had reached their zenith during the visit of the 'Great White Fleet' in 1908, and had been going downhill ever since.

If trade wars rankled, America's political and strategic inconstancy sent shivers through Australia's political class. With Washington increasingly mooting independence for the Philippines, Australia saw the United States abandoning the Pacific to potentially hostile powers like Japan. Even in bucolic Goulburn, the good members of the local branch of the United Australia Party were so worried by this prospect, they proposed admitting the Philippines to the British empire. After Japan invaded Chinese Manchuria in 1931, many were happy to see Japanese aggression funnelled into continental Asia rather than the Pacific, and so ever closer to Australia.

Yet for the time being, Australia's domestic concerns remained more pressing than Asian power plays. Caught in the Great Depression, growing trade with Japan made for one of the few lifelines for a sick Australian economy. With Japan the third largest trading partner, the relationship was considered so important that Tokyo was chosen for Australia's second, after Washington, diplomatic post. Even after Japan's open aggression against China in 1937, Canberra opposed sanctions, as did, for similar reasons, the American and British governments. Australian unions took a more principled stance, but their informal efforts to hamper trade were quickly suppressed by the then Attorney-General Robert Menzies, earning him the lifelong nickname 'Pig Iron Bob', after one of Australia's major exports to Japan.

Even as they continued to send Japan iron to build its warships and warplanes and oil and coal to power them, the anxiety about Japanese aggression kept growing in Australia and the United States. Yet this shared concern spurred little official contact, much less cooperation, between Canberra and Washington. Formal diplomatic relations with the United States were only established in January 1940, three years after Britain finally granted Australia control over its foreign affairs. Australia's first minister in Washington, Richard Casey, took office a month later, and even then only because he happened to be there as part of the British delegation. As war clouds gathered over Europe and Asia, there was still no direct air service between Australia and America, nor a submarine cable connection.

Political isolation, trade competition and cultural differences did not bode well for Australian and American relations. In the inter-war years, few dared to speculate on a different future. One such exception was Nicholas Roosevelt, first cousin of Theodore and a more distant cousin of Franklin, who predicted in his presciently titled 1928 book *The Restless Pacific* that 'As the bonds of Empire weaken, the ties that bind the Dominions to the United States will strengthen.' Grouping together his own country with Canada, Australia and New Zealand, Roosevelt proclaimed: 'We four are of the new world, blessed with the material foundations of cultural greatness and fortunate in having vigorous, healthy populations.'

Responding two years later in his classic history *Australia*, Keith Hancock would have none of it. 'It is absurd to imagine', he wrote, 'that Australia, because she buys American motor cars and submits to the deluge of Hollywood culture, is drifting vaguely towards some new political combination.' Hancock represented the informed consensus of the time. Australia's 'habits, her interests, her sympathies, and her honour, all combine to keep her with the British Commonwealth of Nations', he argued, before asking his readers: 'Could the United States give to Australia the security she now enjoys in virtue of her honourable co-operation with her fellow members of the British Commonwealth?'

A rhetorical question at the start of the decade, by 1939 the answer was far from obvious.

CHAPTER 3

ANSWERING THE CALL

The war in Europe, when it finally came in September 1939, was a shock but not a surprise. Two days after Hitler invaded Poland, Robert Menzies, the prime minister since April, announced that as Britain had declared war on Germany, Australia was now also at war. The 2nd Australian Imperial Force was created on 15 September, initially composed of 20 000 volunteers. With Japan tied down in China and Britain desperate for support, the first units began departing to the Middle East in early 1940 to train, as their fathers in the 1st AIF had done before them in the First World War. The formidable 6th Infantry Division was destined for France, to strengthen the Allied forces there, but to everyone's dismay France fell to the German onslaught before the Diggers could cross the Mediterranean. So the 6th remained in north Africa. With Britain now standing alone against Axis might, Menzies called his countrymen and women for an 'ALL-IN' war effort. Enlistments soared and three more divisions were soon formed.

Reg Evans was among those who answered the call. Upon returning from Solomon Islands to Sydney in June 1940, he tried to enlist with the Royal Australian Navy but, as with his first approach to the Naval College twenty years earlier, he was again rejected. No matter, he would try for the army instead.

The 2/9th Field Regiment, Royal Australian Artillery, was formed in July 1940 and raised at Holsworthy army base, not far from Liverpool, south-west of Sydney. As its official history makes clear, the unit was formed as France fell under Hitler's control and his power extended across most of Europe. Britain was next in his sights. But the gloomy outlook did not deter men from volunteering and the ranks quickly swelled. The threat to the British empire fortified their collective resolve and made up for any lack of military experience. Evans was among the men who lined up to join, most of them other New South Welshmen. At thirty-five, he was older, better educated, and more experienced than an average recruit. These qualities would be noticed by his superiors, and he was soon in line for promotion.

The next month, in anticipation of being shipped over-seas, Evans married his fiancée, Gertrude Slaney Poole. Trudy, as Reg would always call her, came from a distinguished South Australian family. Her grandfather, Frederic Slaney Poole, was a well-regarded lecturer in classics at the University of Adelaide and an Anglican canon of Adelaide for more than a decade. Trudy's father, Thomas Slaney Poole, had been, at twenty-one years of age, a precocious lecturer in Classics who then enjoyed a distinguished career at the Bar before appointment to the South Australian Supreme Court. He frequently acted as chief justice and as governor of the state when the incumbents were absent. He died at only fifty-three and was remembered as the best judge South Australia ever had.

Trudy's mother, Dora Francis Poole, was well known for her community work, including as president of the Adelaide Lyceum Club and the National Council of Women for South Australia.

Throughout the 1930s, Trudy and her two sisters appeared frequently in the society pages of Adelaide papers. The elder one, Katherine, ended up in Solomon Islands as the public relations officer for the British Protectorate. Trudy followed in her sister's footsteps, working as a secretary for Patricia Hackett, a talented Australian artist and actress as well as a ground-breaking female lawyer, who reportedly became the first solicitor to set up office in the Solomons. Hackett was also a poet, writing in a poem dedicated to Solomon Islands and titled 'These Islands', 'I looked upon those islands / With half believing eyes, / For there stretched out as dreams before me / Lay a loveliness that pierced my eyes / And filled me an aching joy'. Reg first met Trudy in Tulagi. If the match was made in tropical heaven, blissful life together for the newlyweds would have to wait.

*

Jack Kennedy was back in London from his European trip when on 3 September 1939 the House of Commons debated the declaration of war on Germany, following Prime Minister Chamberlain's announcement earlier that day. With his parents and brother Joe Jr and sister Kathleen in the Strangers Gallery, Jack watched transfixed as the drama unfolded. Joe Sr and Rose were moved by Chamberlain's sadness and pathos. Jack not so much. He was more interested in the short, pudgy, bald MP wearing a three-piece suit and sporting a bow tie and pocket watch, Winston Churchill.

Jack recognised him. He was a fan and had read his speeches. Churchill, not currently a minister and therefore sitting in the emerald backbench ruck of the Commons, rose with practised theatre and assured a nervous nation that war was right: 'Outside, the storms of war may blow and the lands may be lashed with the fury of its gales but in our own hearts this Sunday morning there is peace ... our consciences are at rest.' But then Churchill thundered, lest anyone dare to forget, 'We are fighting to save the whole world from the pestilence of Nazi tyranny and in defence of all that is most sacred to man.'

It was heady stuff for 22-year-old Jack Kennedy. He knew the occasion was momentous but could hardly have guessed how big a shadow the war would cast over his life and that of his family.

The coming of the war in Europe had solidified Jack's interest in international relations. His Harvard honours thesis 'Appeasement at Munich' was well received and, with the world exploding in war, Jack decided to expand it into a book. Arguing for an American–British alliance in defence of democracy, *Why England Slept* was published in July 1940 to glowing reviews and substantial sales. Jack was delighted with the book's reception, adding as it did to his intellectual self-confidence and growing stature as a young man going places.

He now had sufficient confidence to question Joe Sr's isolationist instincts with a more outward-looking and inter-nationalist stance. The argument between father and son reflected a broad tension within US politics between those refusing to get involved in yet another European bloodbath and those who believed it was not only America's duty to defend democracy on the European continent but also in its national interest. When Joe Kennedy Sr resigned his ambassadorship in November 1940, Jack, who had himself previously harboured doubts about America's proper role in world affairs, now advised his father to distance himself from Chamberlain's failed policies of appeasement.

If the war seemed remote from the United States when *Why England Slept* was first published, by the time his father returned from London, war was increasingly the talk of the nation. President Roosevelt was determined that his country would not be asleep as Hitler took over Europe and ultimately threatened America's security. Public sentiment, too, was slowly shifting away from isolation. Jack Kennedy captured the zeitgeist of the nation on the brink of epochal transformation from a continental power to a global giant.

*

While the dramatic fight against Hitler and Mussolini captivated public attention in Australia and America, the deteriorating situation in Asia was not entirely overlooked. Consigned to following Britain's lead in Europe and the Middle East, Menzies understood that Australia's own backyard was a different matter. 'What Great Britain calls the Far East is to us the near north', he observed, arguing that in the Pacific 'Australia must regard herself as a principal … on the basis that the primary risk in the Pacific is borne by New Zealand and ourselves'. The government soon reintroduced conscription for the Citizen Military Forces, a militia restricted to service in Australia and its external territories, including potential forward defences like New Guinea. War production soared.

This time, the fear of danger from the north was neither paranoia nor xenophobia. On 28 June 1940, Menzies read an announcement from the Japanese foreign minister regarding his country's policy for east Asia and the Pacific: 'The destiny of these regions – any development therein and any disposal thereof – is a matter of grave concern to Japan, in view of her mission and responsibility as the stabilising force in East Asia.' If the prime minister was unsettled, the Tokyo broadcast sent shockwaves throughout the region. Scores of scared evacuees left Hong Kong and Singapore bound for the relative safety of Australia. As events unfolded, they were the prescient and lucky ones.

Japan had by now captured America's full attention as well. Washington finally imposed economic sanctions, hoping a cut in oil and scrap metal supplies might put a spanner in the Japanese war machine and so force Japan to its senses. It had the opposite effect. But however worried the US government was, it continued to be officially committed to non-intervention, a policy that still enjoyed considerable public support. President Roosevelt's re-election for a historic third term in November 1940 at last gave him more room to manoeuvre. The US Congress, stretching the limits of 'neutrality', enacted 'Lend-Lease' on 11 March 1941. With American aid finally on its way to beleaguered Britain, prime ministers Churchill and Menzies (in London since February, and now part of the War Cabinet) collectively breathed a sigh of relief.

*

For the 2/9th, training at Holsworthy was intense. Men from all walks of life quickly learned to work as a team, whether as signallers, gun-layers, drivers, mechanics or others to support the gunners. They fought mock battles up and around country New South Wales and senior officers were pleased with their preparations. Evans' unit called themselves the 'Two-bar-nine' and proudly displayed its insignia, topped by a bulldog astride a boomerang.

By Christmas 1940, there was only one question on everyone's lips: 'When are we going?' The bulldog was keen to bite. Pre-embarkation leave was given just before Christmas and then again in late March. Finally, on Good Friday, 11 April 1941, the 2/9th departed from Sydney Harbour bound for the Middle East. They were lucky, as the ship carrying them was Britain's pride of the seas, fast and, at the time, the largest ship ever built, the 83 000-ton RMS *Queen Elizabeth*, recently requisitioned from the Cunard Line for use as a troop ship.

They arrived in Palestine in May and soon embarked for Egypt, where the regiment spent from 26 May to 25 June at Amariya, near Alexandria. While there, Evans and his mates got a taste of the war when they witnessed the almost nightly German bombing of the ancient port city. Still, troops were occasionally allowed leave in Alexandria and were known to enjoy the Egyptian nightlife.

While the 2/9th trained at Amariya, a new front in the world war was opening several hundred kilometres to the north-east. 'The situation in Iraq had deteriorated because some bozo had overthrown the government and was trying to get German assistance to prop him up', recalled Lieu-tenant Ronald Shea of the 7th Division's 2/2nd Anti-Tank Regiment. 'The Germans were being very helpful and had started pouring aircraft and stores into Iraq through Syria.'

The 'bozo' in question, a nationalist Prime Minister Rashid Ali, was quickly defeated and British control over Iraq restored. Germans, however, continued to use Syrian airfields, forcing the Allies to intervene. In June, 18 000 Australians and 16 000 British, Indian and Free French troops crossed the border into Vichy-controlled territories of Syria and Lebanon.

In late June, while on their way to join the battle in Syria, Evans and his mates stopped near Cairo and spent a night, like the First World War Diggers before them, within the shadows of the pyramids. By the beginning of July, the 2/9th were approaching the border with Syria to relieve their opposite numbers of the 2/5th Australian Field Regiment, supporting a brigade of the Sixth British Division. By then, a young lieutenant of the 2/5th, and much later Governor of New South Wales, Roden Cutler, had begun the series of heroic acts that would soon earn him the Victoria Cross. He was the only artilleryman ever to do so. Cutler lost a leg in action; the future Israeli defence minister, Moshe Dayan, lost an eye and acquired his trademark eye-patch while helping guide Australian troops of the 7th Division.

Evans' regiment soon saw fighting. They were positioned in the foothills that straddled the border between Syria and Lebanon. With the beauty of the snow-capped Mt Hermon to the right and a Crusader fort used by Richard the Lionheart to the left, Australian artillery pounded enemy positions. The Vichy French, most of them colonial troops, and French Foreign Legion gunners fought gamely but the Allies got the upper hand. Australian battle casualties were light, but about four-fifths of the unit became infected with malaria while near the Aammiq Wetlands in Lebanon.

Famous Australian war correspondent and combat cameraman Damien Parer was also in the Middle East at that time to film the 2nd AIF's victories in the Syrian campaign. Parer's renown grew here as he shot footage from ships and planes, as well as on the ground, capturing the fear and courage of ordinary fighting men. Not for the first time, he was nearly killed at Merdjayoun in Lebanon when he was caught by the Australian artillery barrage preceding the 7th Division's attack on Vichy French positions. He later took classic film of Australians taking Fort Khiam and was again lucky not to be killed by mortar fire, this time from Vichy French forces. After the successful Syrian campaign, he filmed *Rats of Tobruk*. And then, like Reg Evans and his regiment, Parer returned to Australia and the war in the Pacific. His brilliant footage of fighting on the Kokoda Track (also known as the Kokoda Trail) was later used for the Oscar-winning documentary, *Kokoda Front Line!*

After several weeks of fighting, on 10 July, with Allied forces about to enter Beirut, the Vichy French sought a ceasefire. After the signing of the Armistice of Saint Jean d'Acre, on 14 July 1941, coincidentally Bastille Day, Allied forces commenced their occupation of the French Levant.

In mid-August, Evans' unit made its way north through Lebanon into Syria and to the ancient city of Aleppo, just south of the Turkish border. With its ancient ruins, bazaars and souks, cafes and antique shops, Aleppo was a long way from Holsworthy army base. At first, Australians wondered why there were no women to be seen. It transpired, the regimental history recounts, that the local women had gone into hiding after 'Lord Haw-Haw', the infamous British traitor William Joyce who broadcast Nazi propaganda from

Germany during the war, described the AIF 'as "Menzies' Bushrangers,"' and had suggested ... that a surer way of destroying a city than by bombing was to give the AIF a week's leave therein'. When after a few weeks of Aussie occupation Aleppo was still standing, the local women began to venture forth and Evans' unit got to enjoy well-attended parties at Madam Lola's.

*

On 13 March 1941, Tatsuo Kawai, Japan's first ambassador (referred to as a 'minister') arrived in Australia. An official reception to welcome him in Canberra was held a week later. Inauspiciously, it ended with a slight, the party cut short as parliament was adjourned without notice and members and senators were hurried off by their handlers and herded on to a special train to Sydney. A bigger and better show beckoned: the United States Navy was back in town.

With seven vessels – two cruisers and five destroyers – and some 2100 men, it was not as formidable or impressive as the 'Great White Fleet', but the Americans nevertheless received, if anything, an even more ecstatic welcome. Sydneysiders lined the foreshore for kilometres as the ships sailed into the harbour. More than half a million watched US Marines and sailors march through the city shoulder to shoulder with Australian soldiers. Relieved and comforted by America's might, the spectators cheered, cried and threw confetti, streamers and flower petals on the visitors. After the party litter was swept away and it was time to leave, Billy Hughes, prime minister during the previous war, reflected, 'I can recall many historic demonstrations of public enthusiasm by Australians' – and as a member of parliament since 1901, he had been an official witness to the 'Great White Fleet' – 'but the farewell to the United States flotilla was the most universally spontaneous and genuine ever given'.

The welcome was even warmer in normally sleepy Brisbane. The city had never seen an American naval squadron up close before, as visiting ships had previously been unwilling to risk the narrow and relatively shallow Brisbane River. This time they docked within a couple of kilometres of the city centre at New Farm and Bulimba. 'We just dropped in', said the commanding officer, Rear Admiral John H Newton, 'to show that we are not so far away from Australia after all. We are on a training cruise and a visit of goodwill.' As they marched from Fortitude Valley down Queen Street and to the City Hall, the Americans were joined by Australian servicemen, and greeted by 280 000 people – 100 000 more than predicted. The biggest crowd in the city's history, nearly 85 per cent of its population, clapped, cheered, whistled and sang, and threw sixty truckloads of paper at the servicemen. It was, argued cultural historian Barry Ralph, 'proportionately, the greatest public display of enthusiasm and emotion in the history of the country, even breaking the previous record set in Sydney only two days before'. The Americans agreed, Rear Admiral Newton calling the reception 'beyond what we had imagined possible'.

By the middle of 1941, international tensions rose a further notch. As German troops invaded the Soviet Union, Japan took the opportunity to finish annexing French Indochina. In Canberra, there were suggestions of negotiating directly with the Japanese. Menzies was urged by some to fly to Tokyo to speak with the Japanese government.

John Curtin, Labor Party leader and a member of the Advisory War Council, championed a conference between the Dominions, the United Kingdom, the United States and Japan. It came to nothing, but anything was worth a try.

If the Japanese attacked south through Singapore, which was now denuded of better quality British and Empire troops, Australia was not confident they could be resisted. With three AIF divisions in north Africa and the Middle East (the 9th and a brigade of the 7th holding the besieged Tobruk against Rommel's Afrika Korps) and only one in Malaya, there was little standing between Japanese forces and Australia's undefended coast. Could our troops be recalled home in time?

As fate had it, this was to be Curtin's decision. Months of Canberra intrigue saw both Menzies and his successor, Arthur Fadden, fall from the top job in quick succession, and on 7 October 1941, precisely two months before the Japanese attack on Pearl Harbor, Curtin was sworn in as Australia's fourteenth prime minister. As a young man growing up in Melbourne, Curtin was a socialist, strong unionist and formidable organiser and advocate, becoming federal president of the Timberworkers' Union while still in his twenties. Leading the opposition to conscription for overseas service during the Great War, he was even briefly jailed for refusing a medical examination by army doctors. Curtin moved to Perth in 1917, becoming the editor of the *Westralian Worker*, the official organ of the union movement in Western Australia. First elected to Federal Parliament in 1928, he became leader of the Labor Party in 1935. Six years later, this former melancholic and alcoholic union organiser and journalist was facing the greatest challenge of his life.

The hour maketh the man. The war would be his cross to bear but also the making of his legend.

By early November, Curtin was advised that 'war between the British empire and Japan must be regarded as a probability'. There were eleventh-hour negotiations. The Americans demanded that Japan withdraw from China and Indochina; the Japanese demanded recognition of their new territories. The talks broke down.

*

In the autumn of 1940, with the introduction of the first peacetime draft in America's history, 23-year-old Jack Kennedy was slated for service in the US Army. Having graduated from Harvard with a Bachelor of Arts in government, for a while he thought of pursuing a commercial career and briefly enrolled at the Graduate School of Business at Stanford University in California. As such, he was allowed to defer until the end of the academic year in the spring of 1941. But intestinal ailments and the return of a lower back injury, sustained while playing football at Harvard, seemed likely to excuse him from the draft regardless. As 1940 was coming to an end, Jack had to return to the East Coast again to nurse his health.

Having regained some strength, he then travelled to South America in early 1941, his future still uncertain. Would he study law? Or was there a life of teaching ahead of him, or perhaps, with a bestseller under his belt and his keen interest in international affairs, a career in journalism? But for now, his thoughts were on military service. Upon returning home, Jack learned that his brother, Joe Jr, had joined the US Navy's aviation cadet program. Not to be outdone, he immediately applied for the army's officer candidate school. He was rejected because of his back problems. Jack then tried the navy. They rejected him for the same reason. By the summer of 1941, willing as he was, Jack was contemplating going to Yale Law School for no other reason than that he could not yet find a way into the armed forces.

But with the help of his father and his contacts, as well as rigorous calisthenics to strengthen his back, Jack finally managed to get a clean bill of health and in September was commissioned as an ensign in the United States Naval Reserve. A few more strings were pulled and, on 27 October 1941, Jack reported for duty at the Foreign Intelligence Branch of the Office of Naval Intelligence in Washington DC. There he collected the latest reports from foreign stations and rewrote them in clear and accessible language for the office's daily and weekly bulletins.

Jack began his service just as events on the global stage were coming to a head. Not seeing a path between honour and survival, in the final months of 1941 Japan committed itself to war against the United States and the British empire. Admiral Isoroku Yamamoto, who knew America well, having hitchhiked across the country with his poker winnings while a young student at Harvard, apocryphally warned his government against 'awaking the sleeping giant'. But if they must, the commander-in-chief of the Combined Fleet advised, Japan must pre-emptively destroy the US Pacific Fleet or face swift destruction itself.

Yamamoto almost succeeded. Commencing just before 8 am on 7 December 1941 local time with the coded signal 'Tora, Tora, Tora', his airmen killed 2403 Americans, including sixty-eight civilians, and sent six battleships to the bottom of Pearl Harbor. It could have been even worse, but three aircraft carriers and their escorts were away from the base that day, patrolling the high seas. The last significant non-combatant had been dragged into conflict; it was now truly a world war.

CHAPTER 4

'AUSTRALIA LOOKS TO AMERICA'

'Pacific Ablaze', ran the banner headline in the Sydney *Sun*; 'Japs Bomb Singapore and U.S.A. Bases'. The news of Japanese attacks on Pearl Harbor and other targets across Asia and the Pacific broke in Australia on Monday morning, 8 December 1941. From the capital cities along the coast to the cattle stations in the great interior, Australians going to work that day confronted the nation's vulnerability. They were no longer simply conscientious citizens and dutiful soldiers called far away to assist the empire in its hour of need – they were now to be active participants in their own defence. They had skin in the game. Their home was in danger.

Addressing a rattled nation later that evening, Prime Minister John Curtin offered no false reassurance. Nor did he pull any punches: 'This is our darkest hour for the nation itself is imperilled.' With the Pacific Ocean 'reddened with the blood of Japan's victims', Curtin foreshadowed the aggressor's next steps: 'These wanton killings will be followed by attacks on the Netherlands East Indies, on the

Commonwealth of Australia and on the Dominion of New Zealand, if Japan gets its brutal way.'

He then asked Australians to stand and to fight. 'Men and women of Australia, the call is to you for your courage, your physical and mental ability, your inflexible determination that we as a free people shall survive. My appeal to you is in the name of Australia, for Australia is the stake in this contest.' Never an orator, though here with a nod to Lincoln and Churchill, the prime minister struck the right note. It was not one of hopelessness or even desperation, but command and resolution. Here was the man who could lead Australia through crisis to victory. Curtin had found his feet and commenced his climb into history.

He had also found a new ally, as a shocked Australia and the United States now moved with single purpose. Japanese aggression finally succeeded where common values, commerce and culture had previously failed. On 27 December, Curtin told his nation in a gloomy but determined New Year's address: 'Without any inhibitions of any kind, I make it quite clear that Australia looks to America, free of any pangs as to our traditional links or kinship with the United Kingdom.' Curtin's statement, wrote the eminent American historian of Australia, C Hartley Grattan, was 'the end of Australia's unswerving allegiance to the dying dogma of "the diplomatic unity of the British Empire"'. Frightened and fearful, Australians now turned their gaze to the east, across the vast ocean, hoping and praying for a new saviour.

*

On Sunday, 7 December, Jack Kennedy and his friend Lem Billings were playing touch football near the Washington Monument. As they were driving back to Kennedy's apartment, the news came over the car radio – the Japanese had attacked Pearl Harbor.

America was at war and Kennedy was now working the night shift from 10 pm to 7 am, seven days a week. To be sure, he was happy to finally be able to play his part. In some ways, as a bright, well-educated, well-travelled and well-connected young man, he was made for intelligence work. But he was not convinced that redrafting foreign reports and analysing data at a desk in Washington was quite what he wanted.

In the end, the decision was made for him. Kennedy was at the time in a relationship with Danish-born journalist and socialite Inga Arvad. Matters were a little complicated as Arvad was still married, though separated. But more than merely raising eyebrows in the straitlaced capital, the relationship soon started raising suspicions and concerns. Arvad had in the past enjoyed access to senior Nazis, attending Hermann Goering's wedding and being Hitler's guest at the 1936 Berlin Olympics. Fearing potential security headaches, in mid-January Kennedy's superiors transferred him to a desk job at the Charleston Naval Yard in South Carolina. If Washington seemed like a sideshow, this move was a clear case of 'two steps back'. Here, in 'Siberia' as naval officers referred to the posting, Kennedy was bored and, he believed, even more wasted and irrelevant. He needed more; he wanted action.

*

There was no panic among politicians in Washington or Canberra. War had been expected and at least now the battle lines were drawn. What came as a shock, however, was 'Japan's rapid, bold and extraordinary success', wrote Curtin's biographer, John Edwards. 'It was that – Japan's success – which would overturn Australia's understanding of the world.'

The Germans had shown the world 'blitzkrieg', but the Japanese were not to be outdone by their Axis partner. The emperor's armed forces moved with a speed that shocked the world and traumatised Australia, ably fulfilling the first part of Admiral Yamamoto's promise and prediction: 'In the first six to twelve months of a war with the United States and Great Britain, I will run wild and win victory upon victory. But then, if the war continues after that, I have no expectation of success.'

And run wild they did. Across a front stretching thousands of kilometres over land and sea, the Imperial Japanese Army and Navy in rapid succession struck targets as far afield as China, Thailand, Burma (now Myanmar), Malaya (now Malaysia), Borneo, Dutch East Indies (now Indonesia), the Philippines and the American-administered Pacific territories of Guam, Wake and Midway. By 23 December, the commander of the United States Army Forces in the Far East, General Douglas MacArthur, began his withdrawal from Manila into the jungle hinterland. On Christmas Day, the British garrison at Hong Kong surrendered, and on Boxing Day, Manila was declared an open city. It fell to the Japanese on 2 January 1942.

Two days later, Australian territory first came under attack when Japanese aircraft bombed Rabaul. Situated on the eastern end of the island of New Britain, Rabaul was the capital of the Territory of New Guinea, the former German colony, taken by Australia at the start of the First World War and now administered by Canberra under a League of Nations mandate. If Rabaul's fall at the end of January was sobering, it was soon overshadowed by an even more shocking debacle.

For nearly twenty years, Australian military doctrine had rested on the 'Singapore strategy' of forward defence, hinging on the ability of Britain's large naval and army base to intercept and repulse a southern thrust by Japanese forces. While some, including MacArthur, considered 'Fortress Singapore' impregnable, Winston Churchill (now the British prime minister) and his generals were no longer certain. Spooked by enemy advances, they gave serious consideration to evacuating troops and armaments. But Curtin would have none of it. He told Churchill that British withdrawal 'would be regarded here and elsewhere as an inexcusable betrayal'. To underscore Australia's seriousness, Curtin sent additional troops to bolster the Singapore garrison.

It didn't help. In the face of fierce bombardment, Allied troops surrendered on 15 February. It was a disaster, especially for Australia. Nearly 2000 Diggers were killed and 17 000 marched into captivity, where a third of them would later die. There could be no sugar-coating the defeat. Chastened, Curtin called it 'Australia's Dunkirk'. But with nary a single Australian soldier rescued, the comparison only held in as much as, in the prime minister's words, '[t]he fall of Dunkirk initiated the battle for Britain' and so now '[t]he fall of Singapore opens the battle for Australia'.

Curtin was right and sooner than he feared. Just four days after the fall of Singapore, Darwin was struck by Japanese bombers. It was the largest bombing attack in the Pacific since Pearl Harbor, killing at least 243 Australians and sinking or damaging more than half the naval and transport ships docked in the port. The first and the deadliest of more than a hundred attacks against Australian mainland targets, Darwin was followed in early March by an air raid on Broome, which killed another seventy people. At the same time, the first Japanese troops landed on the northern coast of New Guinea. Three months on, the war was now right on Australia's doorstep.

*

Reg Evans and his comrades in the 2/9th Field Regiment enjoyed a freezing but joyous Christmas in Aleppo, just over 500 kilometres from Bethlehem itself. City quartering had some benefits. Parts of another Australian unit, the 2/2nd Anti-Tank Regiment, were not so fortunate as they were stationed in the mountains east of Tripoli in northern Lebanon. 'It was an awful place', Gunner Bruce Eglington recalled, 'bleak, and that's when the snow came – by God it snowed! We were living in tents and at Christmas one part of the encampment completely disappeared under the snow. There was nothing else to do so a lot of us just got on the grog.'

Of all the Allies involved, Australia contributed the most troops to the Syria campaign. In some ways it was a sideshow to the more famous campaigns of the war, not least the one in north Africa, and it would be officially downplayed, since Winston Churchill thought it impolite to celebrate a victory over a recent ally. There was nothing minor about it for those who fought and bled there. They had done their duty and won the battle, but their job was now done.

The news of Pearl Harbor and the Japanese onslaught across Asia and the Pacific hit the Diggers in the Middle East and Africa particularly hard. Their home was in danger, and here they were, thousands of kilometres away, unable to help. They felt they should be in Australia, protecting their own country.

Around Tobruk, Italian aircraft dropped leaflets on the Australian positions, aiming to demoralise the Diggers. 'The Yanks are having a good time in your country. You?' asked one. 'These were greatly appreciated by Australians,' recalled one anonymous soldier, 'as they possessed a high souvenir value.' The Diggers were not concerned about the Americans in Australia, certainly not as much as the prospect of the Japanese in Australia. This, rather than the slow and steady build-up of US troops, was playing on their minds and sparking the desire to get back soon.

*

Australia, as John Curtin boldly proclaimed in his New Year message, now 'look[ed] to America' for the security that Britain could no longer provide. Australia first glimpsed a mighty America before the war through the lens of its cinema. Celluloid heroes perhaps, but Australians now hoped the American sheriff would indeed ride to their rescue.

On 1 January 1942, Australia, the United States and twenty-four other countries signed the Declaration by

United Nations, promising to make no separate peace and use all their resources to defeat the Axis powers. From that day on, in war and in peace, Australia and the United States were bound ever more closely by common interests, shared values and mutual dependence. The wariness, the indifference, and the ignorance that characterised the past evaporated as Japan marched to build an empire in Asia and the Pacific.

It wasn't just a one-way street. If Australia needed America's protection, America, as Roosevelt recognised, also needed Australia's strategic location at the foot of south-east Asia. Even before Pearl Harbor, America's military were aware of Australia's value as a base for personnel, equipment and communications in the south-west Pacific. Plans had been made and funds allocated for military infrastructure, especially airfields, in northern Australia. Darwin seemed an ideal staging post for troops and supplies to the Philippines in the event of Japanese aggression. Australia was clearly the best place from which to launch a counter-offensive. We were glad to be of mutually beneficial use.

Back in late November 1941, two US naval transports left San Francisco bound for the Philippines. On their way to reinforce America's military presence on the islands, they rendezvoused in Honolulu with five other transport ships and two escorts including the heavy cruiser, USS *Pensacola*. They carried a brigade of 2000 troops of the US Field Artillery Corps, with all their weapons and materiel, as well as 2700 men of the US Army Air Force, including nearly one hundred pilots and seventy aircraft disassembled in crates. It would have been a significant addition to General MacArthur's forces.

But en route to the Philippines the convoy received word that Pearl Harbor had been attacked by Japan. The news soon got worse: Malaya, Hong Kong and the Philippines too were all under attack. The *Pensacola* convoy, its white navy ships quickly repainted battleship-grey by the crew, circled the mid-Pacific Ocean and waited for orders on where to proceed. Finally, on 12 December, the announcement came: their new destination was Brisbane, Australia. The crew aboard the transport ship *Republic*, reported US Army Captain Howard L Steffy, were stunned and confused: no one had heard of it or knew where it was. It might as well have been the dark side of the moon. 'God created war so that Americans would learn geography,' Mark Twain once quipped. Perhaps he was right.

On 22 December 1941, with relief rather than fanfare, the convoy docked at Bretts Wharf and Newstead Wharf in Brisbane. The first 4700 US servicemen of the war had arrived in Australia, albeit by an accident of circumstance rather than as planned reinforcements. The locals were delighted regardless. And while they tried hard to show their appreciation, cultural sensitivities were inadvertently trodden on. Second-Lieutenant Mark Muller from Kentucky recalled that 'The [Australian] band played "While We Were Marching Through Georgia", a Union victory song from the Civil War.' Commemorating as it did General Sherman's scorched-earth punishment of a rebel state, 'Anyone on board from the South who heard that song would not have thought it appropriate.'

Southerners or Northerners, to Australians they were already all 'Yanks'. Not that the Americans had a mind to care. 'We had been on board that long that we were down to one meal a day', Muller recalled. 'There was nothing left. We were broke and dirty.' Soon they were fed and sheltered, though under improvised conditions, the Australian side caught unprepared for the sudden influx. While the senior officers went to the pride of Brisbane's accommodation, the new Lennons Hotel on Queen Street in the heart of the Central Business District, most troops ended up bivouacking at the local racecourses, Doomben and Ascot (now Eagle Farm). 'You grow rice here?' asked one American confused by the local accent. 'Nah, mate, we run bloody ricehorses 'ere'.

After a few days, Seaman 2nd class John Leeman and some friends were finally allowed to walk into the city:

> We knew nothing of this place. It was like from
> another world. Houses on stumps with red roofs.
> Cable cars in the middle of the roads; the Aussies
> call them trams. The city looked sort of empty and
> quiet. There were plenty of hotels and movie theatres,
> but nothing was open. It was a Sunday, the day after
> Boxing Day, but it was so quiet.

The press were not allowed to report on the presence of American servicemen, though everyone was happy to be hosting the men they hoped would protect Australia from the Japanese. Elizabeth Harland, who had been widowed young after her RAAF pilot husband had been killed over Germany, was typical in her gratitude: 'I remember looking at those ships and the men on them and thinking that we have been saved. I thought "Thank God for the Yanks".' As for the Americans, they might not have known much (if anything) about Australia but were delighted by the warmth of their welcome. Young men from across the United States – farmers, foremen, clerks, factory workers, even priests – sailed across the Pacific to a far-off land. For nearly all of them this was their first time outside of America; for many, the first time outside their state. If not quite as exotic as their intended destination, the Philippines, it was nevertheless still different and a bit strange. And the *Pensacola* convoy was only the vanguard. Soon there would be many more. America and Australia were about to discover each other, and not a moment too soon.

CHAPTER 5

'OUR DARKEST HOUR'

With Japanese troops in northern New Guinea, a mere 700 kilometres from the tip of Cape York and even closer to the Torres Strait Islands, Australia lay virtually defenceless.

True, in the days after the bombing of Pearl Harbor recruiting depots were overwhelmed as men and women sought to join up and defend their homeland. But they would take months to arm and train. In the meantime, the civilian population was thrown into frantic and desperate preparations: children were evacuated to the countryside – 'bomb dodging', as it was called – schools closed, bomb shelters built, buildings sandbagged, and trenches dug in suburban backyards. The invader advancing across Australia would find only a wasteland. Pre-war plans envisaged the destruction of military assets such as airstrips, fuel depots and munitions dumps, but now any potentially useful private property would also be denied to the Japanese. Domestic water tanks were to be drained, crops burned, and any useful machinery evacuated or, failing that, disabled. The times were dire; every Australian would play their part. 'Total war, total citizen collaboration' was the motto.

Not surprisingly, the atmosphere throughout the country was fraught. 'There was more than a touch of panic in the Sydney air', reported the *Bulletin*. And Sydney was far away from the likely Japanese landing sites. When Labor minister and firebrand Eddie Ward claimed in October 1942 that the previous Menzies government had proposed the 'Brisbane Line' to abandon Australia north of Brisbane in the event of a Japanese invasion, he was readily believed. Even after the claims were later examined by a royal commission and dismissed, it didn't matter. The 'Brisbane Line' remains part of Australia's war mythology. Many, perhaps most, Australians were so traumatised at the time by the prospect of imminent invasion, they were inclined to believe the worst. Such a policy made tough sense.

Ceding ground to the enemy was a desperate, though arguably inevitable, tactic. So was destroying the countryside to deny its benefits to the Japanese invader. Far better, of course, if Australia could be successfully defended instead. That was certainly the official intention. 'There will still be Australians fighting on Australian soil,' Curtin told the nation in a radio broadcast on 14 March 1942, 'until the turning point be reached, and we will advance over blackened ruins, through blasted and fire-swept cities, across scorched plains, until we drive the enemy into the sea.' Warning of 'dark and evil days' ahead, Deputy Prime Minister Frank Forde likewise promised that even if Newcastle became 'another Tobruk' and Sydney an 'unconquerable Leningrad', Australians would eventually prevail. Forde was an optimist; unlike Newcastle, the distant Tobruk at least had Australian troops defending it.

For Australia, the deal had always been that it would

fight Britain's wars, even if not under threat itself (the First World War being the best, or the worst, example of this) on the understanding that Britain would come to Australia's aid if it were threatened. A country with a small population and limited resources had no better options. But it left Australia exposed. As a US minister (an ambassador), Clarence E Gauss, reported to Washington more than a year before the outbreak of general war in Asia, 'It can truthfully be said that Australia has weakened her own defences and security for the empire cause in a measure, which unless rapidly repaired, holds the possibility of serious consequences.' Throughout 1940 and 1941, Australian troops fought well, often valiantly, in the Middle East, North Africa, Greece and Crete. There were few trained soldiers left to defend Australia.

Now, with Japan on the march, Curtin wasted no time insisting that two of the three 2nd AIF divisions return immediately home from overseas. Churchill would have liked to see the Australian troops go to Burma instead, to reinforce the British and the Indian units, hard-pressed by the Japanese invader. The two leaders exchanged terse cables. Churchill eventually relented, if not before one last attempt, mid-Indian Ocean, to divert Australian transport ships with the AIF to Asia. It failed. The Diggers were finally coming home.

*

On 7 February, Reg Evans' regiment left Aleppo in convoy moving quickly south. By 10 February the unit arrived in Khassa, in Palestine, just south of Tel Aviv. Here they soon learned that Singapore had fallen. It only increased their desire to return to Australia. But no one was sure. Rumours spread. One day the 2/9th might believe they were heading for India or Burma – which they would have, if Churchill got his way – and the next, Java or 'Home'. Preparations were made to depart but Reg and his mates were not quite sure to where.

On 11 March the regiment made for the coast and boarded the USS *Westpoint*. Like the RMS *Queen Elizabeth*, which brought them to the Middle East the year before, USS *Westpoint* was built as an ocean liner and cruise ship, the SS *America*, but in May 1941 was called in to service as a troop carrier and re-christened. Before it picked up Evans' unit, USS *Westpoint* had already made an emergency landing in Singapore amid Japanese bombing to evacuate troops and civilians, before quickly departing on 30 January 1942, just days before Japanese troops entered the city. Now the USS *Westpoint* was sailing back to Asia with the 2/9th. But where exactly were they going? Evans and his mates still did not know. Rumours started again but were quickly killed. To their immense relief they were told they were returning to Australia.

Unescorted, the USS *Westpoint* sailed quickly south and arrived in Fremantle on 25 March and then Port Adelaide on 30 March. The people of Adelaide were at the wharf to welcome them home and cheer them on to their journey by rail to camp at Angaston. 'Grim-faced, war-scarred veterans', wrote one South Australian newspaper, 'were stirringly welcomed in the hour of Australia's greatest peril.' 'They were not conquerors, returning, their days of danger and campaigning passed, to spend their time in peaceful ease and relaxation, in full enjoyment of the hard-earned joys of victory', reflected one anonymous returnee. 'Victors, yes, but for them was the realisation of tasks ahead, of brief respite with their families and loved ones, before they again took up the fight – against a new foe – the end of which alone could bring them home to stay.'

And while their return was a good start, a couple of AIF divisions would not be enough to defend Australia. In early 1942, only one other country in the world had sufficient firepower to do so. Fortunately, the Americans were willing and able – and they were now on their way.

*

The man who would lead them was General Douglas MacArthur.

Under orders from President Roosevelt to leave the Philippines for Australia, MacArthur left his headquarters on Corregidor Island after sunset on 11 March, the same day Evans and his unit departed the Middle East for home. With typical drama, MacArthur, accompanied by his family and staff, sped across stormy seas in four mahogany-hulled PT boats, for two days dodging the Japanese along the way. MacArthur and his family travelled in PT-41, commanded by Lieutenant John Bulkeley, later awarded the Congressional Medal of Honor for his bravery and soon to meet Joe Kennedy Sr and his son, Ensign John F Kennedy. It was the daring escape of MacArthur and his entourage that gave these small, swift craft a high profile and great glamour, especially among naval recruits.

Travelling by sea, air and then, eventually, land, MacArthur arrived in the Victorian capital on 21 March. 'As the train pulled into Melbourne, cheering thousands lined the streets in a tumultuous welcome,' he recalled later:

> But heartening as the welcome was, it did not disguise
> the fact that a sense of dangerous defeatism had seized
> upon a large segment of Australia's 7,000,000 people.
> The primary problem was to replace the pessimism
> of failure with the inspiration of success. What the
> Australians needed was a strategy that held out the
> promise of victory.

MacArthur's promise to the Philippines, 'I shall return', made earlier at Terowie Railway Station in South Australia, was itself a declaration of confidence and commitment to Australia that the war would eventually be won. But it would be a long haul. MacArthur hardly slept onboard the train. Informed there were only 20000 American troops in Australia so far, he paced up and down, contemplating the challenges ahead. There would not be a counter-offensive any time soon. Manila was a long way away.

MacArthur, at sixty-two still tall and slim, and with his trademark aviator sunglasses, non-regulation cap and corncob pipe, had star quality. In turn vain, brilliant and baffling, he was a deeply polarising figure. Some went as far as to compare him with Alexander the Great – with Alexander coming a poor second. MacArthur himself, never short of self-regard, likely agreed. Australians had never seen anything like it. They were captivated by his charisma and bearing. More than anyone, MacArthur became a symbol of the American people's optimism and spirit. Even before any victories had been won against the Japanese, he projected confidence and determination that, in the end, the Allies would win. Followers, both official American ones and an informal retinue of Australian admirers, soon congregated, like moths to the flame of hope, wherever MacArthur ventured. To a country which viewed the United States primarily through the distorted lens of a movie camera, MacArthur, with his love of the limelight and a sense of the theatrical and dramatic, assumed the role of a lifetime: the star of the Pacific war. Part leading man, part prima donna, he was that and more, embodying the good, the bad, and the larger-than-life of Hollywood's imagined America. It was his show and the Allies fought it on his terms.

As Supreme Commander of Allied Forces in the Southwest Pacific Area, MacArthur also assumed command of Australian troops. General Sir Thomas Blamey was named Commander of Allied Land Forces but in name only, as MacArthur prevented him from commanding any American troops. He was far from the only Australian feeling somewhat left out. MacArthur surrounded himself with his US Army subordinates from the Philippines, dubbed the 'Bataan gang', refusing repeated requests from his superiors in the United States to include senior Allied staff, particularly Australians and Dutch military evacuees from their colonial possessions in the East Indies (present-day Indonesia).

While tensions between the 'Yanks' and the locals, cast to the shadows in MacArthur's glare, would continue to plague the senior echelons throughout the war, there was one notable exception. A few days after arriving in Australia, MacArthur drove to Canberra and met with Prime Minister Curtin. MacArthur recalled, 'I put my arm about his strong shoulder. "Mr Prime Minister", I said, "we two, you and I, will see this thing through together. We can do it and we will do it. You take care of the rear and I will handle the front".' Despite their widely differing temperaments (and political leanings), the general and the prime minister developed a genuinely warm personal relationship.

*

Time in Charleston was not a complete waste for Jack Kennedy. He had plenty of opportunity to ruminate.

In February 1942, his father passed on to him a letter from Clare Boothe Luce, prominent writer and public figure married to the Time-Life publishing mogul Henry Luce, in which she set out her thoughts about the likely progress and conduct of conflict around the world. It gave Kennedy plenty of food for thought. He was struggling to understand the war and how the United States might get through it. His earlier youthful optimism, perhaps naivety, had long evaporated. He no longer echoed his father's old isolationist and defeatist views. Jack knew America had to fight to win the war, not just for Europe's sake – or Asia's, for that matter – but for its own. The country itself and its values were under threat. 'When at long last we realize that what we are fighting for is self-preservation … then and only then, far out on the horizon, will victory be in sight,' Jack wrote in a 'memorandum to self'. Reflecting on Boothe Luce's letter, it explored his own assessment of America's and the democratic world's prospects. For a young man of twenty-four, his view of the horizon was mature if bleak. Jack was not confident, believing 'gloomy alternatives' might soon face the Allies.

Acknowledging that Americans had 'invulnerability bred in their bones by centuries of security behind the broad expanse of the Atlantic and Pacific Oceans', Jack was particularly concerned about the Japanese threat in Asia and the Pacific. 'We could stand up against Pan-Germanism in Europe – a movement which would probably fall apart under three years of peace – but a Pan-Asiatic movement led by militant Japan would be a different story. With the Japs in the driver's seat, the sleepy giant that is Asia would be stirred.' With eerie foreboding Jack prophesied, 'The Japanese themselves would have more than enough to keep them busy, developing Malaysia, the East Indies, the Philippines and Australia.'

As Jack wrote these words in mid-February 1942, the Japanese had taken the first three and the fourth was under direct threat. With Rabaul fallen and Darwin bombed, the 'Battle for Australia' had begun, and few, including Jack Kennedy and John Curtin, were certain that Australia would prevail.

*

The next seven months proved crucial. Between May and September 1942, several battles were fought, on land and at sea, which decided Australia's fate. It was a close-run race.

Soon after the Japanese landed in northern New Guinea in early March, they set their sights on Port Moresby, the capital of the Territory of Papua (now part of Papua New Guinea), on the island's southern coast. Formerly a British colony, Papua was administered by Australia since the beginning of the century, being considered an external territory of the Commonwealth (in contrast to an Australian mandate over the Territory of New Guinea). Only 550 kilometres from Australia's mainland, from Port

Moresby's crucial airstrip Australia's coastline would become ever more vulnerable to Japanese bombers.

There were three possible ways to attack Port Moresby. First, a naval attack through the Coral Sea. Second, by land, over the forbidding Owen Stanley Range or, third, along the eastern coast, past the Australian-held Milne Bay. The Japanese first tried the sea route. As the main convoy with thousands of troops onboard headed south from Rabaul, other Japanese forces sought to eject the Australians and British from Tulagi, the capital of the British Solomon Islands Protectorate. Controlling the Solomons would help disrupt supply and communication lanes between the United States and Australia. Isolated and deprived of American assistance, Australia would be ripe for invasion. But even if not invaded, it would still be rendered useless to America as a staging post for the Pacific war. Either way, Australia would become irrelevant to the war.

Having broken some of the Japanese secret naval codes, the Americans were pre-warned of the enemy's plans, and positioned their forces accordingly. Over the course of several days, Japanese and American flotillas clashed across the expanse of the Coral Sea, with the fighting at times taking place only about 1000 kilometres from the Australian coast. For the first time in naval warfare, the opposing ships never sighted one another, relying on aircraft to attack the enemy.

While the outcome was inconclusive, both Japan and the United States claimed victory, and not without some justification. The Japanese did succeed in taking Tulagi, with Britain's resident commissioner and a small detachment of Australian soldiers fleeing before their arrival on 3 May, but unsure of American strength and lacking sufficient air cover

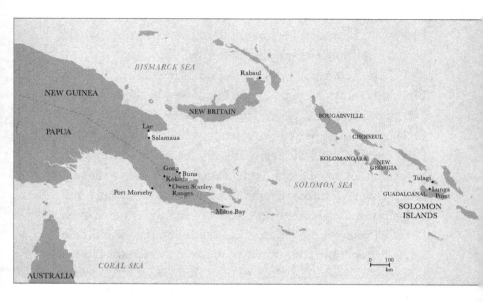

The south-west Pacific theatre of war, 1942–45

the Port Moresby–bound convoy hesitated and the invasion force turned around. After nearly six months of total dominance, the Imperial Japanese Navy failed to achieve their objective. For Japan, it was the first strategic setback of the war. Most importantly, the Battle of the Coral Sea weakened the Japanese fleet at the worst possible time, just a month before the decisive naval engagement of the Pacific war, the Battle of Midway.

The Midway Atoll was a critical strategic outpost for the United States, just 1800 kilometres to the north-west of Pearl Harbor, and as its name suggests, halfway between North Asia and North America. If the Japanese were successful in taking it, reasoned General MacArthur, 'it will be followed by mopping up operations against the islands ... on the line of communication between Australia and Hawaii, in order to isolate Australia from America'.

With so much at stake, the Americans were well prepared and waiting, warned once again by their code breakers. At about 10.30 am local time on 4 June, dive bombers from the US carriers *Yorktown* and the *Enterprise* sighted the Japanese fleet. It was all over in a flash: six bloody minutes ultimately decided the outcome of the Pacific war. Three heavy Japanese carriers sustained lethal hits and soon a fourth, the *Hiryu*, Rear Admiral Yamaguchi's flagship, was ablaze. Yamaguchi, in time-honoured fashion, went down with his ship, a fitting end to a warrior who had commanded forces to bomb Pearl Harbor and Darwin, and was an early enthusiast for invading Australia.

The Imperial Navy never recovered from the disaster; it was still large and formidable, but the days of extending dominion in the south-west Pacific were over. After Midway, Japan was increasingly forced on the defensive. Plans to attack New Caledonia, Fiji and Samoa were scrapped. By 11 June 1942, MacArthur could tell Curtin that 'The security of Australia has now been assured.' We had survived 'our darkest hour'. But the war was far from over. As long as Japan retained a powerful army, no matter what MacArthur thought, the threat to Australia remained.

With the seaborne invasion of Port Moresby turned back on the Coral Sea, Japan would be forced to take the city by land. The Japanese first tried the much shorter and more direct, but also significantly more strenuous route, over the mountains of the Owen Stanley Range. There, along a

single-file trail known to Australians as the Kokoda Track
and to the Japanese as the 'path of infinite sorrow', the two
forces struggled for two months in appalling conditions.

By mid-September, the Japanese had reached ridges
within sight of Port Moresby and were only 30 kilometres
from the city's airfield. But they too were now exhausted and
running low on supplies. Like the apocryphal Wehrmacht
scouts at the outskirts of Moscow who glimpsed the Kremlin
through their field glasses only a few months earlier, the
Japanese had reached their limit and the Australians now
began to push them over the mountains back to their north
coast strongholds of Buna, Gona and Sanananda.

*

After regrouping and awaiting the arrival of their equipment in South Australia, the 2/9th Field Regiment moved
to Arakoon, near Esk in south-east Queensland. Then in
September, they moved again, this time under great secrecy
to Buderim and Maroochydore on the Sunshine Coast, just
to the north of Brisbane.

A total of 1458 men passed through the 2/9th Field
Regiment during its service. Its official history notes with
pride that 'No less than fifty-eight men who joined the Unit
as gunners in the ranks, either gained their commissions in
the Regiment or on transfer to other units – three of them in
the RAN.' Reg Evans was one of them. While life was good
for the regiment on the Sunshine Coast, Warrant Officer
Class 2 Arthur Reginald Evans had had enough of the
artillery. In October he was discharged from the 2nd AIF
and applied to join the navy.

As for the 2/9th Field Regiment, it was subsequently

split up. Of its three artillery batteries, two were sent in mid-1943 to the south coast of Dutch New Guinea (now Indonesian West Papua) to be part of Merauke Force, composed of Australian, Dutch and American troops. The third battery was sent to Cape York. In late 1944, all three batteries re-joined back in Australia. But opportunities were limited for artillery in jungle warfare. The army units now fighting in the Pacific tended to be lighter, smaller and nimbler, preferring not to struggle through tropical terrain weighed down with heavy artillery. The 2/9th Field Regiment ended up stationed on the Atherton Tablelands in far north Queensland and remained there until the end of the war.

Roden Cutler's 2/5th, which fought briefly alongside Evans' 2/9th in the Lebanon and Syria campaign, went on to serve with distinction in Papua at Milne Bay and later Buna-Gona, before their final campaign in Borneo in 1945. By then, Lieutenant Cutler had long gone. He was awarded the Victoria Cross in November 1941 for 'most conspicuous and sustained gallantry during the Syrian Campaign' and was medically discharged in 1942. He later became the longest-serving governor of New South Wales. With hindsight, Evans had chosen a good time to leave his unit. He wanted to see more action, and the 2/9th's garrison duties would have bored him. It was time to test whether he could realise his dream of returning to the sea.

*

All throughout 1942, the Japanese were hedging their strategic bets, pursuing a two-pronged offensive – one in New Guinea, the other in the Solomons – both with the same essential objective: to isolate Australia and thus render it useless for the Americans as their base and launching pad for the eventual counter-attack. The key to supremacy in Solomon Islands was the largest island of Guadalcanal – codenamed CACTUS by the Allies – some 40 kilometres south of the protectorate's capital at Tulagi.

A few months into their occupation, Japanese engineers surveyed an area of relatively flat land on Guadalcanal's north coast for use as an airstrip. They called it 'Lunga Point'. In early July, the Japanese began to build the airfield, using forced labourers from Korea. A major airbase on Guadalcanal would not only give the Japanese command of the skies over the entire archipelago but also the ability to menace Allied bases from Papua New Guinea in the west to New Hebrides and New Caledonia to the south-east.

As construction progressed steadily through July and into August, the Japanese were convinced their work was well hidden from the enemy. The Allies would suffer a nasty surprise once bombs from Guadalcanal-based planes started raining down on their positions and sea traffic all over the south-west Pacific.

What the Japanese did not count on was the Allies' secret weapon: an Australian espionage network, with agents scattered through the region, covertly monitoring and reporting back on their every move.

CHAPTER 6

COAST WATCHERS

Australians had long worried that their vast northern coastline was unwatched and unguarded. Eventually, after the Great War, the Royal Australian Navy created a body of trained volunteer observers to warn of hostile intrusions. By the beginning of the Second World War, the Coast Watcher Organisation had grown to about 800 members, stationed principally on the mainland, but also well established on Australia's forward approaches throughout Melanesia. They were all civilians, though directed by the navy's intelligence division. With the Japanese threat looming over the horizon, Lieutenant-Commander Eric Feldt was given the task of extending coast watching operations in New Guinea and Solomon Islands to better warn Australia of impending attack and to gather intelligence for use against any enemy. By the end of 1941, they were in place.

During the war, some 100 coast watcher stations dotted Australia's sea approaches, their work coordinated by four control stations at Port Moresby, Rabaul, Tulagi and Vila in New Hebrides, and ultimately the organisation's headquarters at Townsville. The job of the coast watcher was first and foremost to gather intelligence. From their jungle vantage points, on mountainsides or in tree houses, they observed and reported by radio enemy aircraft and shipping movements. It was vital work. More than once, a lonely coast watcher in island jungle tapping a message, then relaying the signal to Allied command, changed the likely result of Pacific battles.

The other job was to rescue Allied servicemen who found themselves behind enemy lines in the islands. Coast watchers and Islander scouts working alongside them would seek to locate Allied pilots and sailors who had been downed or sunk and assist them back to the safety of their own lines. By the end of the war, they had rescued seventy-five prisoners of war, 321 downed airmen, 280 sailors, and 190 missionaries and civilians, as well as hundreds of local people and others who had risked their lives for the coast watchers and the Allies. At Choiseul Island, east of Bougainville, coast watchers issued every saved airman with a certificate of membership for the 'Rubber Rafters Association', the only condition being a promise to get drunk every year on the anniversary of their rescue. Many, no doubt, did.

Coast watchers were chosen because they knew the islands and the people, including some native language or Pidgin. Historian John Fahey described them, perhaps a tad unkindly, as mostly 'dislocated "chancers" living in remote places'. Be that as it may, they were just the right people for the job. They were at home in Melanesia; this was their turf. They would not have been able to survive otherwise. As Feldt noted, 'It is easier to teach a man how to operate a teleradio or shoot a submachine gun than to teach him how to live in the jungle.' No novices to the often inhospitable terrain, harsh weather and dangerous environment, coast watchers had before the war worked in the islands' colonial administration, on plantations or in the mines. Some were even men of God, but all had faith in their own ability to help defend Australia.

They were a special breed. They were volunteers, all of them. No one was forced or conscripted to serve as a coast watcher. As the Japanese approached and occupied islands throughout early 1942, most of the Westerners, both military and civilians, were evacuated or fled. The coast watchers stayed behind and stayed put. With the Japanese seemingly unstoppable, they did not know when, if ever, they might be able to leave their posts. What they did know was that if anything went wrong, there was little chance of rescue. If they were caught, as some indeed were, their death would be certain but not necessarily quick – as civilians, they were considered spies by the Japanese. In the faint hope that it might offer some protection, from March 1942 the Royal Australian Navy began to offer coast watchers rank, as well as sending in enlisted Navy personnel to help. It had little impact on the Japanese treatment of such prisoners.

No wonder that a coast watching candidate, after learning of the dangers and the hardships awaiting him, asked Lieutenant-Commander Feldt, 'Are there any special benefits that go with this duty?' 'No', answered Feldt, 'the only thing I can promise you is the promise of certain peril.' Yet Jim Burrowes, who signed up at eighteen in January 1942, recalled, 'Never for a minute was I really scared.' It was 'just excitement and fun. Nothing's going to happen to me', he thought. The bravado, if not naive confidence of youth. Yet the Japanese hunted, chased and harassed coast watchers.

Beheading was a common punishment – after torture. The enemy killed thirty-six coast watchers during the war. 'They watched and warned and died that we might live', reads the plaque on a lighthouse erected in their memory at Madang in Papua New Guinea.

The local Melanesian scouts were essential to the task of coast watching. Every coast watcher knew they could not do their job without the Islanders' support and loyalty. The equipment itself – the radio transmitter and receiver weighing around 150 kilograms, plus batteries, the charging engine, and fuel – took a dozen or more local porters to carry through the jungle to the best vantage points. The scouts also kept a lookout for the enemy and were an indispensable link between coast watchers and the local population, obtaining food as well as valuable intelligence. 'All this hazardous and highly-skilled work', wrote the coast watcher Dick Horton, 'was carried out by the islanders using their initiative and canoes, working in conditions of extreme danger and difficulty, asking nothing and knowing that if they were caught they would be tortured and killed.'

In New Guinea, the vast majority of the population remained loyal to the Allies, despite Japanese bribery and fear of reprisals. In Solomon Islands there was not one recorded instance of a coast watcher betrayed by the Islanders. As Feldt observed of coast watcher work, 'it would be impossible to conduct such operations if the natives favoured the enemy'.

Indeed, much has been made in wartime accounts of Solomon Islanders' loyalty to the Allied cause. But Solomon Islander historian, Anna Kwai, argues that Islanders were not simply blindly 'loyal helpers'. Curiosity and adventure as well as wages, food, propaganda and simply fear all played a part in securing Islander support in the course of what they called 'the Big Death'. 'The Second World War was not our war,' wrote former Solomon Islands prime minister, Sir Peter Kenilorea. But in war the Islanders had found themselves nevertheless, caught between their old white colonial masters and new Asian occupiers. For most Islanders, contact with British colonial overlords had always been slight. Indigenous life continued as it had always, with fishing and farming the mainstays. The arrival of the Japanese at first meant little. Most Islanders, wrote Walter Lord, 'had no conception of nationality, and terms like "Japan" and "America" meant nothing. Both sides were "white", with the Japanese the "new whites"'.

For many years nearly all study of the Solomons campaign was from the Allied perspective, with very little from the Japanese. From the mid-1980s, the oral recollections of Solomon Islanders were recorded, though are not easily available. And even then, few accounts mention the perspectives and experiences of Islander women. What is clear is that the Islanders' relations with Allied servicemen, primarily American (both black and white) soldiers, differed sharply from their pre-war relations with colonial authorities. Americans frowned on British (and other) colonialism but were haunted by their own racist demons at home. For the Islanders, awareness of inequality and race relations were heightened, the experience in time paving the way for challenges to colonial rule.

The scouts, therefore, often trod a fine line. While some were members of the local colonial police force, most were civilians, and all volunteers. Their bravery was unquestioned.

They were vulnerable to capture, torture and death if suspected of aiding the Allied forces. But in some ways their peril was even worse and their bravery even greater. Their family or even their whole village might be threatened with torture or execution too. For coast watchers their work was dangerous for them personally; for scouts, like the partisans and the underground workers in occupied Europe, it was dangerous to everyone they knew.

Given the tough and fraught nature of work behind enemy lines, it is not surprising that the coast watchers were all men, though with one notable exception: the formidable Ruby Olive Boye on inaccessible Vanikoro Island in the Solomons. Her story well illustrates the precariousness, the vicissitudes, and risks as well as triumphs of coast watching. Sydney-born Boye initially took over on temporary duty as a weather reporter, but she quickly learned to operate the teleradio when its male operator left the island. The Coast Watch Organisation chose not to send a replacement, and so she stayed on with her husband, the manager at the Kauri Timber Company, after all other foreign staff were evacuated. 'She always sounded so cheerful and imperturbable', recalled legendary coast watcher Martin Clemens, 'that it did one good to hear her'.

A Japanese officer soon singled out Boye by name in a radio message telling her to 'get out'. She ignored the warning. An American ship stopped in to visit and advised her to use Morse code only, which she did from then on. Boye went on to relay a vital coded signal during the Battle of the Coral Sea and, later, other important messages from Guadalcanal coast watchers. She regularly reported local intelligence to the US naval base in New Hebrides. In recognition of her efforts and bravery she was visited by two US Navy admirals, William Halsey and Aubrey Fitch. Halsey ordered her to evacuate when she developed shingles, but she returned to duty as soon as she could. Long after the war, Boye recalled 'with fond memories' all her 'American friends'.

Coast watchers like Boye were cool characters. They were not, initially at least, meant to be soldiers or guerrillas. As such, their courage was not the kind required to fix a bayonet and charge. It was rarer. To live every day with the tension of uncertainty. To know that your life depended on the loyalty of the locals. To fall asleep and not know if, under cover of darkness, the enemy was silently stalking. 'My God, I was afraid', recalled Martin Clemens. 'I dared not go to sleep, not merely because I thought they might come and catch me unawares but also because I knew I would dream that they had, and the one state was worse than the other.'

In a playful allusion to their hands-off, quiet and covert role in the conflict, the Coast Watcher Organisation was code-named 'Ferdinand', after the placid bull in a popular pre-war children's book who preferred to smell flowers rather than fight the matador. Yet in real life there was nothing fairytale about the coast watchers' lives; the Japanese matadors were indeed after them, deadly and deadly serious, for far from being a harmless irritant the coast watchers often proved to be formidable opponents, trashing their best-laid plans.

*

Reg Evans' time in the arid Levant had not diminished his taste for the sea, and when he applied to join the Royal Australian Navy in October 1942, it turned out to be third time lucky. 'They weren't so fussy this time', Evans later reflected. He was not the only one making a switch between the services. At Flinders Naval Base on the Mornington Peninsula, south of Melbourne, where he trained, they were 'teaching rough Army types how to be Naval gents', he recalled. He was never rough nor would he ever quite be a gent, but he was finally in his element.

Then he got lucky again.

Walter Brooksbank, civil assistant to the director of naval intelligence, sent for Evans. The gnomish Brooksbank, a Gallipoli veteran, was a cultured man. He was a poet and short story writer, and later wrote plays for ABC radio. He was also fond of detail and, having thoroughly checked Evans' background, told him that he was exactly the type of man the Navy was seeking for special operations. If Evans was interested, there was a job going in the Coast Watcher Organisation. Evans had never heard of it, but it seemed right up his alley.

Evans soon met with Commander Rupert 'Cocky' Long, director of Naval Intelligence. Long was a brilliant, stocky, chain-smoking intelligence officer, described by his biographer as 'the intrigue master'. It was Long who, upon his appointment to Naval Intelligence in 1936, tasked Lieutenant-Commander Eric Feldt with strengthening the coast watcher network in the islands to Australia's north. 'The Coast Watching [sic] Organization' wrote Evans, was Long's 'baby'. There were many others, including the Special Intelligence Bureau that Long founded to help break

Japanese codes. Admiral Halsey later described him as 'the best-informed man on intelligence matters in this part of the world'. He was not yet a legend, but his reputation was growing.

As Evans later explained his new role: 'A Coast Watcher's work was not to fight or destroy. His job was to look and listen and gather information; to sit in hiding like a spider, right in the web of the enemy, but unseen and unheard. His duty was to communicate intelligence to headquarters and leave the rest to them.' It sounded intriguing and, more importantly, Evans would be back where he loved best: the islands of Melanesia. He yearned to be, as he saw it, 'the eyes and ears of the Pacific'. He was in.

*

The first months of 1942 saw Jack Kennedy inching closer to active service in his chosen branch, the US Navy. But it was not all smooth sailing. He found his time working in the 'Siberia' of the Charleston Naval Yard in South Carolina immensely frustrating. Worse, his back was playing up again. By April 1942 it was so bad that he was declared unfit for duty and soon sent to the naval hospital in Chelsea, Massachusetts, for evaluation and treatment. Whatever the doctors did seemed to work and Kennedy was declared fit again in late June. By July he was finally granted his request for sea duty and was attending the midshipmen's school at a branch of Northwestern University in Chicago where the navy was now fast producing junior naval officers for combat. They called them 'sixty-day wonders'. Kennedy badly wanted to see action and this was the quickest way to get it. He was 'overjoyed' when he was accepted.

More than anything, Kennedy wanted to captain a motor torpedo boat. After their starring role in General MacArthur's evacuation from the Philippines, PT boats (short for 'patrol-torpedo') were all the rage in 1942. Offering an opportunity for command, active (and dangerous) service as well as no shortage of glamour, competition among Kennedy's fellow junior officers was fierce: more than 1000 applied for just fifty spots available in a specialist eight-week training course at Rhode Island in September 1942. He got in.

The training was basic. Although they were future commanders of Patrol Torpedo boats, the officer trainees never even fired a torpedo in practice. None would until combat. Given the torpedoes were the PT boat's main weapon, the training provided was grossly inadequate. Instead, they spent much time learning about boat handling and maintenance of engines, torpedoes and radios. Jack Kennedy just wanted it over. Years of sailing off Cape Cod had made him comfortable on the water and he was confident he would make a good skipper. He wrote to his friend Lem Billings that 'this job on these boats is really the great spot of the Navy, you are your own boss, and it's like sailing around as in the old days'. In October, Kennedy was promoted to lieutenant junior grade. The dream of leading a boat in combat was nearly within his grasp.

*

On the evening of 6 August 1942, Japanese troops and Korean labourers at Lunga Point on Guadalcanal were given extra saké as a reward for completing the vital new airstrip ahead of schedule.

From his eyrie in the nearby mountains, Martin Clemens knew something was up. Scottish-born Clemens joined the Colonial Service in 1938 when he was twenty-three years old, and was posted to Solomon Islands. In 1941 he was appointed a district officer, but with the outbreak of the Pacific war he volunteered for service in the British Solomon Islands Protectorate Defence Force. Commissioned a captain, he found himself with no company of soldiers to command. Instead, he gathered together trusted Islanders to carry his radio, batteries and chargers and headed for the jungle-covered hills of Guadalcanal, where he became the island's foremost coast watcher.

From up there, Clemens had been keeping the Allies informed of enemy activities. He knew from scout patrols that the runway at Lunga was ready, its red clay and gravel smoothed for Japanese aircraft. He feared that with the airfield operational, the Japanese would bomb New Hebrides and 'we should be too far away to be of any further use'. The prospect made him 'depressed'. 'All I could taste was the bitterness of defeat,' he recalled. 'We were cut off. I would never see home again. I couldn't stand it.' But by early August, with 'many inquiries from "Down South" ... [and] no let up with the teleradio' he also 'could not help feeling that something was about to break'. What Clemens did not know was that the American military, heeding his warning that the airstrip was nearing completion, decided to take Guadalcanal and the airfield before the Japanese could use it. They planned to use it themselves.

In the pre-dawn of 7 August 1942, 6000 men of the 1st US Marine Division launched the Allies' first major land offensive against Japan. It was also the first major Allied amphibious landing of the Second World War, beginning more than six months of ferocious, see-sawing struggle for the island. Things went smoothly at first. Surprising the 2000 Japanese defenders with a large landing force with strong naval and air support, the Marines quickly seized the just-completed airstrip at Lunga Point. They renamed it Henderson Field after a Marine hero, Major Lofton 'Joe' Henderson, who was killed leading a bombing run at the Battle of Midway a month before.

But the success of the operation hung in the balance. The Japanese command knew they had a brief window of opportunity. If they acted quickly, before the Marines entrenched themselves and brought in reinforcements, they could destroy the American beachhead and push the invading force back into the sea. With Guadalcanal and the rest of the Solomons retaken by Japan, it would be a long time before the Americans risked coming back.

It was another two coast watchers, Jack Read and Paul Mason on Bougainville Island, who alerted the US command of the Japanese counter-attacks later on 7 August and then on the following day. Both Australians worked in the territories of Papua and New Guinea before the war, Read as an assistant district officer and Mason as a planter. When the Japanese invaded, Eric Feldt convinced them to remain behind. Mason and Read eventually ended up on Bougainville Island, which was ideally situated along the Japanese flight path between Rabaul and Guadalcanal.

Just hours after the Marines landed on Guadalcanal, the coast watchers observed formations of two dozen Japanese aircraft en route south from Rabaul. 'Twenty-four bombers headed yours' was the crisp warning of Paul Mason's famous signal. Even with the message being relayed through Port Moresby, Townsville, Canberra and ultimately Pearl Harbor, it still gave the Americans two hours' notice of the arrival of Japanese planes, allowing the Marines to disperse and hide around Henderson Field, and the navy to scatter their ships. It also gave the Americans time to prepare a welcome for the Japanese airmen: a barrage of anti-aircraft fire. The Japanese lost at least sixteen planes. Thanks to Read and Mason, the Americans survived the initial air assault and another one the day after, when thirty-six out of forty-four Japanese planes were shot down.

*

For six months the Allies fought, on land, at sea, and near continuously in the air. They endured three major land battles and many jungle skirmishes, seven major naval battles, and daily air combat. Often at close quarters, the fighting was ferocious. The jungle was hot and wet, with insects and rats for unfriendly company, and malaria and dysentery tireless adversaries. Almost half of Allied deaths on Guadalcanal would be due to malaria, dysentery, dengue fever, scrub typhus and other tropical diseases. It was worse for the Japanese. Their supply lines attacked, and their positions increasingly isolated, Japanese soldiers commonly faced starvation. 'I killed some ants and ate them, they really tasted good,' recorded Japanese Lieutenant Akogina.

As 1943 began, Admiral Yamamoto and many others were convinced that the drain on the empire's resources was no longer worth the fight. Better to concentrate on the battles in New Guinea than sacrifice thousands more troops on a lost cause. By the time the last Japanese soldier was evacuated on 7 February, the Japanese had lost more than 25 000 men, 38 ships and 683 aircraft. The Guadalcanal Campaign cost the Allies over 7000 men, 29 ships and 615 aircraft.

Victory at Guadalcanal was the tipping point, or, as a Japanese officer noted, 'the fork in the road'. The United States had won the momentum, albeit agonisingly. After Guadalcanal, the United States remained on the offensive for the rest of the Pacific war. While Japan's navy was never the same after Midway, after Guadalcanal, its air power was diminished and never commanded the skies again. In seeking to recapture the island and then to stop the American advance up the archipelago, Japan had lost its edge. But more than a military victory, Guadalcanal's value was symbolic. It was 'a test of national will and an index of prestige', wrote Rhodes scholar, journalist, international lawyer and Marine veteran of Guadalcanal, Herbert Merillat. It was a test the Allies passed.

Australia soon welcomed back the victors. In January 1943, the Guadalcanal veterans of the 1st Marine Division arrived in Melbourne for rest and refit, or, as the future sportswriter Robert Leckie described it, the 'Great Debauch'. Leckie bunked along with his fellow Marines of the First Regiment at the Melbourne Cricket Ground. Of his first outing into the city, he later recalled:

> The exhilaration of that night! At first I thought
> that it was my strange uniform and deep sunburn
> that marked me out for curiosity. But soon I came
> to realise that there was something more: I was the

deliverer in the land he has saved. The smiles and winks of the Melbourne crowds assured me of it; the street hawkers, too, with their pennants – 'Good on You, Yank. You saved Australia' – told me it was so. It was adulation and it was like a strong drink.

There was plenty of singing, too. 'It seemed that overnight', recalled Leckie, 'everyone had learned at least two verses of "Waltzing Matilda"'. The First Marine Regiment soon adopted Banjo Paterson's iconic bush ballad as their battle hymn and to this day march out to its tune.

It was a fitting cultural borrowing; after Guadalcanal, Australia was finally safe from invasion. The Japanese army would never again get so far south. What Australians would not know until years later, after the war, was the crucial role a few of their own played in the victory on Guadalcanal. Coast watchers supplied the initial intelligence about the construction of the Lunga Point airfield and then provided an early warning of the first Japanese air raids on 7 and 8 August. Over the next six months, they continued to warn of incoming Japanese attacks. 'Had they been able to deliver their many attacks without warning', concluded military historian and naval officer Lt-Commander George Gill, 'the Japanese bombers … would have been able to make the position impossible for Allied shipping'. 'I would get down on my knees every night and thank God for Commander Eric Feldt', Admiral Halsey recalled. 'If it had not been for the Australian Coastwatchers we would not have been able either to mount the invasion of Guadalcanal or to hold the island after we had invaded it in the face of enemy air superiority.' Or as he put it even more succinctly, the coast watchers 'saved Guadalcanal, and Guadalcanal saved the South Pacific'.

Reg Evans was joining an outfit quickly growing in renown and respect, even a certain mystique, in the south Pacific, one which had already earned the gratitude and confidence of Allied servicemen, from the top brass down. Before long, a young American naval lieutenant and his PT boat crew would be joining the list of the grateful.

Tour the South Sea Islands

LANDS of perpetual summer, the Pacific Islands call irresistibly during the Australian winter months. Isles of tropical beauty await you with their palm-fringed golden beaches, quaint native villages and wonderful coral lagoons. Enchanting tours are available to Papua and New Guinea, Solomon Islands, Lord Howe Island, Norfolk Island and the New Hebrides. These round trips occupy from nine days up to five weeks and are no more expensive than many an interstate holiday. Fares are free of exchange, and there are no hotel expenses—you live on the ship throughout. The excellent service and comfort en route will add to the many delights of your cruise. Leave the cold bleak days of winter—follow the sunshine to the South Sea Islands.

At your request we shall be pleased to forward folder No. 6.

-BURNS, PHILP & CO., LTD-

7 BRIDGE STREET, SYDNEY :: 312 COLLINS ST., MELBOURNE
128 ADELAIDE STREET, BRISBANE
& AT ADELAIDE, TOWNSVILLE, Etc.

Young Reg Evans fell in love with the Pacific and its people
in the 1920s. Cruise ships and tourists arrived a decade later.
And then there would be destroyers and aircraft carriers.

Always 'sea-minded' and 'ship-crazy', Lieutenant Reg Evans
was commissioned into the Royal Australian Naval Volunteer
Reserve as a coast watcher in 1942.

Jack Kennedy's lifelong fascination with sailing the seas started
with family holidays at Hyannis Port on Cape Cod in Massachusetts.
By the autumn of 1941, he too achieved his dream, commissioned
as an ensign in the United States Naval Reserve.

Australia's 'eyes and ears in the Pacific': one of the most famous of the coast watchers, Captain Martin Clemens poses with Islander scouts, members of the Solomon Islands Police Force, on Guadalcanal in 1942.

KEN, the coast watchers' local HQ in Solomon Islands at Lunga Point, Guadalcanal, was the centre of an invisible web spanning the islands, watching the enemy's every move.

The only known wartime photograph of Reg Evans (right), here with the legendary New Zealand coast watcher Donald Kennedy (left), talking to a US Marine Corps officer at Kennedy's base, at Segi, on the south-eastern tip of New Georgia, Solomon Islands.

The Solomons coast watchers: the only American in the ranks, Frank Nash, sitting in the bottom row on the right. Also in the photo: Eric Feldt, middle row, fourth from the left, flanked by 'Snowy' Rhoades on his left and Hugh 'Macka' Mackenzie, the boss at KEN, on his right.

Right The Solomons mid-1943: regulation Naval attire be damned, Jack Kennedy already possessed confidence and magnetism that foreshadowed a big future.

Below His crew loved him: Jack Kennedy with his PT-109 men; Lennie Thom (with hand on his knee) next to his skipper.

Above Some called it the 'hooligan navy', but there was something glamorous and romantic about PT boats. For Jack Kennedy it was 'the great spot of the Navy'. 'You are your own boss', he told his friend, 'and it's like sailing around as in the old days'.

Left Eroni (Aaron) Kumana and Biuku (Nebuchadnezzar) Gasa, Islander scouts whose curiosity and bravery made the rescue possible.

Right Just so the Yanks weren't confused: an American poster promotes friendship between the two wartime allies.

Below The *Instructions for American Servicemen in Australia* booklet explains the strange new land, its people and history to the million US soldiers, sailors and airmen who passed through Australia during the Second World War.

This man is your FRIEND

Australian

He fights for FREEDOM

THE AUSTRALIAN

WAR MEMORIAL, MELBOURNE.

DON'T MISTAKE THE EMBLEM ON AN AUSTRALIAN SOLDIER'S HAT FOR A RISING SUN. IT'S JUST THE OPPOSITE. IT'S A RISING RING OF BAYONETS

IN THE FIRST WORLD WAR, AUSTRALIA'S CASUALTIES WERE 226,000 OUT OF 333,000 TROOPS SENT OVERSEAS! THE AUSTRALIANS AND THE AMERICAN A.E.F. LOST ALMOST EXACTLY THE SAME TOTAL NUMBER OF MEN KILLED.

TOP ANZAC GENERAL IN THE FIRST WORLD WAR WAS SIR JOHN MONASH, LAWYER-ENGINEER. HE WAS A JEW. OF GERMAN EXTRACTION. HE DESIGNED THE MECHANIZED ATTACK THAT BROKE THE HINDENBURG LINE. SHARING THE ATTACK WITH HIS MEN WERE THE U.S. 27TH UNDER GENERAL O'RYAN.

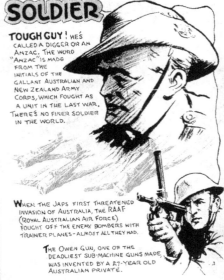

SOLDIER

TOUGH GUY! HE'S CALLED A DIGGER OR AN ANZAC. THE WORD "ANZAC" IS MADE FROM THE INITIALS OF THE GALLANT AUSTRALIAN AND NEW ZEALAND ARMY CORPS, WHICH FOUGHT AS A UNIT IN THE LAST WAR. THERE'S NO FINER SOLDIER IN THE WORLD.

WHEN THE JAPS FIRST THREATENED INVASION OF AUSTRALIA, THE RAAF (ROYAL AUSTRALIAN AIR FORCE) FOUGHT OFF THE ENEMY BOMBERS WITH TRAINER PLANES - ALMOST ALL THEY HAD.

THE OWEN GUN, ONE OF THE DEADLIEST SUB-MACHINE GUNS MADE, WAS INVENTED BY A 27-YEAR OLD AUSTRALIAN PRIVATE.

Gazing down at Salamaua: Australian and American soldiers prepare to eject the Japanese from one of their northern New Guinea strongholds.

'Thank God for the Yanks!' Fearing a Japanese invasion, Australians welcomed their new allies; relations between civilians and servicemen would remain largely positive throughout the war.

Right 'I put my arm about his strong shoulder. "Mr Prime Minister", I said, "we two, you and I, will see this thing through together"': the Supreme Allied Commander in the South-West Pacific, General Douglas MacArthur, and Prime Minister John Curtin developed a genuinely warm personal relationship despite their widely differing temperaments (and political leanings).

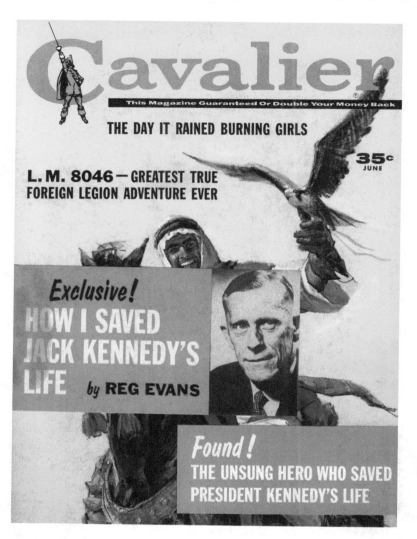

THE DAY IT RAINED BURNING GIRLS

L. M. 8046 — GREATEST TRUE
FOREIGN LEGION ADVENTURE EVER

Exclusive!
**HOW I SAVED
JACK KENNEDY'S
LIFE** *by* **REG EVANS**

Found!
THE UNSUNG HERO WHO SAVED
PRESIDENT KENNEDY'S LIFE

This Magazine Guaranteed Or Double Your Money Back

35¢
JUNE

'And I'm bloody glad to see you, too!' After almost eighteen years,
Reg Evans tells his story of the rescue.

Left Like Gallipoli, but successful: Australian troops disembark from
American ships at Lae, northern New Guinea, 1943, in their largest
amphibious landing since the First World War.

PRESIDENT'S RESCUER

HERO'S WELCOME
FOR REG EVANS

NEW YORK, Fri.—New Yorkers today turned on a hero's welcome for Mr. Reg Evans, the Sydney accountant who 18 years ago rescued President Kennedy from a Japanese-occupied island.

Mr. Evans was besieged by reporters, photographers, newsreel and television cameramen when he stepped from the plane which brought him from Australia.

Interviewers and officials who went to the airport to meet him treated Evans like a hero.

But he insisted that the credit for President Kennedy's rescue belonged to the Australian coast-watching organisation.

Mr. Evans told interviewers at the airport: "If I had not been on the spot to rescue him someone else in the organisation would have been there.

"So the credit goes to the organisation. However I was very pleased to be the one to do it."

Mr. Evans was a Navy lieutenant in the coast-watching service when he rescued President Kennedy in 1943.

He operated a watching post and wireless in jungle on a Japanese occupied island in the Solomons, to warn Allied forces of movements of Japanese planes and ships.

He organised a rescue craft for President Kennedy (then a U.S. Navy lieutenant) when he landed on a nearby island after his PT boat had been cut in two by a Japanese destroyer.

The President had always believed his rescuer was a New Zealander named Wincote until the Sydney Daily Telegraph correctly identified Evans in a Ray Castle interview last January.

Australian Consolidated Press and Cavalier Magazine brought Mr. Evans to the United States for his first meeting with President Kennedy since they said farewell on a wartime beach 18 years ago.

In New York, Mr. Evans showed the letter on White House stationery, dated April 8, he received at his home in Avalon Beach.

It read: "Dear Mr. Evans:

"I understand that you are coming to the United States in early May.

"I would be delighted if it would be possible for you to drop by the White House on May 1st at 11.30 a.m.

"I look forward to the opportunity of re-living the hectic days in the Solomons with you.

Not something a middle-aged suburban accountant is accustomed to: Reg Evans surrounded by a media scrum on his arrival in the United States in April 1961.

From the Gomu beach to the Oval Office, the coast watcher
and the PT skipper reunited in May 1961.

Reg Evans and Bob Curran, editor of *Cavalier*, present President Kennedy
with a framed illustration of his rescue used in the *Cavalier* article.

Watching the Australians challenge the Americans in the
America's Cup yacht race: President Kennedy and the First
Lady onboard USS *Joseph P Kennedy Jr*, September 1962.
The Americans won the series, four races to one.

Mr Kevu Goes to Washington: Benjamin Kevu meeting with President
Kennedy and PT-109 crewman George 'Barney' Ross in the Oval Office,
September 1962. Prime Minister Robert Menzies was kept waiting outside.

On the set of *The Jack Paar Show*, Reg Evans and Benjamin Kevu share
the spotlight with the surviving crew of PT-109, September 1962.

Reg Evans DSC at his last
ANZAC Day ceremony,
April 1988.

Biuku Gasa in 2003, two years before
his death, with the bust of the man
he saved sixty years earlier, presented
to him by a grateful Kennedy family.

CHAPTER 7

SOLOMONS-BOUND

Guadalcanal was not the end, though, to borrow from Churchill, it was the end of the beginning. Even before the Allied victories of early 1943, it was obvious that retaking New Guinea and the Solomons would be a hard slog, requiring more troops, more resources and new plans. Operation Ferdinand also had to take stock and consider new strategic imperatives. Certainly, additional coast watchers would be needed for the long haul to recapture the islands from the Japanese.

After leaving the army, Reg Evans undertook general naval officer training at Flinders Naval Base, south of Melbourne. By December 1942, he was in Guadalcanal, as a newly commissioned sub-lieutenant in the Royal Australian Naval Volunteer Reserve (RANVR). Here, at the edge of Henderson Field, the site of furious fighting just weeks before, Reg entered the coast watcher control station call-signed KEN, after its buoyant boss, Lieutenant-Commander Hugh Mackenzie. In this rough dugout Evans 'learned the ropes', mainly how to use radio. As a former soldier he already knew how to use weapons. Soon, specialist training schools were built for naval intelligence officers in Refuge Bay, north of Sydney, as well as near Cairns and on K'gari

(Fraser Island). But coast watchers like Evans trained on the job. He spent the next three months as a general assistant at KEN, learning from the best.

Mackenzie was a classmate of Eric Feldt's and Rupert Long's at the very first intake of cadet-midshipmen at the Royal Australian Naval College in 1913. Barely teenagers at the time, they became lifelong friends. Now, thirty years later, having left the navy in the 1920s for a life in the south Pacific, 'Macka' Mackenzie returned to it to fight the Japanese in the islands. A friend later recalled Mackenzie 'knew no fear, and no organization either'. He would stand in the open during Japanese bombing raids, preferring to bark orders at terrified soldiers and enjoy the 'view'. It was 'Macka' who, arriving just after the Marines had taken Lunga Point, decided to set up local coast watcher headquarters right next door to the airfield so as to expedite critical communications between the Australians and Americans.

In February 1943, the Allies learned that the Japanese were building an airstrip at Vila Plantation, the only relatively flat land on the southern shore of Kolombangara Island in the central Solomons, some 400 kilometres from Henderson Field. Meaning 'Water Lord' in the local language, the island is an almost perfect cone some 30 kilometres across, its volcanic peak rising over 1800 metres above the surrounding sea. The Japanese wanted the airstrip to support their larger base to the south at Munda, on New Georgia, and the coast watchers needed to monitor it. So Evans was sent in.

Easier said than done. Getting to his post at Kolombangara was dangerous and fraught with risk. First Evans travelled to the American Flying Boat base at Florida Island. From there, he hitched a ride aboard on old Catalina flying boat to Segi, on the southern tip of New Georgia. This was the domain of the all-seeing, all-knowing Donald Kennedy, a legendary New Zealand coast watcher whom the Japanese singled out for particular attention. Walking a thin line between intelligence work and guerrilla activity, Donald Kennedy built up an army of seventy Islanders and a fleet of six barges, with which he protected his fiefdom. He had managed to escape death many times already, all the while killing any Japanese soldiers who chanced within a perimeter of his hideout. His toll was said to be 100.

While Donald Kennedy went to Guadalcanal for a conference Evans relieved him for a couple of weeks. Upon Kennedy's return, Evans made for Kolombangara accompanied by a young English-speaking Islander, Malanga, recruited as his general assistant. It was a nerve-racking journey. Evans and Malanga canoed up the western coast of New Georgia by night and hid by day. 'We took hours to pass Munda airstrip', Reg later recalled, 'always close enough to hear Jap truck engines.' The Japanese, too, were taking advantage of the darkness, working to reinforce their defences.

On 21 March, Evans and Malanga finally reached Kolombangara Island, landing their canoe at Kunji, about 15 kilometres west around the coast from Vila Plantation. 'It was no picnic', recalled Evans, 'but we made it.' Not only that, he was royally received by the local chief, Rovu, and local scouts who had been told by a former district officer, now coast watcher, Dick Horton, to expect him. Evans was taken to Hiruka hilltop, his new lair, with a leaf house and two lookout posts built in trees providing a good view of the airstrip and the sea approaches. Rovu told Evans that his forebears had used the same spot as a lookout for their enemies. Now Evans would use it for the Allies to spy on theirs.

From the time he arrived at Kolombangara, Evans enjoyed the Islanders' trust and support. They remembered him from before the war. He was no stranger. 'They were in my corner from the start', Evans recalled. 'I had their goodwill.' It was just as well he did; he estimated that the Japanese 'could have combed that jungle in two weeks'. He was only as safe as the Islanders made him. As it was, Rovu told him that even the Islanders − there were only 500 of them on Kolombangara, living in coastal villages fed by eighty rivers and creeks that flowed down the slopes of the volcano − only very rarely ventured beyond the beach and settled areas. They had no reason to, the ocean and their gardens providing all their needs; besides, it was dangerous, and they might get lost. While the people of the island, the Dughore, believed they were descended from a couple who lived inside the crater, they had long ago abandoned the inland; Rovu was the only one who knew the secrets of the island's interior. Don't worry, Rovu assured Evans, you will be safe here.

Evans sent his first message on 22 March 1943, adopting GSE, his wife's initials, as his call sign. A few weeks later Evans moved his camp to a nearby hilltop he called 'Square Top', which was slightly nearer Blackett Strait, along the southern coast of Kolombangara, and gave him an even better view of Japanese operations. 'From his position', wrote Feldt, 'Evans was able to report all vessels approaching Vila and Bairoko [on the north coast of New Georgia] … His teleradio, in the hut, kept him in contact with Mackenzie at Lunga and his scouts were in contact with Horton's to the south, Kennedy's to the east and Henry Josselyn's to the north-west.' Evans was now part of an invisible web spanning the islands, watching the enemy's every move. Before the era of satellites, drones, and high-altitude spy planes, the coast watchers were all that and more. Combined with the effect of their codes being broken and read, the Japanese fought well but, compared to the Allies, they fought blind.

*

Next to Guadalcanal and Solomon Islands, New Guinea has over the years become somewhat of a forgotten campaign in the American memory. Not so for Australians. Alongside Gallipoli and the Oxford laboratory where Howard Florey developed penicillin, the Kokoda Track is officially recognised by the Australian government as one of only three overseas locations of national significance. But if Kokoda continues to be evoked, remembered and celebrated, it was only the first of many more jungle hells in this 'bastard of a place'. For the next three years, some of the most brutal fighting of the Second World War would bring more Australians and Americans together than at any time before in either country's history.

Their bloody road together began at Milne Bay, a beautiful inlet on the easternmost tip of Papua. The coastal strip, hemmed in on three sides by hilly terrain, allowed small but rich coconut plantations and native gardens. In mid-1942 it was also the site of a newly built Allied airstrip, with two others under construction. By mid-July, codebreakers informed General MacArthur that the Japanese were preparing to land at Milne Bay later the next month. From there, as their comrades ground their way down the Kokoda Track, the Imperial Army would strike towards Port Moresby along the southern coast of Papua. Pre-warned, MacArthur ordered reinforcements. By contrast, military intelligence and aircraft reconnaissance had failed the enemy. The Japanese believed that Allied soldiers numbered only a few hundred men. In reality, by mid-August the Allies had mustered 9000 troops at Milne Bay – about 7500 Australian, the rest American. They were ready and waiting.

Even before they could disgorge the troops, Japanese transport ships were hit by United States Army Air Forces (USAAF) and Royal Australian Air Force (RAAF) aircraft, though the damage was minor. Landing at Milne Bay by dawn the next day, 25 August, Japanese soldiers, supported by two light tanks, moved quickly towards the all-important Allied airstrips, about 10 kilometres to the west. They were stopped by Australian infantry while Allied aircraft bombed their staging base on the northern shore of the bay.

Fighting continued through the jungle mud and mangrove swamp, often in pouring rain and at night. 'The Aussies were fighting mad', wrote American war historian Rear-Admiral Samuel Eliot Morison, 'for they had found some of their captured fellows tied to trees and bayoneted to death, surmounted by the placard, "It took them a long time to die".' No quarter was given. 'From then on the only good Jap was a dead one,' recalled Sergeant Arthur Traill of Australia's 2/12th Infantry Battalion. The Japanese were tenacious fighters but by 1 September the Australians and Americans had their measure and the Japanese ashore knew they could not capture the airfields. They sought reinforcements, but learning they would take too long, the Japanese infantry withdrew to the bay, where the navy evacuated the last of them on 7 September.

The Australians and Americans had done what no one had yet done: bested the Japanese on land. It was a full-scale defeat. The Japanese had withdrawn and abandoned their campaign. They could not pass through Kokoda, and they could not bypass Kokoda through Milne Bay. By the end of September, both roads to Port Moresby had been shut.

Just as important as the strategic outcome was its symbolic value. Even before the victory at Guadalcanal, there was now a glimmer of hope that the Pacific war was turning; that, perhaps, it could be won. Morale lifted, and not just in Australia. In far-away Burma, where British and Indian troops were slogging away against the Japanese in similar harsh conditions, the Allied commander of Burma Corps (and later governor-general of Australia), Field Marshal Sir William Slim, later recalled: 'Some of us may forget that of all the Allies it was Australian soldiers who first broke the spell of the invincibility of the Japanese Army; those of us who were in Burma have cause to remember.'

*

Jack Kennedy was desperate to see combat, commanding the craft that the Japanese dubbed 'devil boats'. But just when he thought he was finally off to fight the foe, there was another setback: he was made a PT boat instructor instead. Kennedy could not believe it. He had performed well on his course and was assuming that active service awaited. Whether it was because of his lauded ability to communicate or because his father had intervened to keep him from harm's way, Jack could not be sure. Refusing to take 'no' for an answer, he got his influential maternal grandfather, John Francis 'Honey Fitz' Fitzgerald, to pull strings through Massachusetts senator David Walsh and have him reassigned to a combat role.

It still wasn't a straight march to the front lines. Sent first to Jacksonville, Florida, Jack was assigned to patrol duty at the Panama Canal. Again, he asked Senator Walsh to intervene and, finally, by March 1943, he was on his way to Solomon Islands.

Many men will do what they can to stay away from combat. Jack Kennedy never had to go to war, least of all serve in harm's way. His older brother, Joe Jr, was the one destined for politics; Jack did not need frontline heroism to enhance his CV. To enter active service he had to badger and plead repeatedly, ask others to intercede on his behalf, put up with constant back pain while at the same time convincing a succession of army medics he was fit to serve, and last but not least defy, or at least circumvent, the wishes of his parents. No one could argue that he did not want to play his part at the point of the spear. But now that he finally had his wish, his posting did not seem like a promising arena for valour. After the ferocity of the early fighting on Guadalcanal and the ejection of Japanese troops from the southern Solomons, some thought that it was now just a mopping-up operation. How wrong they were.

Kennedy made his way across the Pacific aboard the transport ship *Rochambeau*. Originally built for the French Merchant Marine as *Marechal Joffre* and then crewed by Vichy French forces after France's surrender in 1940, it found itself in the Philippines at the outbreak of the Pacific war from where it was hijacked by downed US Navy fliers and taken to Australia. Jack then took another vessel for the last leg from New Hebrides to Guadalcanal. On 7 April 1943, as he approached the destination, the Japanese launched their largest air raid since the climax of the battle for Guadalcanal. On a transport ship carrying fuel and high explosives, Kennedy's war nearly finished before it had begun. Bombs landed so close to his 'tub' – as he described it in a letter to Billings – that it lifted the stern out of the water. Other nearby US ships and their crew were not so lucky. Neither was the Japanese pilot who attacked Kennedy's ship. He was shot down and, having parachuted into the water, started firing his revolver at the bridge of the transport, 'battling an entire ship' by himself until he was killed. As Kennedy wrote to Billings, 'it brought home very strongly how long it is going to take to finish the war'.

Five days later, the Americans counter-punched. Deciphered Japanese communications having placed Admiral Yamamoto at Bougainville, American fighters were sent in and shot down the plane carrying him. There were no survivors. Kennedy was at Henderson Field to see the pilot responsible do a roll over the airstrip in celebration. The breaking of the Japanese codes was considered so secret at the time, the American top brass encouraged the rumour that Yamamoto's movements were traced by coast watchers. '[Most] of the fliers', wrote Walter Lord, 'who by now believed these guardian angels could do anything, were happy to give them credit for one more miracle.'

*

After the defeats on the Kokoda Track and at Milne Bay, the Japanese retreated to their strongholds in northern Papua. The 25-kilometre stretch of the coast they controlled was bracketed in the east by their base at Buna and by Gona in the west, with Sanananda in the centre. It was in retaking these towns that Australian and US forces would forge their most significant partnership of the war, assisted in the task by several thousand Papuan labourers and porters and the troops of the Papuan Infantry Battalion.

Throughout 1942 and 1943, Australia shouldered much of the land war against Japan. 'In this period', wrote American military historian Eric Bergerud, 'Australia's war ... was largely fought by the AIF, the best infantry in the Pacific.' If the AIF was lacking anything, it was in support and logistics, where they quickly learned to make use of the US Army. The Americans were willing and able partners in the New Guinea campaigns, supplying the Australians where their own army could not. Henrietta Drake-Brockman, who chronicled the Americans in the Pacific in her novel, *The Fatal Days*, wrote that while in Australia 'there was comparatively little fraternization between troops ... [i]n the islands they were cobbers and buddies in arms. The Yanks admired the Australians as fighters; the Australians admired and envied the superb American mechanical equipment.'

Bergerud goes as far as to say that 'It is one of the curiosities of war that the AIF and the US Army, if one looks below the controversies that continually revolved around MacArthur, cooperated better than did the US Army and the Marines.' And while the Australian infantry and the US Marines never fought on the same battlefield, they did come to enjoy mutual respect. 'I think we were the best. Period', opined Donald Fall, of the 1st Marine Division, the heroes of Guadalcanal, 'Except for maybe the Aussies. If anyone could fight as well as the [Marine] Corps it was Aussies. If it was up to me they would have all been inducted into the Marines then and there.'

As October turned into November 1942, the Australian 7th Division and the US 32nd Division closed in on the Japanese beachheads in northern Papua. Weeks of ferocious fighting followed against a well-entrenched and desperate enemy. It poured with rain every afternoon, making progress even more difficult. 'The Japanese constructed some of the finest field fortifications in World War II at Gona-Buna', wrote Bergerud. Conditions were so miserable that the battle was likened to tropical trench warfare.

The Allies finally took Gona on 9 December, with a regiment of the US 32nd Division fighting under the Australian 7th Division in echoes of the First World War and the battle of Hamel. The remainder of the 32nd Division, meanwhile, fought in the hellhole of Buna − a 'nightmare', as their commander, General Michael Eichelberger, called it. 'I want you to take Buna, or not come back alive,' MacArthur ordered Eichelberger. Eichelberger had earned the Order of the Rising Sun and several other Japanese military decorations while fighting alongside Japanese troops against the Red Army in 1919, during the Western intervention in the Russian Civil War. Now he would need to use his talents against the former allies.

The 32nd entered the Buna township on 14 December, though the approaches were littered with Japanese fortifications that had yet to be taken. Mopping up would take weeks and hundreds of Allied lives, but the arrival of

Australian light tanks on 15 December 'was doom for the Japanese'. Aggressive Australian jungle fighters also helped to 'orient the 32nd Division into the nightmare world of jungle warfare'. 'Australian soldiers were kind and good people,' reminisced American infantryman Ernest Gerber. 'The Aussies knew more than we did. Australians were the best.' Eichelberger recalled this bright spot of US and Australian cooperation:

> It was a spectacular and dramatic assault, and a brave one ... American troops wheeled to the west in support, and other Americans were assigned to mopping-up duties. But behind the tanks went the fresh and jaunty Aussie veterans, tall, moustached, erect, with their blazing Tommy-guns swinging before them. Concealed Japanese positions – which were even more formidable than our patrols had indicated – burst into flame.

'No American Division in the South Pacific faced a worse military situation,' observed Bergerud. But they held on, with Australian assistance. Eichelberger, meanwhile, would go on to command the liberation of the Philippines less than two years later, helping MacArthur fulfil his promise to return.

While victorious, the battles for control of the northern coast were costly. The Japanese defenders were tenacious, if not fanatical, and displayed a bravery and fortitude that was a grim prelude to later battles in the Pacific war. In a depressing calculus, Australian and US soldiers were three times more likely to be killed at the battles for the Papua and New Guinea beachheads than were troops fighting in Guadalcanal. The brotherhood in arms had been sealed with blood.

CHAPTER 8

CARTWHEEL

Once on the ground in the Solomons, things moved fast for Jack Kennedy. With few commanders available, on 25 April 1943, he was given charge of PT-109, the oldest surviving PT boat of the Guadalcanal campaign. He had finally made it. It was to prove both a blessing and a curse.

There was something romantic, no doubt, about PT boats. They had a freebooting, buccaneering image that harked back to Lieutenant John Bulkeley's daring rescue of General MacArthur from Corregidor in the Philippines through 900 kilometres of enemy waters in March 1942. For his undoubted bravery, Bulkeley received the Congressional Medal of Honor and was soon fictionalised in William White's popular book *They Were Expendable*, the movie of which was released at war's end starring, among others, John Wayne. Bulkeley even enjoyed a private audience with President Roosevelt, where he extolled the virtues of the plywood craft. MacArthur, not surprisingly, was also an advocate. Most of the US military, however, was not.

PT boats were about 24 metres long, with a crew of a dozen men, though often with a few more later in the war, once equipped with superior armaments. Powered by three Packard Marine gasoline engines generating

4500 horsepower, they had a top speed of 45 knots, or about 85 kilometres per hour. But however handsome, with their plywood hulls, sleek dimensions, and romantic history, they were less attractive as weapons of war. Their wooden hulls offered virtually no protection and their tanks filled with aviation fuel proved highly combustible, while onboard guns, dismissively nicknamed '50-calibers-at-50-paces', were near useless. Worse, as PT boat historian William Doyle writes, 'their torpedoes didn't work'. Their principal weapon, if not their reason for being, was noted for its 'stunning ineffectiveness', with the result 'PT boats fired many hundreds of the underwater missiles at Japanese targets and only very rarely hit anything.'

The PT fleet was the light cavalry of the seas: colourful perhaps, but its time had long passed and it had no place in brutal mechanised modern warfare. 'The only thing they were really effective at', PT skipper Leonard Nikolovic later reflected, 'was raising War Bonds' (a means for patriotic civilians to invest their savings in the war effort). Not surprisingly, many in the US Navy had little respect for PT boats and their disdain often, rather uncharitably, extended to their officers and crew. Some called it the 'hooligan navy'. No PT officers ever achieved flag rank during the war – that of rear admiral or above. It might have been glamorous, but it was a career dead end.

Perhaps not even glamorous. The bestselling novelist James Michener, who spent the war travelling around the Pacific as a navy historian, vented in his Pulitzer-winning debut *Tales of the South Pacific* (subsequently turned into a musical by Rodgers and Hammerstein): 'I have become damned sick and tired of the eyewash written about PT boats ... It was just dirty work, thumping, hammering, kidney-wrecking work. Even for strong guys from Montana it was rugged living.' And often deadly. Built for speed, not comfort, the PTs were more dangerous to their own crew than to the foe, producing high casualties onboard without the compensating enemy kills. 'Those of you who want to come back after the war and raise families need not apply,' Bulkeley warned potential recruits. 'PT boat skippers are not coming back!'

Yet for all the trouble they caused him, Kennedy would remain an advocate of PT boats. Writing nearly two decades later, he argued they 'filled an important need in World War II in shallow waters, complementing the achievement of greater ships in greater seas. This need for small, fast, versatile, strongly armed vessels does not wane.' The former two attributes were undoubtedly correct, the latter two at best questionable. But Kennedy's nostalgia was perhaps understandable – PT boats made his war and they helped to make his post-war career.

Through May 1943, Kennedy's crew was learning to work together as a team. They practised drills and manoeuvres of varying sorts, including as part of a formation of PT boats. Much time back at the base was spent worrying about food, primarily what to create from the ubiquitous Spam and baked beans. According to some, everything tasted better with a wicked brew of drinking alcohol covertly made from the 190-proof fluid supplied to assist in the firing of torpedoes. A cynic might say this was the only thing the PT torpedoes were good for.

For all the challenges, Kennedy loved it. Photos of him at the time show a young man, looking younger even than his 26 years – he celebrated his birthday on 29 May – skinny, gangly even, with a broad smile and audacious presence. Often shirtless, but with sunglasses and non-regulation headwear perched on luxuriant hair he refused to cut, Jack Kennedy found individual flair even in the US Navy. Arguably, it was the only branch of service where he could get away with it.

Already he possessed a confidence and a hint of the magnetism that in only three years' time would lift him into the US Congress. Kennedy's friend and hut-mate at Tulagi, Johnny Isles, recalled, 'It was written all over the sky that he was going to be something big. He just had that charisma … He loved to win … He was good-looking, had a fantastic smile, the tone of his voice, his sense of humour.'

An old man to his crew of teenagers and twenty year olds, Kennedy's men 'liked him', wrote one of his biographers. 'They found that he treated them much more like equals than some other officers treated their crews. He was never dictatorial.' His intellect, charm and good humour set him in good stead. The character of the president was already evident in the young navy lieutenant. People knew who Jack Kennedy was. He stuck out. 'Kennedy's identity sooner or later became known practically wherever he went.'

Soon he acquired a nickname, 'Shafty'. Whenever Kennedy or his crew got a raw deal from senior officers, he would complain in his distinctive Boston-Harvard accent of being 'shafted'. The name stuck in the south Pacific, so much so that 'Shafty' ended up being painted on the head of one of the PT-109's torpedoes. Even when he became president, his old mates at PT-109 reunions still referred to Kennedy as 'Shafty'.

The shape of Kennedy's crew on PT-109 shifted and changed until late July. He was lucky with his second in command, Ensign Leonard Jay Thom, a blond giant of a man who played American football for Ohio State University. They had first met at the PT boat training squadron at Melville, Rhode Island, where Kennedy had been his instructor. There were ten others – machinists, gunners, torpedomen – a cross-section of American youth, most of them working class from small towns and rural districts, from Massachusetts all the way to California, a microcosm of a vast country, now at war.

If it was often rough at sea, back at base was not much better. There was little sleep, fresh water or nutritious food. Often exhausted and in poor health, Kennedy and his men had to contend with the heat, malaria, dysentery, and a string of tropical skin diseases. It wasn't the family holiday idyll of Hyannis Port. Books were an escape. Kennedy read whenever he could, often retreating into his bunk with his current favourite, most notably *War and Peace*. Engrossed in Tolstoy's epic of Napoleon's failed invasion of Russia, he could not have known that another unwise invader of Russia was now preparing for his last roll of the dice some 500 kilometres south of Moscow, what in August 1943 would become the largest tank battle in history. But Kursk was a world away from the Solomons. Kennedy even brought along with him a portable Victrola turntable on which he would play old showtime favourites along with a new star named Frank Sinatra. There were also cards, usually poker or cribbage, and plenty of time to talk.

In May, in one of the never-ending debates on base, Kennedy took the side of Australian coconut plantation owners. There was a rumour that they would seek compensation from American authorities for the war damage Americans did to their crops. Controversially, Kennedy argued that destruction to private property should be compensated if American shells were responsible. Few Americans, particularly servicemen, would have shared his opinion.

On base, Kennedy and his crew were subject to frequent attacks by Japanese aircraft. On one occasion, he was reading on his tent bunk and got tangled in a mosquito net as he scampered for the slit trenches outside. He just made it as shrapnel hit the tin roof of the plantation house they were temporarily staying in. As he wrote to Inga Arvard, 'I asked for it honey and I'm getting it.'

At sea, while night-time patrols provided some breathtaking sights with flying fish and phosphorescent water, they could also be deadly. The most feared enemy were the Japanese floatplanes, which in the dark of night would seek out the PTs' long, glowing, V-shaped wake before dropping a flare followed by a bomb. Still, for the ever-present danger, PT-109 saw little action. April and May brought a lull in fighting in the Solomons as the Americans regrouped after taking Guadalcanal. But the calm was not going to last.

*

While Kennedy itched to go into battle, it wasn't long before Evans had his first taste of making history – the official *History of United States Naval Operations in World War II* no less – even before he set his eyes on the future president.

On the night of 7 to 8 May 1943, a convoy of four Japanese destroyers struck mines in Blackett Strait. 'Next morning', wrote American maritime historian Rear-Admiral

Samuel Eliot Morison, Evans 'stared in delighted amazement at the two cripples flaming and floundering' and relayed the good news to Guadalcanal, which responded by sending out sixty aircraft to finish the job. Though hampered by poor weather, American aircraft located and sank three destroyers and badly damaged the fourth. Just another day on the job for a coast watcher. 'When it was all over', Evans wrote, 'we used to get the cricket scores'.

With the Allies setting their sights on the Japanese stronghold of Munda on New Georgia, Evans' post on nearby Kolombangara became increasingly important. To help him out, Mackenzie at KEN sent Evans an assistant. His name was Benjamin Franklin Nash, 'Frank' to Reg and the coast watchers. What was unusual, unique in fact, was that Nash was a corporal in the US Army.

A 188-centimetre-tall 25-year-old from Colorado, Nash was a radio operator with the 410th Signal Company (Aviation), initially stationed in New Hebrides. In January 1943, the 410th were re-deployed to Guadalcanal, where Nash helped install and operate the first Allied radio control tower on Henderson Field. It was there he also learned of the vital but dangerous work of the Coast Watch Organisation. He wanted to be part of it, particularly as his unit was soon being transferred back to New Hebrides. 'This was not my idea of the war,' Nash explained his reluctance to leave for the rear.

But it wasn't easy. Mackenzie was at first reluctant to take Nash onboard. A third-generation cattle grazier, good in the saddle and handy on the ranch, Nash had no experience on the islands. And besides, he was an American and not a member of the Australian military. But so keen was Nash that he did not wait for a formal transfer – it would have taken months to clear – telling American historian Walter Lord that he 'sort of deserted'.

The young Coloradan soon proved popular at KEN. While the coast watchers received plenty of praise for their work, they were desperate for supplies, from light bulbs and stationery to toilet paper. Being an American had its advantages, and Nash happily scrounged his way into the affections of the Aussies. If nothing else, he was a good radio operator, was clearly resourceful, and had been commended for his cool head under fire from Japanese bombers, which later earned him a Bronze Star.

But Nash wanted to see real action, behind enemy lines, and so when Evans needed an assistant, he volunteered. Mackenzie was eventually persuaded. Nash left Henderson Field on 8 May, and after stopping in at Segi (now Seghe) for one of Donald Kennedy's famous briefings, he was delivered by Islander scouts to Kolombangara in a dugout canoe on 17 May. Evans and Nash 'hit it off immediately', wrote American historian Ron Soodalter, 'and Nash could not have had a better mentor'. Evans was 'glad to have him' and he soon 'became one of us'.

From their island hideaways, Evans, Nash and other coast watchers nearby never stopped reporting on enemy movements. Armed with this intelligence, American fighters and bombers as well as PT boats searched for targets and blasted away at the Japanese supply lines. Whenever a plane or PT boat was hit by the enemy in battle, coast watchers were asked to stay on the lookout for American survivors. It was busy in Blackett Strait and who knew who might turn up.

But still concerned that '[t]oo much movement was going on that we knew nothing about', Evans decided to move camp to the tiny island of Gomu (now known as Makuti), halfway between Kolombangara and Wana Wana Island (now Vonavona), where he was confident he would be better placed to report on Japanese comings and goings. Evans was still awaiting approval for his request to relocate when, in his words, 'there was some strife around Gizo', another island in Blackett Strait.

*

The road to Tokyo began with a 'Cartwheel'. Having first stopped the Japanese advances in the south-west Pacific in the first year and a half of war, it was now time for the Allies to go on the attack to push the enemy out of the Solomons and New Guinea. Under the leadership of General MacArthur and Admiral Halsey, the offensive of that codename commenced on 30 June 1943.

This was the reason for the 'strife'. Halsey moved first against Japanese positions in the New Georgia group of islands to the north-west of Guadalcanal. With two aircraft carriers, six battleships, nine cruisers, and at least sixteen destroyers, the Japanese were pummelled in their entrenched positions.

They responded by launching constant naval and air raids from Rabaul to support their southerly bases. Kolombangara, with its port facilities at Vila, was the key to the Japanese stranglehold over the nearby New Georgia and surrounding islands. The Japanese used the cover of night to ferry supplies and reinforcements from Bougainville down the western coast of Kolombangara to Vila, from where in turn these were shipped across the narrow Kula Channel to Munda on New Georgia. The Japanese admiral in charge called it 'Rat operations'; the Americans nicknamed these night convoys the 'Tokyo Express'. They tried to take Munda in July, but the initial assault failed. Halting the 'Tokyo Express' became the prerequisite to future success.

With the USAAF winning the battle during daylight hours, PT boats were now called forward to take on the Japanese convoys at night. PT-109, which was initially based at the Russell Islands to the south-east of New Georgia, was in July transferred to Lumbari (now Lumbaria), a tiny island off the northern tip of Rendova Island, which gave its name to the new PT base. Jack Kennedy and his men were now right on the front line of the fight for New Georgia.

Throughout the second half of July, Kennedy's PT-109 and other PT boats had been repeatedly sent out on patrols to intercept the Japanese transports. More hunted than hunter, Kennedy never spied a Japanese vessel, but was seen by Japanese aircraft and was lucky to survive several close calls. When, in the afternoon of 1 August 1943, the Rendova PT-boat base was bombed for the first time, he and his crew mates had to jump into fox holes just outside the tents where they had been playing poker only moments before. That night, all serviceable PT-boats were dispatched to patrol Blackett Strait, hoping to derail the Tokyo Express once and for all. The fifteen boats were divided in four 'divisions'; PT-109 deployed furthest to the west in the strait as part of Division B. Kennedy's boat had one more man onboard that night than the standard twelve, with unassigned Ensign George Ross volunteering for the ride.

Right from the start things did not go well. It was, recalled Lieutenant Dick Keresey, skipper of PT-105, 'a screwed-up action'. The Japanese convoy was first sighted after midnight. In all, thirty torpedoes were fired without scoring a single hit against enemy ships. The only PT boats equipped with radar, primitive though it still was, were the four division leaders. But the leaders were the first to fire their torpedoes and, inexplicably, returned to base leaving the other eleven PT boats in the lurch. Leaderless and radarless, they went on searching blind and in mandated radio silence for Japanese craft, having to rely instead on regular eye contact with one another on a pitch-black night. It was a shambles and a disaster waiting to happen; as the US Navy's official history later conceded, 'the most confused and least effective action the PT's had been in'.

The Tokyo Express, meanwhile, docked unharried at Vila at 12.30 am and began unloading its cargo of about 1000 men and munitions. By that time, many of the remaining PT boats had already returned to base. At about 2 am on Monday, 2 August 1943, Kennedy's PT-109 and PT-162 had linked up and were slowly heading north-west up Blackett Strait, unaware of the current location of other PT boats and equally unaware of the location of the Japanese destroyers and transport ships of the Tokyo Express. By chance, they soon joined up with another boat, PT-169. But despite their best efforts, the three PT boats drifted further and further apart in the darkness and poor visibility.

Just before 2.30 am, while manoeuvring into position to lead the Japanese convoy back to base, the crew of the leading destroyer escort, the *Amagiri*, saw an unidentified craft moving slowly at about 1000 metres directly to the front of their bow. The *Amagiri* watch quickly determined it was an enemy PT boat. PT-109, unaware of the looming Japanese giant, did not change course and steadily approached. Travelling fast, the *Amagiri*, which translates as 'Heavenly Mist', hit the PT boat less than a minute later. There was nothing heavenly or soft about it.

Dispute would later erupt as to whether the *Amagiri* deliberately ran into PT-109. The commanding officer, Captain Katsumori Yamashiro, claimed that he tried to pass to the stern of the PT boat, while the skipper of the *Amagiri*, Lieutenant-Commander Kohei Hanami, maintained that with poor visibility and a small and fast target, ramming the enemy boat was the best option for destroying it. Either way, the outcome of the collision was beyond doubt.

CHAPTER 9

ADRIFT

It was the dead of night and there was fire on the water.

Moments earlier, a helluva noise, as the steel bow of the 112-metre-long, 2000-tonne Japanese destroyer smashed into the 24-metre, 57-tonne plywood hull of a PT boat at about 30 knots, or 55 kilometres per hour. It was like a truck hitting a billy cart. The PT boat was sliced diagonally just behind the cockpit, where Jack Kennedy stood at the wheel. Igniting on impact, the highly flammable aviation fuel used to power the boat exploded in a 30-metre fireball.

Destruction came with little warning. There was no moon, and to make matters worse, fog had crept in over Blackett Strait earlier that night. In the milky darkness beyond the cockpit windows, the sea and the sky merged into one impenetrable mass. Without radar, PT-109 was virtually blind. The *Amagiri* burst out of the gloom at close to top speed, giving the PT crew only seconds to react. For an instant, Kennedy – as well as those onboard the nearby PT-162 and PT-169 – thought the intruder was another PT boat. As the dark shape loomed larger and clearer, Kennedy realised his mistake. Instinctively, he spun the wheel to position the torpedoes for firing. But it was too late.

Having smashed the hapless PT-109, the *Amagiri* for good measure fired two machine gun bursts back at the wreckage. Even with their target brightly lit by the flaming gasoline slick, they missed. But it did not matter; the PT boat was destroyed and its crew, floundering in the water in the pitch black, surely as good as dead.

Miraculously, eleven of the thirteen members of Kennedy's crew survived the collision. Most were injured by the impact or by fire, including Kennedy himself, who slammed his back against a metal brace that reinforced the cockpit. But he was lucky; the destroyer's steel hull passed just a few feet away. Andrew Kirksey, the torpedoman's mate, who was on watch on Kennedy's right, died instantly, as did another crew member, Harold Marney, the master machinist's mate. 'Some men are killed in a war and some men are wounded and some men never leave the country,' Kennedy later reflected. 'Life is unfair.'

Maybe so, but, damage done, it was now Kennedy's duty as skipper to make sure no one else would perish on his watch. His first priority was to keep the crew together. While most of the boat's starboard, including the gun turret and the engine, soon sank to the bottom, intact watertight compartments kept the forward section of the hull afloat. Kennedy got the survivors to hold on to it, while Quartermaster Edgar Mauer shone a light to attract the surviving crew. Remarkably for men of the navy, some could not swim, while those injured had to be tethered to stop them from falling back into the dark sea and drowning. Some were hallucinating, some shouting, some quietly praying, all desperate and all looking to their commander, John F Kennedy. Through those first crucial minutes of bewilderment and panic, Kennedy cajoled, encouraged and ordered his crew to keep them focussed on the task immediately at hand: survival.

They knew there was at least one other PT boat in the vicinity. Expecting a swift rescue, they chose not to fire a flare gun lest it attract the attention of the Japanese. A reasonable fear, it was, nevertheless, an unfortunate call. PT-169, nearest to Kennedy's boat, and PT-162, further away, both witnessed the explosion but inexplicably failed to follow up. PT-162 believed all aboard PT-109 must have perished and, having lost contact with PT-169, returned to base. PT-169 likewise made no attempt to look for survivors and sailed away. By the time its commander had second thoughts and returned to the crash site an hour later, they could not see anyone, the wreckage and the men having already drifted some way away.

As far as Kennedy and his men were concerned, their comrades had given up on them. They were right. There would be no search and rescue mission, now or in the morning. But it was worse than that. Unbeknown to the wretched survivors, back at Rendova preparations instead would soon be underway for a memorial service in their honour. Convinced that the crew were all dead, the base commander, Lieutenant-Commander George Warfield, requested the Air Force bomb any remains of PT-109 that might still be afloat, so as to prevent the boat's codebook falling into enemy hands. Missing and – on little evidence – presumed dead, Lieutenant John F 'Shafty' Kennedy and his ten surviving crew were now well and truly shafted.

*

Clinging to the bow of the boat, the crew of PT-109 floated down Blackett Strait through the night, undisturbed by either friend or foe. Occasionally Kennedy would call out 'Kirksey' and 'Marney', hoping the two might have somehow survived and were still somewhere nearby. Patrick McMahon, the engineer, was badly burned and William Johnston, motor machinist mate, was delirious and vomiting, having swallowed petrol and inhaled its fumes. The others, fortunately, were in better condition, though shaken and in fear of lurking sharks, crocodiles and barracuda – not to mention the Japanese enemy.

As the initial shock wore off, in the harsh light of day the full extent of their predicament became clear. At dawn, as Kennedy peered through binoculars, he could clearly see Kolombangara Island just 4 kilometres to the east and Gizo Island 6 kilometres to the west. He and his crew knew there were Japanese encampments on both islands – 100 or more Japanese soldiers at the Gizo anchorage and perhaps 10000 on Kolombangara. Flanked on two sides by the enemy, they were now drifting slowly south-east. If the Japanese came looking, as they might at any moment, the wreckage of PT-109 would not be hard to find.

The problem, however, soon became moot. As the morning wore on, watertight compartments finally gave way and all that remained of the boat's bow began to sink. Just as well, since with no rescue ship or search plane in sight, there was no longer any point holding on to what was left of PT-109's hull in hope it would be spotted and recognised by friendly eyes.

Kennedy and his crew knew they had to get to land, particularly for the sake of those seriously injured, before they were sighted by the Japanese and before nightfall. By about 2 pm, after more than eleven hours of drifting down Blackett Strait, Kennedy decided to abandon the wreckage and make for a small island to the east of Gizo and some 6 kilometres due south of their current position. They hoped it was too small to attract a Japanese presence but big enough to sustain the crew with coconuts, if not fresh water. Known to the locals as Kasolo, to the British as Plum Pudding Island, some years later it would be renamed Kennedy Island in recognition of the skipper's fateful decision.

*

When Kennedy and his crew peered at Kolombangara from the wreckage of PT-109 they saw danger. What they could not see was a carefully camouflaged hilltop lookout, well positioned to view events in Blackett Strait. From there, in the early hours of 2 August, Reg Evans and his American assistant Frank Nash looked down on the 'strife' below: a flaming flotsam bobbing on the dark waters in the wake of that night's Tokyo Express. One of the Japanese destroyers swept the sea with a searchlight before it sailed off with the other escorts and the transport ships.

Peering through his French 15-power telescope, Evans thought he could see survivors moving around the wreckage. But he wasn't sure. It was hard to know at that distance and in the dark. After the Japanese gave up the search and left, he thought he might have imagined the figures in the water. Later, he reported the incident to KEN and waited for further news. At 9.30 am he received word that PT-109 was lost in action. So this must have been the unfortunate boat whose burning remains he saw at night. At 11.15 am Evans replied, 'No survivors so far. Object still floating between Meresu and Gizo.' At 1.12 pm HQ requested Evans and Nash to be on the lookout for any Americans who might nevertheless still be alive.

Evans passed the word to his Islander scouts. They would be extra vigilant but had to be careful, sneaking around as they did under the watchful eyes of the enemy stationed nearby. In any case, they found nothing except for a large number of dud American torpedoes, which had washed ashore after the previous night's debacle.

*

As Evans was instructing his scouts, Kennedy and his crew lashed two mates to a coconut log which had been used as a cannon brace onboard PT-109. While seven of them swam slowly, pushing Johnston and Mauer on the log towards the distant island, Kennedy and the badly burned McMahon made their way ahead of them, with Kennedy holding on to the straps of McMahon's life vest with his mouth as he swam breaststroke for land. Kennedy must have had good teeth and a strong jaw, as it took him four hours to bring McMahon to the safety of Kasolo, the famous Kennedy smile unchipped in the process. He had swum on the Harvard University team, but this surely was his toughest race yet.

Kennedy and McMahon reached the island just before sundown. Kasolo was tiny, a mere 40 metres in diameter and not much bigger than a football field. But it was firm land at last and it seemed safe. They crawled exhausted up the sandy beach and lay there, glad to be alive. Moments later, remembering the threat of Japanese spotters, they hid under casuarina trees. Some time later, the rest of Kennedy's crew made it to the shore, nine exhausted men with a few pistols, a ship lantern, and knives, but no food or water. They had by now spent almost fifteen hours in the water, dragged by currents, battered by waves, and in constant dread of the enemy and the equally deadly wildlife. They were beyond exhaustion.

But Kennedy would not stop. After a brief rest, he entered the water that night holding aloft PT-109's lantern, hoping the light might attract any rescue boat that was searching for them. Little did they know that none was. Kennedy's actions seemed, even to his crew mates, foolhardy – it was night-time and he knew nothing about the currents, reefs or enemy movements, let alone lurking predators – but no one had a better idea. Kennedy himself was not totally comfortable in this endeavour, as he recalled a grim warning against such saline sallies in the Solomons. 'Barracuda will come up under a swimming man and eat his testicles,' a crewman had once warned him. An accomplished freestyler, Kennedy quickly improvised with backstroke, and with some trepidation swam back out into Ferguson Passage. He knew that this stretch of water, through which they had entered Blackett Strait the day before, was frequently patrolled by PT boats. Unbeknown to Jack, PT boats took a different patrol route that night, avoiding the passage. After an hour or so of treading water he decided to return to his crew mates resting on Kasolo Island.

But he could not get there. Battling a strong current and suffering dehydration and exhaustion, Kennedy could do no better than collapse on an islet to the south-east of Kasolo and crawl into the bushes to sleep. His crew were relieved when Kennedy eventually emerged from across the reefs late the next morning. While he has been criticised for this and other dangerous exploits from the comfort of a professor's study or a journalist's lair, Kennedy's crew loved him for it. He would not give up, ever.

Kennedy asked Barney Ross to try again on the night of 3 April. An unenthusiastic Ross did have a go but became increasingly hesitant on his swim after spying sharks. Much worse, he lost the lantern in the waters of Ferguson Passage. PT boats from Rendova again used a different patrol route that night. It seemed like a comedy of errors, but no one was laughing. With every passing hour, the crew's anger grew. Their base was not looking for them. They had been left for dead. But more pressing for now was hunger and thirst. With hope fading of an early rescue, the men had to find water and sustenance soon, and then try to find their own way home.

*

By 4 August, with Kasolo's coconuts too high in the trees to dislodge, Kennedy led his weary crew back into the water.

They set out for Olasana Island, just over 2 kilometres to the south. Olasana was larger than Kasolo and had more abundant vegetation. Importantly, it was closer to the usual PT patrol route through Ferguson Passage. After another three-hour swim, fighting currents much of the way, with Kennedy again clenching his teeth around a strap from McMahon's life vest, the weary men made it to Olasana. Here, nature's bounty did indeed prove more accessible, and they finally feasted on coconuts, devouring their flesh and drinking their milk, before falling into exhausted sleep. Too tired after the day's exertions, Kennedy did not swim out that night to look for rescuers. Had he done so, he might have run into PT boats, which were back patrolling the passage.

Next morning, 5 August, Kennedy and Ross swam out to the southernmost island of the small chain, closest to and with the best view of Ferguson Passage. Arriving about noon at Naru Island, also known to cartographers as Gross Island or Cross Island, they gingerly snuck across its length under cover of bushes and trees. On the far shore they made a happy discovery: a small Japanese crate with biscuits and hard candy. And nearby, they spied a local lean-to hiding a one-man canoe and a tin of water. Water! They did not know it, but they had accidentally come across an emergency stash, secreted away by one of Reg Evans' scouts. Whatever their provenance, all these priceless provisions would nicely supplement the crew's coconut diet.

Delighted with their discoveries, Kennedy and Ross made their way back, this time along the beach, when they saw what appeared to be a Japanese barge caught on the reef a few hundred metres offshore. Soon they noticed two Solomon Islanders in a canoe, paddling around and also examining the wreck. Quickly, Kennedy waved to the men, hoping they might help save him and his crew. Instead, startled by the two rough-looking men, and 'thinking [they] were Japanese', the Islanders paddled swiftly away, heading north-west.

Kennedy and Ross did not know what to make of it. Might the locals inform the Japanese and betray their presence on the island? Or were the two scared because they thought that Kennedy and Ross were Japanese? Better the latter, but only time would tell. Again that night, Kennedy ventured out into Ferguson Passage, this time in the one-person canoe, hoping to flag down a passing PT boat. Again, no PT boats appeared, and Kennedy went back to Naru Island. He decided to return to his crew on Olasana with the treasure cargo of water, biscuits and candy. Ross had to stay behind as there was not enough room in the canoe. He would swim back to join his crewmates the next morning.

Arriving at about midnight, Kennedy was startled. Who should he find sitting around a campfire, smoking cigarettes with his crew, but the same two Islanders he and Ross had startled only hours before?

The two Solomon Islanders fraternising with the PT crew were 25-year-old Eroni (Aaron) Kumana and twenty-year-old Biuku (Nebuchadnezzar) Gasa, both scouts for Evans. Running away from Kennedy and Ross, they headed for their home base at Kolombangara, but decided to stop on the way at Olasana Island to fetch some coconuts. There they ran into the Americans.

Both parties were frightened at first and kept at a distance. Neither knew if the other was friend or foe. The Islanders thought the Americans might be Japanese – or German – or otherwise working for them. If so, and they were caught, torture and execution as spies was likely.

Conversation was halting and nervous, with little under-standing. Lennie Thom said 'Come help. I'm an American.' He then pulled up his sleeve and said to Gasa and Kumana 'Look at my skin. It's white.' Gasa was still not impressed, replying in Pidgin 'No mata yu waet skin, yu Japani.' It was not until another PT-109 crew member mentioned the name of an Islander scout he knew about, Johnny Kari, and then Thom pointed to the sky, saying 'white star', the insignia on American aircraft, that the scouts were finally convinced the strangers were the missing American sailors they had been told to look out for and came ashore. Kumana recalled many years later that the first thing the bedraggled Americans asked for was cigarettes. No one had any matches, but Kumana enthralled them when he made a flame by rubbing two sticks together. They quickly struck up a friendship. The scouts told the Americans they saw two 'Japanese' on Naru, but no one made the connection with Kennedy and Ross. When a few hours later Kennedy joined in with biscuits, sweets and water, he and the two Islanders quickly realised they had already seen each other earlier on Naru. The circle was closed, with much relief.

CHAPTER 10

THE RESCUE

On 6 August, the day after they discovered Kennedy's men on Olasana Island, Gasa and Kumana returned to Naru with Kennedy and picked up Barney Ross, who was swimming back to join the rest of the crew. Again, there was no sign of American boats anywhere along the way. Before they returned to Olasana, the Islanders showed Kennedy where they had hidden a larger, two-man canoe.

Kennedy now wanted the scouts to take a message back to the PT base at Rendova to spark a rescue mission but had no idea how to put it in writing. Gasa came up with a simple yet brilliant suggestion: a coconut. Grabbing a green one, Kennedy took his sheath knife and, with elan, carved crude letters into its husk. The famous message read:

NAURO [SIC] ISL
COMMANDER NATIVE KNOWS POS'IT
HE CAN PILOT II ALIVE NEED
SMALL BOAT
          KENNEDY

Gasa and Kumana now started off on their 60-kilometre journey, first stopping by Olasana to tell the rest of the

Kennedy men about their mission. Kennedy's deputy, Lennie Thom, happened to have found a blank invoice (numbered 2860) from – of all places – Burns, Philp & Co, Reg Evans' pre-war employers. In a more traditional manner, he wrote a note reiterating the call for help from Rendova.

Leaving Olasana in rough seas with an inscribed green coconut husk and a weathered Burns, Philp invoice, the two scouts decided to cross Ferguson Passage to Wana Wana Island. It was a fortunate decision, for there they met Benjamin Kevu, Evans' principal scout. Before the war Kevu had been clerk to the district officer at Gizo and spoke good English. He knew that Evans had finally been given permission to move his observation post from Kolombangara to Gomu Island, just north of Wana Wana, and was due there that very evening. He would need to be told the good news about the American survivors as soon as he arrived; Kevu would see to it.

*

Back at Olasana, Kennedy and Ross again went out into Ferguson Passage, this time in the small two-man canoe formerly secreted on Naru Island by the scouts. Searching in vain for a PT boat patrol, instead they found wind, rain, and a pounding on the reef. In the squall, Ross was lacerated against the coral and nearly drowned. His troubles were far from over; back on land he soon developed a serious infection from the wounds.

Kevu, meanwhile, passed the word about the survivors to another scout, who went straight to Gomu to await Reg Evans' arrival. At about 11 pm, Evans arrived at Gomu and was walking towards his new observation post when he 'heard the snap of a twig and whirled about with the tommy gun at the ready'. Happily, it was the scout, who greeted him with the news about the eleven Americans stranded on a small island off Ferguson Passage. Evans was delighted. From his charts, he soon worked out that the survivors must be on Naru Island, though he would later learn that it was in fact Olasana; Kennedy and Ross only ever visited Naru briefly.

Having just arrived at his new hideaway, Evans had not yet set up his radio, so he pencilled a note that night to be carried to the survivors first thing in the morning. At first light, Kevu made for Naru with a crew of several Islanders and provisions as well as the request for the senior officer to return with Kevu to Gomu to plan the rescue.

By 9.20 am Evans established radio contact and alerted KEN to the thrilling news:

ELEVEN SURVIVORS PT BOAT ON GROSS IS X [Note: X
is used in messages as a full stop] HAVE SENT FOOD
AND LETTER ADVISING SENIOR COME HERE WITHOUT
DELAY X WARN AVIATION OF CANOE CROSSING
FERGUSON

*

Having moved to his new base at Gomu on the night of 6–7 August, Evans missed out on a spectacle that unfolded just north of his old island home at Kolombangara. Fed up with the ineffectiveness of the PT boats in slowing the Tokyo Express, Admiral Halsey ordered a force of six destroyers to intercept the enemy flotilla. The American ships, which were all fitted with the latest radar technology, unlike the PT boats, soon found their quarry just north-west of Kolombangara and sank four enemy destroyers carrying 900 soldiers and 50 tons of cargo headed for the base at Vila. While of no comfort to Kennedy and his crew, two of the four had been in action the night PT-109 was sunk, though not the *Amagiri* itself. Karma would take longer to strike; Kennedy's nemesis went on to survive having its own bow sheared off a few months later in a collision with another Japanese destroyer, before being finally sunk by a mine in April 1944.

Later dubbed the Battle of Vella Gulf, after the thrashing on the night of 6–7 August, the Japanese never again sought to use precious destroyers to supply their southern Solomons bases. The Tokyo Express was no more, replaced with much slower and more cumbersome barge convoys. The Japanese days on New Georgia were now numbered.

*

At about 11.30 am on Saturday morning, 7 August, Kumana, Gasa and Johnny Kari, who also happened to be at Wana Wana, arrived at Roviana, a small island not far from Munda. There they came across men from an American artillery unit. To the scouts' surprise and consternation, their story, notwithstanding Kennedy's coconut and the note from Thom, was treated with scepticism; the artillerymen, perhaps not surprisingly, knew nothing of a PT boat lost several days before in Blackett Strait. After paddling for over 24 hours, the scouts were becoming increasingly desperate and angry. The commanding officer on the island, Colonel George Hill, later recalled that Kumana, in exasperation 'started swinging his machete in my direction indicating I was not acting fast enough'. 'Bot wea? Man ya hemi siki! (Where is the boat? The man is sick!)' Gasa yelled at the American. Hill did notify the team at Rendova and put the scouts on an American-crewed boat for the final leg of their journey, saving them more rowing.

Even when they finally arrived at Rendova later in the afternoon, they were at first met with suspicion. As it happened, Evans' 9.20 am message to KEN had been relayed and reached the PT base before midday, just before Colonel Hill's from Roviana. Three PT boats would be sent out later that night to check Evans' story. But the base command, having convinced themselves right from the outset that all PT-109 crew had perished together with their boat, remained unconvinced. Surely, Kennedy and his men could not still be alive. It must be a mistake. Or perhaps it was an enemy ruse to draw the PT boats out into an ambush, Evans having been played by double-dealing Islanders. It was uncomfortable for the Rendova brass to contemplate that they might have been wrong all along, having too easily given up on their comrades.

It was only when the scouts showed the coconut that the penny finally dropped. The carved message seemed too elaborate to be part of a Japanese or Islander ploy. It suggested that at least some crew members survived the sinking of PT-109. Perhaps the only thing more inexcusable than failing to search for survivors on 2 August would have been failing to search for them now. The command could not risk more embarrassment.

*

Arriving first on Naru Island in the morning on 7 August, Kevu and his crew found no one. So they paddled on to Olasana to check if Kennedy and his men were there. Eventually, they found them in a jungle clearing. Any fear Kennedy and his crew might have felt as several unknown Islanders suddenly emerged from the jungle was immediately overcome by the clipped vowels of Benjamin Kevu, who stepped forward to announce in perfect English, 'I have a letter for you, Sir.' Kennedy opened it and read:

On His Majesty's Service

To Senior Officer, Gross Is.

Friday, 11pm. Have just learned of your presence on Naru Is. + that two natives have taken news to Rendova. I strongly advise you return immediately to here in this canoe + by the time you arrive here I will be in communication with authorities at Rendova + we can finalise plans to collect balance of party

A R Evans, Lt

RANVR

P.S. Will warn aviation of your crossing Ferguson Passage.

'You've got to hand it to the British,' Kennedy smiled, as he passed the note to Ross. Kennedy might have been confused by the note's header, but in this way misidentification of

Evans had already begun before the two had even met. It would plague him for almost two decades. The coast watcher's illegible signature did not help either; it too would later play havoc with Kennedy's memory of events.

But none of this mattered now. Kennedy was elated, as were all his crew. A rescue was finally underway. He would have to return with the scouts to Evans on Gomu and work out the evacuation details, but – despite Evans recommending urgency – first things first. A feast.

The scouts prepared local yams and paw paws, rice, potatoes, boiled fish, and the ever-reliable C-rations of canned corn beef and hard tack biscuits. For Kennedy's men it was an unforgettable banquet followed by a bump of nicotine from army-issued Chelsea cigarettes.

At Gomu, Evans had by now received a reply to his earlier message to KEN. Not only had the coast watch HQ on Guadalcanal excitedly received his 'great news' but Evans' scouts, Kumana and Gasa, had also made it to the PT base at Rendova with Kennedy's coconut and Ross's Burns, Philp invoice confirming Evans' radio message. The rescue was underway. For now, all Evans could do was wait.

*

By mid-afternoon, after the splendid lunch, it was time for the scouts to ferry Kennedy across Ferguson Passage to Gomu Island to meet with Evans and plan the evacuation of Kennedy's crew from Olasana. Cautious about travelling in broad daylight, the scouts hid Kennedy under palm fronds on the bottom of the canoe so that he could not be seen from the air. As it was, three Japanese planes soon buzzed them. But with a friendly wave from Kevu, they soon flew off. The palm fronds did their job, but it was a close call.

Evans and Malanga nervously awaited the arrival of the 'Senior Officer, Gross Is'. Scanning the sea, they wondered what was holding them up. Perhaps they were waiting for the safety of nightfall, thought Evans. He checked with Malanga: had he asked the scouts to come back without delay? Yes, Malanga assured Evans. The scouts were told to return straight away. Anxiety mounting, Evans sent another message at 12.45 pm:

COULD ONLY MAN ONE CANOE SUITABLE FOR CROSSING
X NO SIGN ITS RETURN YET X GO AHEAD SEND
SURFACE CRAFT WITH SUITABLE RAFT OR DINGHIES X
IF ANY ARRIVE HERE LATER WILL SEND OTHER ROUTE
X PLEASE KEEP ME INFORMED.

At 2 pm, Evans received a message from Rendova: 'THREE PT BOATS PROCEED TONIGHT AND WILL BE AT GROSS ISLAND ABOUT IOPM X THEY WILL TAKE RAFTS ETC X WILL INFORM YOU WHEN WE RECEIVE ADVICE OF RESCUE'. Trying to ease the tension, Evans now sought comfort in routine, ordering groceries for his new base.

At about 6 pm, in the softening daylight, Evans and his scouts saw the small ripple of a canoe approaching Gomu. Surely that must be it. But peering with binoculars through bushes near the beach they could see no white man onboard, only Islanders. What had gone wrong, wondered Evans.

But as the scouts in the canoe came closer, he could see they were beaming, Ben Kevu 'wreathed in smiles', reassuring Evans that perhaps all was well. And just as they reached the shore a tall, skinny young man jumped from under coconut leaves onto the beach. Sporting the famous smile he said, 'Man, am I glad to see you!' Evans, as he subsequently recalled, looked at him and said, 'And I am bloody glad to see you, too.'

Some later American and English retellings made the famous encounter sound like a comedy of manners, a Southern Seas staging of *The Importance of Being Earnest*, with Kennedy simply saying, 'Hello, I'm Kennedy' and Evans politely replying – you can almost picture him bowing – 'Come to my tent and have a cup of tea.' Evans' own recollection certainly rings truer.

This much, however, all versions have in common: both men were greatly pleased to finally meet and, after greetings, Evans did invite Kennedy for tea. He was delighted that, after the nerve-racking delay, Kennedy had made it to Gomu. As for Kennedy, he finally knew the whole thing was not some sort of elaborate trap. 'He was relieved,' Evans later reflected, 'He looked it. It was only natural. He didn't know those natives ... and he took a risk when he went with them. They could have been leading him to the enemy'.

As they talked over a cup of tea, Evans was surprised at how youthful Kennedy seemed, guessing he was about twenty. Kennedy was bare-chested and barefoot, and had sustained coral cuts to his legs and feet. His hair was matted, and he'd gone six days without a shave. Even after the passage of twenty years, Evans still 'recall[ed] the day very, very clearly'. Kennedy 'looked like a very tired, very haggard and a very, very sunburned young man. It looked as though he'd been through an awful lot.' Even so, Kennedy said little about his ordeal and when Evans suggested he be taken from Gomu straight back to Rendova, he would

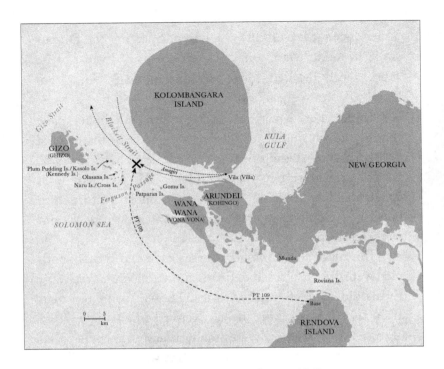

The crash and the rescue, August 1943

not hear of it. He would not be the first one off to safety while his men were left behind. After Evans told him Rendova was sending three PT boats to Gross Island, Kennedy asked Evans to send a message requesting he be picked up instead from Patparan Island (now Patuparao) on the eastern side of Ferguson Passage, from where he would guide the rescuers to his crew through treacherous coral and currents he now knew well. Evans agreed and at 6.50 pm he radioed the PT base:

LIEUT KENNEDY CONSIDERS IT ADVISABLE THAT HE
PILOT PT BOATS TONIGHT X HE WILL AWAIT BOATS
NEAR PATPARAN ISLAND X PT BOAT TO APPROACH
ISLAND FROM NW TEN PM AS CLOSE AS POSSIBLE X
BOAT TO FIRE FOUR SHOTS AS RECOGNITION X HE
WILL ACKNOWLEDGE WITH SAME AND GO ALONGSIDE
IN CANOE X SURVIVORS NOW ON ISLAND NW OF GROSS
X HE ADVISES OUTBOARD MOTOR X PATPARAN IS
ONE AND A HALF MILES AND BEARS TWO ONE FOUR
DEGREES FROM MAKUTI [GOMU]

An hour later, at around 8 pm, Kennedy said goodbye to
Evans. They shook hands on this small island behind enemy
lines, having spent a couple of hours in each other's company.
Winds of war had blown them together to this lonely spot
far from their homes and they never expected to see or hear
of each other again. For Evans, the operation was 'no glory-
and-haloes stunt ... just a routine job'. For Kennedy, it was
all about saving the lives of men under his command. He
did not see himself as a hero, and he could not have foreseen
that this would be a pivotal moment of his life, the story
which would later help launch his political career.

Kennedy would not meet Evans again until nearly
twenty years later in the Oval Office, in May 1961. He forgot
Evans' name and could not decipher Evans' signature on the
OHMS stationery letter he kept as a memento. He misread
'AR Evans' for 'A Rinhaus'. Worse, after initially mistaking
him for a Brit, Kennedy subsequently thought that the coast
watcher was a New Zealander. A most egregious error, if not
an unusual one for an American to make or an Australian
to suffer.

Before they parted, Kennedy was forced to 'borrow' some of Evans' property. By this stage of the ordeal, Kennedy was wearing only tattered shorts so Evans gave him a pair of his 'coveralls'. Kennedy also suddenly realised that while Evans' message to Rendova said he would fire four shots in recognition to his rescuers, he only had three bullets left in his .38 revolver. With no time to alter arrangements, Kennedy asked to use Evans' Japanese rifle. No problem, said Evans. He never saw the rifle again, but it didn't matter; he soon acquired another one. When Evans visited President Kennedy in the White House, Kennedy was quick to apologise, one historian noting, 'The rifle disappeared'. As had the 'coveralls', perhaps just as well.

*

By 11 pm, on Patparan, Kennedy was becoming impatient. Where was the rescue team? Where were the PT boats? He worried that again he and his men were being neglected. Then, out of the darkness, came the rumble of PT engines not far away. Followed by four gunshots. Quickly, Kennedy stood up in Ben Kevu's dugout canoe and replied with his snub-nosed .38 pistol, bang, bang, bang, and, grabbing the rifle, the final BANG. The recoil was powerful, and Kennedy nearly ended up in the water.

For a second, bubbling with frustration after a week waiting for rescue, even now an hour late, Kennedy lost his famous cool. 'Where the hell have you been?' he shouted. Who could blame him? Still, he soon recovered his trademark poise, replying waspishly when offered food, 'Thanks, I've just had a coconut.'

Once aboard, and after some medicinal brandy, his

spirits soon lifted. Old friends from the base, as well as Kumana and Gasa, greeted him as PT-157 snaked beside the coral towards Olasana and Kennedy's waiting men. The scouts insisted on going onboard despite the dangers, saying, 'It's OK. If they die, we die, too'. At about 12.30 am Kennedy arrived on the island to find his crew asleep. So much for keeping watch. But before long all were aboard PT-157 and heading back to Rendova.

They were elated. The eleven who had survived the initial impact would all make it back. There was much backslapping and carrying on. And after that, there was sheer relief. Kennedy had done what a good commander should; he had looked after his men under the most trying of circumstances. In turn, writes one historian, his crew 'all admired, and in some cases revered, Kennedy for his skill and leadership in averting their capture and death at the hands of the Japanese'. He had salvaged their lives and their futures. And he had salvaged his own too.

As the tattered survivors made their way back, Motor Machinist William Johnston threw his arms around the two Islanders and they sang. It was no heavenly choir, but it was a hymn to God's grace, 'Yes, Jesus Loves Me!', that both the devout American and the mission-raised Kumana and Gasa knew well:

Jesus loves me! This I know,
For the Bible tells me so.
Little ones to him belong;
They are weak, but He is strong.
Yes, Jesus loves me! The Bible tells me so.

CHAPTER 11

AUSSIES AND YANKS

Whether on the streets of Australia, in the jungles of New Guinea, or even on the beach at Gomu Island, wartime encounters between the Australians and the Americans would prove momentous. For some, like Reg Evans and Jack Kennedy, the impact was life changing. For most others it was less dramatic, but few remained unaffected. Australia itself was transformed.

Over a million Americans would pass through Australian ports, cities and towns before the war was over. They constituted just under 1 per cent of the US population at the time, but for Australia, a nation of little more than 7 million, their presence was a shock to the system – economic, cultural and social. The Americans arrived in a country that was insular, somewhat staid and straitlaced, and consciously very British, though, needless to say, not for around 2 per cent of the population who were Indigenous Australians and other people of colour. Observing American visitors caused Australians to look more closely at themselves. The war was to be a turning point in the development of an Australian national consciousness, of a unique identity.

As American units began arriving in Australia in early 1942, the United States military thought it prudent to publish an information booklet for their enlightenment. Prepared by anonymous writers at the Special Service Division of the US Army, it was titled simply *Instructions for American Servicemen in Australia – 1942*. Along with a pocket Bible (with a personal message from President Roosevelt) and the *Army Song Book*, the *Instructions* were issued to every American GI entering Australia. It is an introduction to Australian life, culture, history, heritage, food and even currency that the average American soldier could understand. This story of Australia is simple, funny and well crafted. It finds much in common, starting with a jocular appreciation of the Australian accent and vernacular but concentrating on similarities in history, outlook and values of the two countries.

Even today, the booklet makes for fascinating reading. The *Instructions* reflect the temper (good and bad) of the time. Australia's Indigenous people who 'roam the waste lands' are quickly passed over in favour of cultural reflections on singing and sport. Thus, 'Australians, like Russians, are natural group singers. It's one of the great differences you'll notice between American camps and Australian – the singing.' To that end, the booklet contains the words of 'Waltzing Matilda', explaining that 'The swagman (hobo) of the song represents the common man struggling against the oppressive exploiter. He prefers death to slavery and it is this defiant attitude which the Aussies hold dear.'

There are also curious culinary explanations. 'Meat pies are the Australian version of the hot dog, and in Melbourne, the substitute for a hamburger is a "dim sin" [sic], chopped meat rolled in cabbage leaves which you order to "take out" in Chinese restaurants.'

138 SAVING LIEUTENANT KENNEDY

The booklet also addresses our mutual love of sport. The authors ungraciously describe cricket as not a 'very lively game to watch', whereas Australian Rules Football is heartily endorsed as 'rough, tough and exciting' and creating the 'desire on the part of the crowd to tear someone apart, usually the referee'. Now, that's better.

Dim sims and cricket might have been amusing curiosities, but to some of the visitors, perceived differences in character and temperament were more profound. A few Americans, for example, were surprised that Australians did not always share their passion for hard work and excellence, preferring the mediocre, optimistic cry of 'she'll be right'. 'The people here aren't as ambitious as Americans', wrote 22-year-old army medic Dean Andersen to his parents in Iowa. 'They like to sit around and talk and drink tea.' The American ambassador to Australia from 1941 to 1945, Nelson T Johnson, summarised it like this: 'the average Australian desires a high standard of living but he expects the State to give it to him, while by contrast the American desires a high standard of living but expects to work for it'.

Australian lackadaisy particularly rankled when it affected the conduct of war. American conscripts sent to the other side of the world to stop the Japanese advance and defend Australia were confounded by the rule that restricted their Australian counterparts in the militia to service only at home or external, Australian-administered territories, such as Papua and New Guinea. Worse still was the shock when, with national survival at stake, Australian wharfies from time to time went on strike. Outraged American servicemen were forced to unload containers themselves, appalled at what they saw as betrayal of the war effort.

Such predicaments, however, were outliers; the quest for a shared understanding was far more common. Commenting on their 'kindred ideas', American Charles Schroeder wrote to Australian Charles Tutt (the two had met in Townsville), 'though 11,000 miles may separate our ideals we can still see eye to eye in problems that mold our happiness'.

*

If Australians seemed strange to Americans, the feeling was mutual. For a start, for the discerning Australian, the Americans did not look like 'us'. They were more diverse. They were more European, with plenty of Polish, Scandinavian and Jewish names in the mix. There were many German and Italian ones too. And there were African-Americans, with a few Native Americans as well. Indigenous Australians served in both world wars, more than 1000 of them in the first and more than 3000 in the second, but Australia's armed forces, like the population in general, were overwhelmingly Anglo-Celtic in their makeup. According to the 1933 census, the last before the war, of 900 000 residents born outside of Australia, 760 000 were born in Great Britain or New Zealand; all together only about 113 000 outside of the British empire. All but around 150 000 out of the population of more than 6.6 million were considered European by race. Back then, Australians by and large simply said they were British.

The Americans also presented differently. For Australians, they seemed rich, modern and most of all glamorous. 'Those first United States troops are probably as fine a body of young men as the world had seen,' gushed novelist Henrietta Drake-Brockman. 'They are polite, but walk with easy assurance, unselfconscious. Their good manners impress the women, their clothes and equipment catch male eyes.' The media and official publicity emphasised the friendship and cooperation between Australians and Americans. This was largely true, especially in relation to Australian civilians. In the dark days of late 1941 and early 1942, Americans were nearly universally regarded as Australia's saviours. Australian civilians remained overwhelmingly grateful for their presence until the end of the war, if not blind to the frictions that inevitably accompany any such mass encounter between different peoples.

As elsewhere that Americans made their presence felt in large numbers – not least in Britain itself – they soon became the subject of the biting quip 'overpaid, oversexed, and over here'. Australian troops often felt themselves poor relations to the exuberant guests from overseas. In the lower ranks, Americans earned twice the pay of their Australian peers and the disparity increased with rank. An American lieutenant-colonel received nearly three times the salary of his Australian counterpart. Just a generation before, it was the Diggers who were the best-paid troops of the First World War and were disparagingly dubbed 'six bob a day tourists', earning more than an average worker. Now the tables were turned. American money made for easier access to luxuries like cigarettes, alcohol and stockings, which in turn enhanced the GIs' ability to woo local women. It didn't help that the 'Yanks' scrubbed up well too. While the Australian soldiers were dressed in Great War fashion, wearing a 'fluffy green blanket', as the slang had it, the Americans paraded around in their smart, well-cut and well-made uniforms. 'Yes, we were jealous of their fancy uniforms and taking out the girls and what have you,' recalled the coast watcher Jim Burrowes. 'But I have gratitude for what they did.'

The American authorities were aware of this and issued instructions to US servicemen forbidding them, for example, to hold hands or indulge in long embraces with Australian women. There were pleas not to grab taxis ahead of locals and not to demand dishes unavailable to civilians in restaurants. In short, American officers wanted their soldiers to lower their profile and to move through Australia more quietly and considerately. But with hundreds of thousands of men, many still teenagers, high on testosterone and the exhilaration of youth, this was often easier said than done. This is a story as old as war itself.

*

Tensions sometimes boiled over, as in retrospect they were bound to, when American bravado met Aussie tall poppy syndrome. The locals, feeling themselves outdone by the visitors, shared drink and resentment with their mates. Inflamed by alcohol and alight with indignation, it took but a spark to cause a fight, and a gunshot to fuel a riot. As in Britain, there were brawls, even stabbings, in Melbourne and Townsville and other towns around Australia.

But it was Queensland's capital, first to welcome the Americans in December 1941, that was destined to become the scene of the most notorious incident involving Australian and American service personnel. Truth be told, no Americans were needed for tempers to be excited. Brisbane had already seen riots by Diggers unhappy about their conditions as well as pitched battles between Australian soldiers and sailors, fuelled by inter-service rivalry. But it was the sheer numbers and the very ubiquity of Americans that stood Brisbane apart from all other Australian cities.

In July 1942, MacArthur and his general headquarters (GHQ) moved from Melbourne to Brisbane. It made sense – Queensland was closer to the Pacific front line. MacArthur's office, on the eighth floor of a sandstone building in the city centre, is now a museum and the former AMP Building has been renamed MacArthur Chambers in honour of its most illustrious occupant. Its largest tenant is now Apple – testament to continuing American influence in Australia. But in 1942, it was soldiers and sailors and airmen who were the face of the new alliance – though, ironically, another American premises was to be the epicentre of the drama that became known as 'the Battle of Brisbane'.

To some locals, the 'Yank' influx felt like an invasion, if friendly enough at first. Brisbane's population quickly rose from a little over 300000 to nearly 400000 at the peak of American presence. In addition, many thousands more stationed elsewhere in south-east Queensland regularly poured into the city while on leave. For American service-men, Brisbane became a cross between a sub-tropical boarding house and a bawdy house, a place you might let off steam if you stretched the rules. After all, after the safety of Brisbane, who knew what might happen in combat. Donald Friend, later a famous Australian artist and diarist, noted that Brisbane was popularly called 'the American village'. '[A]nd the name is justified', wrote Friend, 'The Aussies are very much in the minority.' It was an exagger-ation, but in certain places and at certain times – like the CBD on a Saturday night – it hardly seemed so. The city could not cope. Pubs, restaurants and even theatres were overcrowded, queues long, and amenities cracking under demand.

On 26 November 1942, Thanksgiving Day, the American PX ('post exchange') store was proving popular. Celebrating the first harvest of their Pilgrim forebears, American servicemen were drinking up. Just 100 metres down Adelaide Street was the Australian military canteen. It was full of Australians who were also drinking, though, never needing an excuse for a beer, not celebrating anything in particular. By 7 pm, soldiers were drunk, and tempers simmered.

The Diggers never liked military police, their own or anyone else's. Officious and cowardly, was the general view. This night, they attacked US military police, who retreated to the American PX and quickly called on reinforcements. Within an hour, around 4000 soldiers were running riot in the streets of Brisbane.

Then a shot rang out. An Australian soldier was killed when an American military policeman's rifle he was trying to grab discharged. Eight other Australian soldiers suffered gunshot wounds and eleven Americans were injured – one seriously. But these were the official findings. In the broader skirmishes and brawling, hundreds may have been injured on both sides. Many of them were recently returned Australian troops from the Middle East.

'The Australians ... had very solid reasons to be aggrieved', reflected Major Bill Thomas, a member of General Blamey's staff. 'The Yanks had everything – the girls, the canteens and all the rest of it – and our blokes were completely ostracised in their own city.' But it was in no one's interests, and to no one's credit, to dwell on the 'Battle of Brisbane'. Curtin agreed, believing that the less publicity given to the brawl 'the better for everyone concerned'. With both Australian and American authorities desperate to censor the event, the riot inevitably became mythologised. The numbers of killed and injured climbed with the years and the retellings.

*

Not all violence was a matter of tension and competition between Australians and Americans. Some problems that were to haunt Americans in Australia – as they would also in Britain and elsewhere – they brought from home.

In late April 1942, President Roosevelt sent a three-man team to report on the war effort in the south-west Pacific. One of them was a serving congressman from Texas with a lieutenant-commander's commission in the Navy, Lyndon Baines Johnson. On his arrival in Australia in mid-May, Johnson met first with General MacArthur, before setting off to survey the war effort in Sydney, Brisbane and then Townsville. From Townsville he flew to Port Moresby and was lucky to survive enemy action when his B-26 bomber was hit by Japanese Zeros.

On his return to Australia, flying between Darwin and Cloncurry over what Johnson referred to as 'El Paso desert country', his party was forced to land near Winton, in western Queensland, after they lost their way. Robert Caro, Johnson's acclaimed biographer, writes that Johnson told everyone that the locals he encountered are 'the best damn folks in the world, except maybe the folks in his own Texas'.

Caro then tells of Johnson's visit to Garbutt Field airbase, near Townsville, in early June 1942 to look over the facilities and speak to the airmen of the 22nd Bomb Group about their missions to New Guinea. But there is no mention of an event that had occurred just two weeks prior and may better explain why Johnson took three whole days from his busy schedule, from 6 to 8 June, to remain in Townsville.

On 22 May 1942, African-American servicemen based at Kelso airfield near Townsville fired machine guns into the tents of white officers who had reportedly mistreated black soldiers. The matter only came to public attention in 2012, seventy years after the event. There are widely varying reports of the subsequent siege and resulting casualties. But it is certain that Australian soldiers were called in to roadblock the rioting soldiers and help restore order. A journalist for *Time*, Robert Sherrod, was embedded with American troops and wrote a report of the episode, which was handed to Lyndon Johnson during his investigation in Townsville. The report was suppressed, a copy only recently emerging in the US National Archives and Records Administration. 'The Townsville mutiny' was the most serious explosion of racial tension in Australia within the still segregated US armed forces, but it is far from the only one.

In his memoir of childhood, celebrated Australian author David Malouf wrote, 'When Brisbane became a garrison town in 1942 ... the city was segregated to propitiate American fears of race riots, and the South side, our side, was declared black.' If Indigenous Australians were more familiar, until the war few Australians would have encountered men or women of African and African-American origin. In his boyhood memoir of the war years, writer Graham Smith related how his two-year-old brother, on a train journey from Toowoomba to Brisbane, first encountered an African-American sergeant in his late twenties. 'Robin got down from his seat, walked up to the soldier and reaching up ran a finger down the soldier's cheek … Taking in the look of surprise on my brother's face, the sergeant said in a deep southern drawl, "Noooo boy, it don't come off".'

Australia, of course, had its own issues with race. There was little enthusiasm to recruit Indigenous soldiers into the 2nd AIF in 1940, though some were selected. By 1942, with Japan threatening Australia, Indigenous Australians were made more welcome and several thousand served in the war, including nearly 900 Torres Strait Islanders in the famed Torres Strait Light Infantry Battalion. In November 1944, Reg Saunders became the first Indigenous Australian to be commissioned as an officer in the Australian Army. Coming from a family that had served in the Boer War and the First World War, Saunders volunteered with the 2nd AIF and fought in north Africa, Greece and Crete, before returning to Australia in October 1942. He then served in New Guinea (where his younger brother Harry was later killed), including alongside the Americans in the Salamaua–Lae campaign in mid-1943. Though refused a place with the British Commonwealth Occupation Service in Japan after the war because of his Aboriginality, he did later serve in the Korean War where he rose to the rank of Captain. 'Australian soldiers I met in the Army were not colour-conscious towards the aboriginal [sic]', Saunders later said, but Indigenous soldiers earned less and were rarely granted the war pensions and benefits that others received. Interestingly, Indigenous Australians were often invited to segregated African-American armed forces clubs, including the Doctor Carver Club in South Brisbane, named after the distinguished African-American scientist, George Washington Carver. It held dances and film nights, and in September 1943 welcomed the First Lady, Eleanor Roosevelt. Indigenous and other Australians volunteered to work there.

*

It would be easy to exaggerate the differences and conflicts that accompanied the first mass encounter between millions of Australians and Americans. Some more recent historical reassessments fall into this trap, with their claims that after the first six months or so the Americans had worn out their welcome. Or, worse, that relations between the two countries were permanently scarred because of negative wartime experiences.

The reality was more complex. As the authors of the introductory booklet for American servicemen reminded their readers, for all the cultural differences and potential irritations with Australians 'the main point is they like us, and we like them'. The Americans might have been 'overpaid' but they overspent locally. 'I had five prices for a melon,' was a perhaps apocryphal recollection of one fruit seller, 'Australian civilian, one bob. Australian army, two bob. American, three bob. American soldier with a girl, four bob. Marine with a very pretty girl. Sky's the limit.' Some called it 'Ned Kellying', others called it the 'khaki gold rush'. More selflessly, countless Australian families invited American soldiers into their houses to offer a brief respite from homesickness and monotonous military chow.

'My brother was away with the Royal Australian Air Force', recalled a Brisbane resident, Marjorie Robertson, 'and my mother's contribution to the war was to give anyone else's son a bit of ordinary home comfort.' Lifelong friendships were formed and love blossomed, with some 15 000 Australian women becoming 'war brides', the first one getting married as early as the day that Darwin was bombed.

'I like this country', wrote Dean Andersen to his family back home. 'The people like us and try to make our stay a pleasant one.' A comprehensive study of the Australian-American wartime encounter, informed by exhaustive reference to diaries and interviews with veterans and civilians, concludes that, 'The experience of having so many Americans in their country over several years was marvellous; it was akin to sustained travel abroad and could not help but disturb the insularity of the inhabitants and redraw the image of Americans held by Australians.' The American experience was not only necessary, but largely positive.

While there was no one attitude expressed by the GIs towards Australians or by Australians towards the GIs, there is no doubt that on the whole American servicemen felt welcome in Australia. And Australians were grateful to welcome them as defenders. As the introductory booklet reminded the GIs:

> The Australians need our help in winning this war,
> of course, but we need theirs just as much. You might
> remember this story when you get into an argument
> about 'who's going to win the war': Not long ago
> in a Sydney bar, an American soldier turned to an
> Australian next to him and said: 'Well Aussie you

can go home now. We've come over to save you.'
The Aussie cracked back: 'Have you? I thought you
were a refugee from Pearl Harbor.'

Tensions over rates of pay, rations, fraternisation and
race relations would persist for the rest of the war, but in
jungle foxholes such concerns seemed petty. Side by side,
individual to individual, the Diggers and the GIs got on
well after some initial glitches. They were in it together.
This is what ultimately mattered the most. 'There's no finer
soldier in the world,' the authors of the *Instructions* booklet
wrote about the Australians. The Americans would find this
out time and time again on the battlefields of Papua and
New Guinea. In the Solomons, Australian coast watchers
might have been numerically insignificant compared to the
scale of the American war machine, but their importance
to the course of fighting was far out of proportion to their
numbers. None of the Americans who came in contact with
coast watchers – including hundreds of shot-down pilots
and shipwrecked sailors like Jack Kennedy and his crew –
would ever forget them.

CHAPTER 12

TO THE END

Reg Evans remained in the Solomons for only the opening stages of Operation Cartwheel, the Allied offensive to retake the rest of the archipelago as well as the northern coast of New Guinea from the Japanese. After the rescue of Jack Kennedy and his crew, he grew increasingly frustrated with his own side's carelessness. His scouts and their families were much more at risk from 'friendly fire' than from the wrath of the Japanese occupiers.

'The difficulty of finding hidden Japanese barges, the accuracy of the charts and the inexperience of the new pilots led to many friendly villages being strafed,' wrote Eric Feldt. 'This had always been a problem, both in New Guinea and the Solomons, but probably the natives of Kolombangara suffered worst from it.' The island, thought Evans, 'seemed to be jinxed'.

After Munda fell to the Americans on 4–5 August, the remaining Japanese scrambled to get off New Georgia. Evans left Frank Nash and the scouts to watch over the Vila airfield, while on Gomu he concentrated on monitoring the barge traffic evacuating the enemy.

Shortly afterwards, despite repeated pleas and warnings from Evans, American aircraft again bombed his scouts' hideaway. Evans was exasperated: 'Because Kolombangara was a Japanese-held island the American fliers weren't too particular who they strafed and bombed there. It was probably a combination of green pilots and poor briefings. Our work was dependant [sic] on native help and these air attacks were devastating to the morale of my scouts.' Evans could not in good conscience keep asking his scouts to risk their lives for the Allied cause. He felt he could 'no longer call on [their] co-operation'. He asked to be relieved.

Evans was briefly replaced by HA Forbes Robertson. Nash, who initially remained the lone coast watcher on Kolombangara, eventually joined Robertson on Gizo. Nicknamed 'Dry Robbie' for being the only total abstainer among the coast watchers, Robertson compensated with his comprehensive knowledge of local flora and fauna and excellent cooking skills. Nash no longer had to subsist on Spam and army rations like he did with Evans. But the good times did not last long. After the Japanese succeeded in evacuating 12000 of their troops from Kolombangara over a fortnight in late September and early October 1943, there was no longer a need for a coast watcher presence in the area. The station was closed soon afterwards, Nash and Robertson heading for Munda, where the local coast watch headquarters had shifted to from Rendova.

Evans, meanwhile, returned to Australia and continued his service with the navy. After the danger and the excitement of coast watching behind enemy lines, the rest of the war passed safely and uneventfully back home. But his work in the Solomons had not been forgotten. On 20 February 1945, King George VI approved the award of the Distinguished Service Cross to Evans for 'bravery in reconnaissance operations'. Reg Evans was discharged on 16 May 1946.

*

The battle to eject the Japanese from New Georgia, in which both Evans and Kennedy played their role, was just the opening parry of Operation Cartwheel. These actions were followed by a series of carefully coordinated manoeuvres to neutralise Rabaul on the eastern tip of New Britain, Japan's biggest and most important base in the south-west Pacific. Its large airfield and deep-water harbour made Rabaul the key to Japanese defences in the region. With Rabaul 'reduced' – encircled and cut off – Allied troops would be able to break through the New Guinea–Solomons archipelago barrier and strike north to the Philippines and beyond.

This strategy of avoiding a costly head-on assault worked. By early 1944, Rabaul was rendered impotent. Relentless Allied bombing had destroyed nearly all the base's aircraft, with the last hundred or so evacuated to make up for heavy losses of carrier aircraft elsewhere in the Pacific. By the Japanese surrender in August 1945, nearly 70 000 Japanese troops remained at Rabaul, unbowed and undefeated, but also diseased, hungry and irrelevant.

The Australians' role in Operation Cartwheel was vital. Their task was to capture Japanese positions on the north-eastern coast of New Guinea, across the Bismarck Sea from New Britain, helping to further isolate Rabaul. First, in a pincer movement with the Americans, the Australian 3rd Division captured the coastal town of Salamaua. Salamaua, in fact, was not so important. It was a diversion from the more strategically important Japanese base at Lae, one of the main objectives of Operation Cartwheel.

Planning the action took six months. It was intense and exacting and both MacArthur and Blamey as well as their senior officers were involved. A complex operation and a valuable preview of D-Day in Normandy a year later, for Australia it was also the first opposed amphibious landing since Gallipoli. Fortunately, this one was far better planned and executed, cost far fewer lives and, best of all, was successful.

On 4 September 1943, Australia's famed 9th Division hit the beaches about 30 kilometres east of Lae. Veterans of Tobruk and El Alamein, the 'Magnificent 9th' had retrained in Australia for jungle warfare and amphibious operations. Following fierce bombardment from five US destroyers, the first wave of around 1500 Australians with their arms and supplies was carried to the shore in the landing craft of the US Navy's VII Amphibious Force. The Japanese defenders quickly retreated and, despite bomber counter-attacks, the Allies secured a beachhead. After a further 6500 Australians made their landing, two brigades of the 9th Division headed west for Lae, while the third one remained to hold the beach.

Meanwhile, on 5 September, 1700 US paratroopers along with the Australian 2/4th Field Regiment were airlifted to Nadzab airstrip about 30 kilometres to the northwest of Lae. Having secured the airstrip with little resistance, the Americans improved the rough tarmac to receive the Australian 7th Division. They landed, on schedule, the following day. During the Siege of Tobruk in 1941,

Field Marshal Erwin Rommel wistfully, though perhaps apocryphally, had remarked, 'Give me two Australian divisions and I will conquer the world for you.' The 7th and the 9th were now both in place, this time with the Japanese firmly in their sights.

Lae was a complicated logistical operation, perhaps Australia's most difficult of the war, but it was simple in aim. The Japanese garrison was to be taken in a pincer movement with the 9th advancing along the coast and the 7th by land from Nadzab. It was hell, as always, with New Guinea's creeks, rivers and jungle a miserable test for the Aussies. But it wasn't just the terrain. The Japanese were well entrenched and offered fierce resistance even as the Allies started to overwhelm their positions.

A race soon started as to which division would enter Lae first. As it was, they both reached Lae on 16 September, with the honour of first going to the 7th Division. Lae had been captured faster and, with several hundred Allied soldiers killed in battle, there were fewer casualties than the Allied command had expected. Not so for the Japanese. The 'kill ratio' the Allies achieved against the Japanese in New Guinea, wrote American military historian Eric Bergerud, reached 'levels rarely seen in modern war'. Australians were earning a reputation as fearsome jungle fighters. If Lae was not a complete rout – around 9000 Japanese soldiers managed to escape north through appalling conditions and fight again later in the Huon Peninsula campaign – it was a vital spoke in Operation Cartwheel, securing the Allied grip on the northern New Guinea coast.

Huon Peninsula, the New Guinea mainland's closest point to New Britain, was to be the Australian Army's last strategically significant campaign of the war. The control of the peninsula was vital to further isolate Rabaul. For months, through the misery of torrential rain, heat and humidity, stinking mud, dense jungle and dangerous slopes, the Australians pursued the enemy along the coast and the hinterland. By April 1944, they were victorious.

In the eight months it took to fight across the Huon Peninsula from Lae to Madang, Australians and their American allies had soundly beaten a Japanese land force only slightly smaller than that which so triumphantly took Malaya and Singapore in early 1942. The hard lessons of combat experience, combined with superior air power and better supplies, provided the recipe for victory. A particular loathing of the ferocious foe added to the desperation to succeed. 'More than any of his western allies in Europe-Mediterranean theatre, the Australian soldier fighting the Japanese was confronted by primaeval savagery,' wrote historian John Robertson. 'For no belligerent was there a sharper contrast between its cosy domestic environment and the horrors its fighting men had to endure.'

In the end, the Allies proved they could beat the Japanese on the ground too, the one theatre of the Pacific war where the Imperial forces were most competitive. 'In July 1942 the Japanese Army was invincible,' wrote Bergerud. 'In the fall of 1943 both Australians and Americans ripped it to shreds in every encounter.'

MacArthur, wrote historian Joan Beaumont, was only too happy to attribute success to '"Allied" troops when Australian troops were doing the fighting and to American troops when Americans were involved.' It's true, wrote the conqueror of Buna, Lieutenant General (later General)

Robert Eichelberger, in his post-war memoirs, '[O]ur Air [Force] made it possible, our Amphibs did much of the fetch-and-carry … but the main responsibility was borne by the 7th and 9th Australian Divisions. Because of the term "Allied Forces", which the censors then employed, many Americans still believe erroneously that our troops carried the burden of that back-busting advance.' Those who were there on the ground knew better. 'When brought up to strength, and given flexibility and firepower that modern sea and airpower provided,' wrote Bergerud, 'the invincible Australian killing machine of 1943 developed smoothly from the AIF of late 1942. Few armies in modern times have combined the steadiness, savvy, and ferocity the way the Australians did. It was an extraordinary performance.'

After Cartwheel, the island barrier was finally broken and broken through. Determination born of earlier humiliation drove General MacArthur as he, in turn, drove his army towards the Philippines. With spectacular amphibious landings he now seized bases in Dutch New Guinea in April 1944, while the US Navy pushed quickly westward. By October 1944, MacArthur's army and Nimitz's navy joined to begin the liberation of the Philippines. MacArthur did return, as he'd promised more than two years before at a dusty backwoods train station in South Australia.

*

Jack Kennedy was young and didn't take long to mend. In a hospital at Tulagi, the fatigue lifted, the coral lacerations soon healed, and by 16 August he was ready to serve again. 'I am alive,' Jack wrote to his parents. 'It was believed otherwise for a few days … Fortunately they misjudged the durability of a Kennedy.' Joe Sr had kept the news of Jack being missing from his family all throughout the ordeal, Rose only alerted to the drama by a newspaper asking her to comment on her son's rescue. His parents wanted him back and Jack was offered a transfer to the US, but he desperately wanted to return to combat duty. There was unfinished business. He had lost his boat and two members of his crew. He still had something to prove.

By now, some of the romance of PT boats was gone, particularly for those who had served on them. Senior brass, too, found it increasingly difficult to justify the effort in building and transporting them from the US, and then provisioning, crewing, arming and maintaining them at the front, in light of their disappointing record in action. To recoup the enormous past investment and improve their future performance, PTs were now armour-plated, equipped with radar, and given much greater firepower, 'so many muzzles, [they] bristled like a porcupine'. Gone were their nearly useless torpedoes and depth charges. No longer were they torpedo boats; they were now gun boats.

Kennedy took command of one such improved PT boat in early October as he was promoted to full lieutenant. In an indication of the respect in which Kennedy was held, five of the young men he had commanded on PT-109 volunteered to serve on his new boat, the former PT-59 officially renamed Gunboat No 1. With Japanese destroyers now a rarity around New Georgia, Kennedy and his crew could contemplate confronting enemy shipping with confidence that the contest would be more equal. The opportunity came in early November, when Kennedy's gunboat opened up on three Japanese barges at Moli Island, destroying the lot. A few days before, Kennedy and his crew had, under fire, rescued wounded Marines trapped on Choiseul, a large island to the north of New Georgia. One of the marines, a badly injured corporal, died on Kennedy's bunk on the way back to base. Until the end of his service, Kennedy was volunteering for missions undaunted by the risks.

But by now the war was moving away from him. The successful progress of Cartwheel, with Rabaul firmly in the Allies' sights, was dragging the war westward. Kennedy's new base at Vella Lavella Island, just to the north-west of Kolombangara, was becoming a backwater.

While he still enjoyed the camaraderie of his men and shared in their mission and challenges, he was growing weary of the war. He could see little point in what he was now tasked to do. Never much impressed by military rank nor martial flummery, his experiences in the Pacific would shape Kennedy's unawed response to military advice when president. He caught the first whiff of scepticism in the Solomons.

But above all, his ailments were getting worse. Jack Kennedy was sick of being sick. His ongoing health problems made continued active service nearly impossible. First it was stomach pain. Painfully thin – at 185 centimetres tall weighing in at only 65 kilograms – and with a grey pallor, by late November he was diagnosed in the Tulagi military hospital with an 'early duodenal ulcer'. By January 1944, he was back in the United States on leave, before reporting back to the PT training facility in Melville, Rhode Island, where it had all begun with such hope and anticipation two years earlier.

But it was his back pain that finished his military career, as it would continue to plague him for the rest of his life. Reassigned to a PT base in Miami, Florida, in March he agreed to surgery. The operation, which took place in June, was not a success. He was in and out of hospital for months. The back pain rarely left him. When it did it was because he had been given painkilling drugs or due to the onset of other competing pain, usually in his stomach. By November, the Chelsea Naval Hospital, in Boston, declared him permanently unfit for military service, and after debate among doctors about the origins of his incapacity, Kennedy was placed on the navy's retirement list on 1 March 1945.

He again went to Arizona to convalesce. But it was useless and, refusing further medical treatment on his back, he worked briefly as a journalist covering the conference establishing the United Nations in San Francisco, the British elections that saw Churchill defeated, and the Potsdam Conference in Germany, which divided conquered Germany into four zones of occupation.

By now, Jack Kennedy was already one of the best-known war veterans of his generation. Back in June 1944, while at the Chelsea Naval Hospital, he was awarded the Navy and Marine Corps Medal for courage and leadership, in addition to a Purple Heart for injuries sustained when PT-109 was rammed. The dramatic story of his heroism and the rescue had been widely publicised in American media. Soon, a political career would beckon the charismatic young war hero.

*

As the war moved away from Australia, Australia now started to move away from the war. From mid-1943, the Curtin government began reassessing Australia's military role. In 1942, an Australia in peril needed as many men in uniform as possible. A large army was considered vital in those desperate days to secure the frontier and fight the forward defence in New Guinea and the Pacific islands. But now, with the nation safe – Curtin waited until June 1943 to finally dismiss the threat of invasion – the Australian government looked to a more efficient fighting force and a better use of resources, including human resources. Curtin termed it a 'balanced war effort'.

With MacArthur's agreement, men were released from active service to work on supplying Allied countries to defeat Japan. The Australian Army, which in August 1942 had a strength of 476 000 men, was progressively reduced by half. Curtin's plan was resoundingly endorsed at the general election held on 21 August 1943. It was a landslide to Labor, and a personal triumph for Curtin and his handling of the war.

Not all have judged Australia's diminished role generously. British military historian Sir Max Hastings wrote that 'Australia seemed almost to vanish from the war after 1943. Australian soldiers played a notable, sometimes dazzling, part in the North African and New Guinea campaigns. Yet the country's internal dissensions, together with American dominance of the Pacific theatre, caused the Australian army to be relegated to a frankly humiliating role in 1944–45.'

The truth was that Australia was no longer necessary. MacArthur, wrote Bergerud, knew that 'Australia was, when all was said and done, a small country. In 1942 and 1943 Australia's war effort was central to Allied success. When the American war machine appeared in strength in 1944 and the war moved into the Central Pacific and

Philippines, this ceased to be so.' The United States could, and surely would, complete the defeat of Japan without Australian help. But Australia could not afford to rest just yet either. The fight against Japan was predicted to last years more, and with tens of thousands of Japanese soldiers still on Australian territory in New Guinea as well as thousands of Australian soldiers held as POWs, the country had to fight on.

There was also politics. Australia could not be seen as a redundant ally. Curtin was already contemplating the post-war world. If Australia was to have an influential voice in Pacific affairs, the prime minister knew his nation must not only fight but be seen to fight. And while American power was vital in saving Australia in 1942, Curtin was not keen for the United States to claim territory in the south Pacific, Australia's immediate neighbourhood and its assumed sphere of influence. North of the equator was a different matter, with both Australia and New Zealand encouraging American engagement. After the war, Australia's forward defences would once again lie across south-east Asia, but this time guarded by the Americans, and not just the British.

While the RAAF and RAN remained active in support of the Americans through the rest of the war, after the Huon Peninsula the army's large-scale operations were over. MacArthur had assured Curtin and Blamey that Australian troops would serve in the Philippines, but in the end it never happened. The refitted 7th and 9th Divisions were installed on the Atherton Tablelands in north Queensland ready for such deployment. There they trained and there they languished.

Only in late 1944 were Australian Army divisions called to combat in New Britain and then, in the dying days of the war, in British Borneo (now part of Malaysia). Many thought the fighting unnecessary. The strategy of bypassing isolated Japanese garrisons, which had worked so well in 1943, was ditched just as the end of the war was clearly in sight, possibly for political rather than military reasons. In Borneo, as well as in the last few Japanese redoubts around Rabaul, the price was paid in Australian blood. The Diggers were not impressed with these 'mopping up' operations. 'The evident futility of these embittered many men', wrote Hastings, and 'drove some to the edge of mutiny and beyond'. And while it's true that MacArthur's plan to invade Japan did include an Australian division, the dropping of the atomic bomb made even that plan redundant. If tragic for the victims, it was undoubtedly fortunate for the thousands of young Australian men spared the horror of fighting and dying in Japan's last stand, including the POWs, who were to be executed in case of invasion.

Some Australian troops, however, did in the end get to Japan. Of the 45 000-strong British Commonwealth Occupation Force, about a third were Australian. There, they were responsible for the military administration of Hiroshima Prefecture, where the first atomic bomb was dropped. As years went by, the Australian soldiers had been warily and wearily accepted by the Japanese as their occupiers. By the time the last of them departed in April 1952, and with war raging on the other side of the narrow Korea Strait, they even came to be seen as Japan's protectors. All within a few years. Such are the shifting sands of history.

CHAPTER 13

SAILING TO THE WHITE HOUSE

He sat by himself that first morning as president, surveying the walls of the Oval Office, pressing the buzzers, and checking the drawers of his desk. A gift from Queen Victoria to President Rutherford B Hayes, the desk was made from timbers from HMS *Resolute*, a British warship abandoned in the Arctic during the unsuccessful search for the English explorer and former Lieutenant-Governor of Van Diemen's Land (now Tasmania), Sir John Franklin. The first lady, Jacqueline Bouvier Kennedy, universally known as Jackie, whom Kennedy had married in 1953, discovered it in the White House broadcast room. Ever with a decorator's eye, she insisted it be restored to its rightful place. As it happened, the drawers were empty, except for the dire instructions in the event of a nuclear attack, but the desk itself was to centre the look of Kennedy's office as that of a 'navy man'.

With paintings and photos of ships and yachts, model boats and whale teeth etchings, and even a plaque with the Breton fishermen's prayer, 'Oh God, Thy sea is so great, and my boat is so small', the nautical décor recalled Kennedy's lifelong love of the sea. It was, however, his personal mementos scattered around the desk that had the most profound meaning: his navy ID card encased in a glass ashtray, a 25-centimetre glass ornament in the likeness of PT-109, and the *pièce-de-résistance*, a paperweight made of the coconut etched with the famous message that helped rescue his crew.

These were, as one biographer put it, 'talismans from the event that paved his path to power'. Kennedy would look at them every day while in office, reminding himself of the fecklessness of fate: some die in war, while others live. And some even reach the highest office in the land. Life is chaotic and unpredictable. Like the proverbial flapping of the butterfly's wings, albeit much louder, the crash of a Japanese steel hull through an American plywood bow in Solomon Islands set off a chain of events culminating nearly eighteen years later in the fireworks of a presidential inauguration in Washington DC. The sinking of PT-109 nearly cost Kennedy his life, but it also sparked and propelled his career. He could not have known it at the time, but the first step to the Oval Office took place in Blackett Strait that dark night in August 1943.

*

From the day of his rescue until the end of his life, John Kennedy wore the mantle of war hero. Whatever the claims sometimes made that Kennedy behaved recklessly in allowing his nimble craft to be rammed by a Japanese destroyer, his bravery and leadership after the crash were unquestionable. His crew recognised it, as did all others, even the sceptics. Those dramatic few days lost and left for dead in the south-west Pacific also shaped Kennedy's character, maturing him and instilling a loathing of war and scepticism of generals. War made both Kennedy the man and Kennedy the legend; in it 'the seeds of his presidency were sown'.

PT-109 was certainly a motif for bravery, but it became so much more. It stood also for vigour, energy and over-coming. It became a symbol for all those now assuming the mantle of leadership in the United States, a 'new generation of Americans', as President Kennedy described them in his inaugural address, 'born in this century, tempered by war, disciplined by a hard and bitter peace'. Nineteen-sixty saw a change of guard in American politics and more broadly in American life. While General Dwight Eisenhower had come to the White House eight years previously on the strength of his command at war, Kennedy was the first president to have fought it. This fighting generation – 'the greatest', as it would later be called – would occupy the Oval Office for the next thirty-two years. PT-109 set sail the values and mythology of the New Frontier and beyond.

If the collision was unexpected and Kennedy's reaction genuinely heroic, the tale of survival and rescue was shrewdly marketed and sold for the world of politics.

It all began with a lucky coincidence. Onboard PT-157, which was sent out to pick up Kennedy and his crew, were two leading war correspondents, Leif Erickson of the Associated Press and Frank Hewlett of United Press. Between them, their syndicated columns were read in hundreds of newspapers across the United States. Erickson and Hewlett, who through sheer coincidence happened to be in Rendova at the time, had been separately tipped off that PT-157 was going out to rescue Ambassador Joseph Kennedy's son and both recognised it would make a good story. Not only that, senior officers at the PT base also approved their presence on the mission, knowing that a successful rescue would be good publicity for the war effort.

They were right. After making the front page of his hometown's *Boston Evening Post* as well as the august *New York Times*, the PT-109 story ran again in nationally syndicated newspapers upon Kennedy's return to the United States in January 1944. There was no mention of Ensign Lennie Thom's note or the role of the coast watcher and the scouts – in fairness, their work in the south Pacific was still classified – it was all Kennedy, his heroism, and his coconut. No doubt it helped that some of the articles were written by Jack's former girlfriend, Inga Arvard.

But it was Kennedy's first love, Frances Ann Cannon, who had, albeit indirectly, a more profound impact on the story. Jack had wanted to wed Cannon, but she married journalist Jack Hersey instead. The two stayed friends, however, and Jack attended the nuptials. In February 1944, Kennedy travelled to New York, where he caught up with Cannon and Hersey. Hersey, who would later be one of the first Western journalists to report from the ruins of Hiroshima and who published a classic book about the tragedy, was fascinated by Kennedy's tale and decided to write about it.

The resulting article was rejected by the influential mass-market *Life* magazine as too long, but then another publication that Hersey worked for, the *New Yorker*, stepped in and on 17 June 1944 ran it under the title 'Survival'. It was a pioneering piece of what became known as 'New Journalism', a new writing style which dramatised news reporting with literary techniques drawn from fiction.

Not surprisingly, Jack Kennedy was once again the hero of the story, but at least Hersey introduced to the reading public a new character: the coast watcher. He wrote of the English-speaking 'native' passing a note to Kennedy – Evans' note to 'the commanding officer', written on 'On His Majesty's Service' letterhead – which in Hersey's retelling inexplicably ends with an invented sentence, 'I am in command of a New Zealand infantry patrol operating in conjunction with US Army troops on New Georgia' and is signed by 'Lt. Wincote'. The article not only misnamed Evans – Hersey referred to him again as 'Wincote' when writing about the eventual meeting on the Gomu beach – but also managed to change Evans' nationality.

Years later, Hersey insisted that 'The wording and signature of this message are as Kennedy gave them to me in Boston in 1944.' Whether it was Kennedy's or Hersey's memory that was at fault here, Evans has a good claim to be an early victim of New Journalism, with its relaxed attention to accuracy. The original mistake was soon amplified when Joe Kennedy Sr pulled strings to have the *New Yorker* article reprinted in *Reader's Digest* in its August 1944 issue. Unlike the *New Yorker*, beloved by the sophisticated but numerically insignificant urban elites, *Reader's Digest* was read in over 3 million households, hairdressing studios, and doctors' waiting rooms. Lieutenant Jack Kennedy – and Lieutenant Wincote – were now truly famous.

It was from *Reader's Digest*, in fact, that Evans got the full story of the rescue. He read the August issue towards the end of 1944, when it eventually made its way to Australia. Here, for the first time, Evans learned that the shaggy young man he helped save and whose name he soon forgot was the son of the former United States Ambassador to the United Kingdom. More intriguingly, Evans read of a 'Lieutenant Wincote', a New Zealand army officer, who was credited with rescuing the commander and the crew of PT-109. Misidentification aside, like millions of others, Evans must have thought it was a great story. And he left it at that. Always modest and unassuming, he felt no need to correct the record and attract the spotlight. For the next seventeen years, Evans later recalled, 'I've kept my trap shut. I could have bought in long ago, but why?' For Evans there was nothing special about the events of August 1943 and his role in them; it was just another day in a long war.

*

Misidentification was not a problem that Kennedy suffered from. He was the star of the PT-109 story, and everyone knew it. And there it would have all ended, Jack's heroism just one among countless ripping yarns spun from the upheaval of the bloodiest conflict in human history. But then a family tragedy struck.

One could argue that two accidents – one at sea, another in the air – shaped Jack Kennedy's destiny and put him on the path to the White House: PT-109 made him a hero, while the death of his older brother made him the heir apparent of his father's political ambitions. Less than a fortnight after the August 1944 issue of *Reader's Digest* hit the newsstands, Joseph Kennedy Jr, a pilot with the US Navy, was killed when his plane exploded mid-air over England. His father had hoped that as the oldest of nine Kennedy siblings, Joe Jr would enter politics and perhaps, eventually, run for president. Suddenly, Jack found himself the oldest surviving son. The Kennedy destiny was now his to fulfil.

He first stood for Congress only two years later, in 1946. Joe Sr arranged for 100 000 reprints of the *Reader's Digest* article to be distributed to Massachusetts voters. Jack won, still in his twenties, and commenced his trek to the White House.

In every political contest from then on until his victory over Richard Nixon in the 1960 presidential election, the exploits of PT-109 were central to his campaign imagery. Kennedy's status as a war hero distinguished him from his opponents. The whole episode, said a Kennedy aide, Richard Donohue, 'was the entire basis of his political life'.

Perhaps the most critical use of Kennedy's wartime heroism took place in the West Virginia Democratic primary race in May 1960. For Jack Kennedy and his team, it was victory in the West Virginia primary that opened the doors to the Democratic Party's nomination of him for the presidency. Forever after, a certain hierarchy existed among his supporters: those who supported Kennedy before that primary election, and those who only came onboard after.

After thirteen years in Congress, first in the House of Representatives and then in the Senate, Kennedy was emerging by early 1960 as a Democratic front-runner. But the West Virginia primary had long worried the Kennedy campaign with fears of anti-Catholic bigotry in a heavily Protestant state. Weeks from the poll, Kennedy was trailing Minnesota senator, Hubert Humphrey, by up to 20 points. But West Virginia was also an intensely patriotic state that had suffered disproportionately high casualties in the war. War service meant a lot, bravery even more.

For that, PT-109 was a trump card, and it proved to be the winning one. A former president's son, Franklin Delano Roosevelt Jr, and other Democrat luminaries stumped West Virginia for Kennedy, contrasting for voters Kennedy's war record and heroism with Humphrey's lack of military service. Cowardice was all but implied. In fact, Humphrey tried to enlist but was rejected for medical reasons. Politics is a rough game, and the truth did not matter. Some of the anti-Humphrey leaflets even went so far as to claim he was a draft dodger. Less controversially, hundreds of thousands of copies of Hersey's *Reader's Digest* article were once again distributed to voters. 'In the newspapers Kennedy advertisements drummed away at the record of their war hero ... TV opened with a cut of a PT boat spraying a white wake through a black night,' Theodore White wrote in his classic *The Making of the President 1960*. 'With a rush one could feel sentiment change.'

It was over quickly. Kennedy won the West Virginia primary with 60.8 per cent of the vote, a stunning turn-around. Humphrey pulled out of the race, clearing Kennedy's run for the Democratic nomination, which he would win on the first ballot in July 1960.

The contrast was not as stark in the year's ultimate contest, the November presidential election against Republican nominee Vice-President Richard Nixon. Nixon had also served as a naval officer in the Pacific during the war but without the combat heroics of the Senator for Massachusetts. Even later, writing in *RN: The Memoirs of Richard Nixon*, Nixon did not try to embellish his war record. His duties in the south-west Pacific were broadly, if unexcitingly, described as 'Ground Aviation Officer'. By all accounts he had been a good poker player during the war, his winnings helping to fund his first campaign for Congress in 1946. But as a narrative of wartime service, it was nothing to compare to PT-109 and in 1960 it certainly did nothing to help him against the photogenic, charismatic war hero.

'Joseph Kennedy's dream had finally come true: a Kennedy would be president,' wrote Jack's biographer, William Doyle. 'It was the culmination of an 18 year quest ... [in which] the mythology of PT 109 played a central, and possibly decisive, role.' 'Without PT 109', Doyle quoted longtime Kennedy friend and political aide Dave Powers, 'there would never have been a President John F Kennedy.'

*

While Jack Kennedy was fast becoming a public figure and launching his political career, for Reg Evans the taste for adventure lingered and he yearned to return to his old life in the Pacific.

But it was not to be. After the war, Burns, Philp & Co did not resume operations in Solomon Islands. Rather than settle into an ordinary life in Sydney, Reg answered an advertisement in a veterans' magazine for the British Colonial Service. He hoped to work in Fiji or Malaya but when a job was finally offered it was in Ghana – or the Gold Coast as it then was – on Africa's west coast, in the Gulf of Guinea. Confident it would make an 'interesting change', he accepted the appointment as an inspector of cocoa plantations, attached to the British Department of Agriculture.

In July 1947, Reg and Trudy departed Australia for a new chapter in Africa. While he no longer had to dodge the enemy, life was again eventful. In a letter to her mother, who then passed it for publication to the Adelaide *Advertiser*, Trudy wrote that not long after their arrival on Gold Coast there were riots in the capital, Accra. The high cost of cloth led to people boycotting and then looting European stores in the city before the army, including reinforcements from Nigeria, was called in to restore order. But despite the occasional violence and the 'appalling' cost of living, there were apparently compensations for the Evanses: 'There are quantities of French wines and liqueurs but flour is rationed.'

Reg and Trudy stayed on Gold Coast for twelve years. Conditions improved over time even as political instability continued, with nationalist politicians like Kwame Nkrumah calling for independence. In 1957 the Crown Colony broke from Britain and became the independent nation of Ghana, the first in sub-Saharan Africa to do so. Nkrumah became Ghana's first prime minister and later president.

During their African sojourn, Reg and Trudy enjoyed holidays in London and Australia but now it was time to head back home for good. Evans retired from the British Colonial Service in mid-1959, and they returned to Sydney and built a house at Avalon Beach on Sydney's northern beaches. Evans then took up work as an accountant for the organisation that ran the War Veterans' lottery.

There he would have likely led a quiet life but for Jack Kennedy's rising political star. After receiving the Democratic Party's nomination for the presidency, interest in Senator Kennedy grew – as did interest in the identity of the man who had rescued the young Lieutenant Kennedy.

In October 1960, *Pacific Islands Monthly* (*PIM*), a small Sydney-based magazine, published a piece titled 'Who was the Kiwi who gave wartime aid to Kennedy?'. 'There has been speculation in New Zealand regarding the identity of Lieutenant Wincote,' the article reported, 'as the NZ army has no record of the incident and cannot identify the officer.'

By the November issue of *PIM*, with Kennedy the victor of the presidential election, the quest to track down his rescuer was becoming ever more topical and tantalising. Under the heading 'Who was that who Helped President-elect Kennedy?' the 'Editors' Mailbag' ran a response to the October article from Eric Feldt. Feldt, the acclaimed author of *The Coast Watchers*, the definitive history of the service, replied that he 'had no record of that particular rescue because it was one of many, but by the time and place he thinks the Coastwatcher would have been Sub Lieutenant Reg Evans who had withdrawn from Kolombangara about that time. With him was Sergeant Nash, the only American to operate behind the lines with the Coastwatchers.' In any case, Feldt said that, contrary to Hersey's version of the story, he had no recollection of any New Zealand forces operating in New Georgia at the time and suggested that 'Perhaps Reg Evans can settle the problem – if anyone knows where he is.'

It was fortunate that Evans, on account of his long association with Solomon Islands, was a regular reader of *Pacific Islands Monthly*. Evans, who had last thought of Kennedy when he read Hersey's *Reader's Digest* article in late 1944, lately 'began hearing again of Kennedy – but this time of Kennedy the politician, Kennedy the racket buster, Kennedy the Senator and finally Kennedy the US President-elect'. However, it was only when *PIM* started asking questions about the 'mysterious Lieutenant Wincote' that Evans decided to break seventeen years of silence.

Evans phoned the magazine in late November 1960. He did not at first introduce himself but announced that in relation to the 'October issue about Kennedy and the Lieutenant Wincote who is supposed to have rescued him – I can give you some more details about that'.

He was then asked if he had read the November issue where Eric Feldt identified Reg Evans as the coast watcher likely to have rescued Kennedy and his crew. He said he had not, but went on to say, 'That's me. I'm Reg Evans.' Still in no rush, he said he would come in in a few weeks, 'to give … his version of the story – maybe for the January issue'.

Curiously, this was not the first time Evans made his story public. On 25 November 1960, Evans attended the 'Niddites' dinner, the annual celebration of former members of the Naval Intelligence Division. He told his colleagues about his role in the PT-109 rescue and one of them passed the story on to Alan Nicholls of *The Age*. On 29 November, Nicholls first published Evans' story in print in a small article on page 2. But no one followed up Nicholls' article. No one joined the dots. Reg Evans' involvement in the saga continued to remain unheralded.

Evans, meanwhile, kept his word. Just before Christmas 1960, he walked into the modest office of the *Pacific Islands Monthly*. Now fifty-five, still trim and energetic, he brought with him his coast watcher log book, which included the messages he had sent from Kolombangara, to back up his story.

The result of the visit was a three-page article in the January 1961 edition titled 'US's 35th President – by Courtesy of "Ferdinand"'. Here, finally, was the full and accurate story of the dramatic events of August 1943. Evans is quoted as saying he was 'impressed' when he met Kennedy, who he initially took to be about twenty or twenty-one years old. The article goes on to say that Evans was interested to learn that Lieutenant Kennedy was the son of the US ambassador, but 'even more interested that the man who had organized his rescue was a "Lieutenant Wincote", and a New Zealander to boot'.

Yet for all its hard work in raising the questions and chasing the answers about the rescue, *Pacific Islands Monthly* did not end up getting the kudos it so richly deserved. They were beaten to it by Ray Castle of the *Daily Telegraph*. In his piece, published on 21 December 1960, Castle added insult to injury by claiming that 'As far as I know, this is the first time this historic story has come into the open.' Traversing much of the territory of *The Age* article a month earlier, though without mentioning it, Castle wrote that he had learned of Evans' story from the Naval Intelligence annual reunion dinner. He then met with Evans who said he remembered Kennedy so well because 'he was the only person I rescued up there'. Evans recounted the events leading to the rescue of the PT-109 men, concluding that Kennedy 'was certainly a nice guy. The first thing he thought about was his crew.'

Castle's piece was the tipping point. In the United States, it was picked up by the North American Newspaper Alliance, with Kennedy's hometown daily, the *Boston Globe*, running the story on 3 January 1961. Wincote was out, Evans was in. The truth was finally emerging.

CHAPTER 14

REUNITED

Seventeen days after the *Boston Globe* article hit the newsstands, on 20 January 1961, John F Kennedy was sworn in as the 35th President of the United States.

A centrepiece of the inauguration festivities was a replica of PT-109. To Kennedy's surprise and delight, surviving crew members rode on the PT-109 float. As they passed the presidential review stand, recalled Pat McMahon, 'Kennedy stood up, grinned, whipped off his silk top hat, and gave us the skipper's signal "Wind 'em up, rev 'em up, let's go!"' McMahon's burns had long healed, but he still bore the scars as well as gratitude to the man who towed him to land and saved his life that night back in 1943.

Sadly, the two men most responsible for Kennedy's rescue, Biuku Gasa and Eroni Kumana, missed the ceremony. They were invited to the inauguration but were denied permission to board the plane at Honiara International Airport – formerly Henderson Field. Lacking sufficient English, colonial officials cancelled their trip. Ironically, in the spirit of post-war reconciliation, the skipper of the *Amagiri*, Kohei Hanami, who had previously endorsed Kennedy's 1952 Senate campaign, was invited and happily attended the inauguration.

Neither Gasa nor Kumana ever got to see Jack Kennedy again. Disappointed, as he had every right to be, Gasa nevertheless penned a note to Kennedy. 'This is my joy that you are now President,' he wrote. 'It was not in my strength that I and my friends were able to rescue you in the time of war, but in the strength of God we were able to help you.' Kennedy replied warmly. 'Like you, I am eternally grateful for the act of Divine Providence which brought me and my companions together with you and your friends who so valorously effected our rescue during time of war.' He concluded, 'You will always have a special place in my mind and my heart.' Kennedy never forgot those rescuers who first laid eyes on him and his weary crew in August 1943. He always hoped to meet them again one day.

Also missing from the inauguration was Evans himself, but at least his absence from official history was about to finally come to an end. On 25 February 1961, the president's press secretary, Pierre Salinger, officially confirmed to the media that the identity of the president's rescuer had been established to the satisfaction of the White House. He explained that the initial misidentification had come about because Evans' 1943 signature was so hard to read. Kennedy first thought that the signature read 'A Rinhaus' before Hersey complicated matters further by giving the coast watcher the name Wincote.

Evans took it all with grace. When eventually told of Salinger's explanation, he laughed and said that the 'next time he writes any note to any Navy Lieutenant he is going to sign it with a thumb print and a cross'. As for Kennedy himself, he was delighted to finally learn the true identity of his rescuer and hoped he might soon meet him again.

Just the day before, on 24 February 1961, the Australian prime minister, Robert Menzies, had lunched with the new president. They had not met before. Menzies, a conservative politician in the old mould, did not think he would be impressed by the young and telegenic Kennedy. But, rather unexpectedly, they hit it off. Graham Parsons, then Assistant Secretary of State for East Asian and Pacific Affairs, who was present at this 'completely informal, completely relaxed … most memorable occasion', described both principals as 'Two of the greatest spellbinders that I had ever encountered … Menzies is just a fascinating figure and a man of immense stature – he would have been in any country, let alone Australia – and a very colourful and persuasive talker and relater of anecdotes. And, of course, the President … a man of great humor, great presence, great wit.'

The two reminisced about the war, especially the sinking of Kennedy's PT boat and the coast watcher who rescued him and his crew. The president, reported the *New York Times*, told Menzies 'that he had just learned that Australia was responsible in a way for the present administration'. Kennedy and Menzies were to meet several more times over the years ahead, growing quite fond of each other. Reflecting after Kennedy's death, Menzies had long abandoned his initial scepticism: 'I have no doubt that President Kennedy had the stuff of greatness in him, a stuff which had yet to be woven into its full fabric.'

By the time the February 1961 edition of *Pacific Islands Monthly* (*PIM*) carrying the Reg Evans exclusive was finally published, his story was already well and truly out. In a slightly peevish tone, its editors noted that the Sydney *Daily Telegraph* was claiming to have discovered the identity of the person who had rescued the new president of the United States. *PIM* quickly reminded readers that Evans had contacted them 'weeks before the *Daily Telegraph* had anything to say on the matter'.

But life is not fair, not least in the cut-throat world of the media, and thanks to the *Daily Telegraph*, Evans was now a hot international commodity, the press trying to 'squeeze just a bit more out of the story' that *PIM* thought of as its exclusive. He had been run ragged by reporters and, private person that he was, was reported as being 'browned off with everyone in the journalistic profession'.

One of those who noticed the *Daily Telegraph* story, via the *Boston Globe*, was Bob Curran, the editor of *Cavalier*. What would nowadays be called a 'lad mag' and what Curran described as 'a men's adventure magazine', *Cavalier* traversed similar territory to *Playboy*, minus centrefolds. The titillating story of disaster and survival in the South Seas involving the current president, an Antipodean intelligence officer, and Islander scouts, all in the ever-present shadow of a Japanese threat, was exactly what readers of *Cavalier* would enjoy. It had been told before, but never from the rescuer's perspective. No one had bothered to find him. 'When I talk to prospective journalists, I tell them this story to illustrate how a big story can go practically unnoticed', Curran later reflected. Curran would now grasp the opportunity and run with it. He would make Evans a star.

Pacific Islands Monthly, meanwhile, continued to fight for recognition of its work. By the April edition, *PIM* reported that it had sent copies of all its recent articles relating to President Kennedy and his Solomons Islands rescuers to Pierre Salinger. Not expecting a reply, they were surprised by a 'charming letter' Salinger sent to *PIM*, revealing that the president would soon write directly to Evans 'that if Evans ever gets to the United States there will be a welcome mat out for him at the White House'.

Events now moved fast. With Evans' story scheduled to come out in the June 1961 issue of *Cavalier*, Curran stitched up a deal with Sir Frank Packer's Australian Consolidated Press and American Airlines to sponsor Evans' visit and a publicity tour. Aware that Evans was coming soon, President Kennedy wrote to him on 5 April 1961 with an invitation to 'drop by the White House on May 1st, at 11:30am'. The president 'look[ed] forward to the opportunity of re-living the hectic days in the Solomons' with Evans. He concluded with the words, 'I am certainly happy that all the confusion about the true identity of my rescuer has been cleared up.'

*

'"Here he comes!", shouted the crowd of newspaper photographers. "Don't let those television people steal him", cried the assemblage of reporters. "We must get him first and immediately", screamed the television cameraman.' So the *New York Herald Tribune* reported the arrival of Reg Evans at Idlewild Airport (now the John F Kennedy International Airport) in New York.

Evans touched down in the United States on 27 April 1961 as something of a celebrity. 'New Yorkers today turned on a hero's welcome', reported the *Daily Telegraph*. 'Mr. Evans was besieged by reporters, photographers, newsreel and television cameramen when he stepped from the plane which brought him from Australia.' Not something that a middle-aged suburban accountant was used to. Ever modest and unassuming, even in the middle of a media scrum, Evans had no regrets about not setting the record straight with Kennedy any earlier: 'As far as I was concerned there was no reason to contact him. If I hadn't been on the spot, someone else in the [Coast Watch] organisation would have been. Besides, Mr. Kennedy was too busy doing other things to bother him.'

He wasn't too busy now. Shortly before noon, on 1 May 1961, Evans and Curran, who accompanied him to the White House, entered an anteroom to the Oval Office and were ushered into the president's White House study. President Kennedy himself opened the door, greeting Evans with a handshake and introducing him to Vice-President Lyndon Johnson, who was on his way out. Sounding much as he had in 1943, Kennedy told Evans, 'I am extremely glad to see you today,' adding later, 'I am very grateful for what you did.' And employing Kennedy humour, he apologised for not leaving Evans' Japanese rifle in the canoe, as promised. For his part, Evans said he 'was amazed to find [Kennedy] scarcely changed in appearance from our last meeting in the Solomon Islands ... But as I told him he was better dressed this time.'

Eighteen years on from their two-hour tea and conversation on Gomu Island, the rescuer and the rescued – or the Sydney accountant and the American president as they now were – hit it off immediately. Evans 'felt at home with President Kennedy from the first moment'. 'We chatted on like two old cobbers,' the Australian veteran said, paying the American president the ultimate compliment.

They both shared a love of the sea; the president pointed to models of ships in the Oval Office and paintings on the walls and said, 'You notice the maritime atmosphere here.' Kennedy picked up the now-famous framed message and read Evans' words back to him. Hastily scribbled in a jungle hideaway, they were now the stuff of history. Kennedy then presented Evans with a PT-109 tie clip, while Evans and Curran gave the president a painting by a magazine illustrator of the moment Kennedy stepped ashore on Gomu from the canoe paddled by the Islanders. It would appear in the pages of *Cavalier* accompanying Evans' exclusive story.

Later, Kennedy took Evans outside to the White House verandah, as Reg called it, but light rain deterred them from taking a quick stroll through the gardens. All in all, they chatted for half an hour, twenty minutes of it in private. There is no official transcript of the meeting, and only a minute-long piece of silent black-and-white footage of the two in the Oval Office supplements Evans' brief recollections.

As he began to walk Evans out to the steps of the White House and the waiting media, Kennedy said, 'I am all for Australia.' His last words to Evans were, 'I will see you tonight. I think you will enjoy it.' For a second Evans was puzzled, but then remembered he was scheduled to appear on television in *The Jack Paar Show* in New York that night. The president would be watching.

This was not, however, to be Evans' debut on American TV. Earlier in the evening, at 7.30 pm, he was the 'mystery guest' on the CBS game show *To Tell the Truth*, hosted by Merv Griffin. Evans and two imposters claiming to be him were asked questions about PT-109 and Kennedy's rescue by a panel of four celebrities, including Don Ameche and Betty White. At the end of the show, the panel was evenly split as to who was the 'real' Reg Evans. Sadly, Ms White chose an imposter.

The Jack Paar Show was in a more traditional television format, a high-rating night-time chat show, in later years hosted by Johnny Carson, Jay Leno and Jimmy Fallon. Himself an army veteran of the south Pacific, albeit as an entertainer for the troops, Paar hit the big time in the late 1950s, hosting his show under the *Tonight Show* franchise for NBC. Airing at 11.15 pm – Kennedy must have stayed up quite late that night – Jack Paar's guests that evening included comedian Stan Freberg, comedian Cliff Arquette, and singer Peanuts Taylor of Nassau, as well as Evans. Having met the president earlier in the day, Evans now told his story to Jack Paar with a viewing audience that doubled Australia's then population of 10 million. With his modesty and unassuming manner, no doubt assisted by his Australian accent, Evans was a hit.

Evans was busy for the rest of his stay in America, attending Battle of the Coral Sea commemorations and a garden party at the residence of the Australian ambassador, Sir Howard Beale, where he was a guest of honour, as well as PT officers' events in Manhattan and Chicago. A keen trotting fan, Evans even made a presentation to the owner of the winner of the International Pace at Yonkers Raceway in New York. There is no doubt, however, that the half an hour with the former Lieutenant Kennedy was the highlight of his American trip, which *PIM* celebrated as a 'happy ending' to this saga. While *PIM* were delighted for Evans, they noted, perhaps with some satisfaction, that despite a burst of 'exclusive' articles by 'press interests' that sponsored Evans' trip, 'they added little' to the story as first published by *PIM* in their issues from September 1960 through to April 1961.

Once Evans returned to Sydney and normal life, the media scrum might have dissipated but interest in him was set to continue. In June 1961, *Cavalier* published its article, 'Found! The Unsung Hero Who Saved President Kennedy's Life'. On a daffodil-yellow cover, an attached red sticker highlighted the drama: 'Exclusive! How I saved Jack Kennedy's Life by Reg Evans'. In the telling, Reg was assisted by D'Arcy Niland, a well-known Australian novelist married to writer Ruth Park. Evans' story was that month's feature article. Sharing pages with a 'Special' on 'The Man Who Would Bring Back Hitler' and 'True Adventure' with 'The Day It Rained Burning Girls', it played well to the magazine's readership, telling the story of adventure, heroism and wrongs righted. The article remains an important source on the rescue of Jack Kennedy and a rare reference on Reg Evans' perspective. It is now a collector's item.

In late 1961, Robert J Donovan published his book *PT-109: John F. Kennedy in WWII*. It became a bestseller. He commenced his research by speaking to Evans in Sydney. Reg's log book and recollections provided the chronology for the rescue. The book was serialised in a mass-market weekly the *Saturday Evening Post*, again putting the PT-109 story in the public eye. This time, Reg Evans and the Solomon Islanders, including Biuku Gasa, Eroni Kumana and Benjamin Kevu, were all correctly identified. History stood corrected.

And, as it would transpire in the following year, Jack Paar wasn't finished with them yet either.

CHAPTER 15

MR KEVU GOES TO WASHINGTON

President Kennedy came to office as the Cold War threatened to turn hot. In his thousand days in the White House, he was preoccupied by security concerns that might at any time turn to armed conflict, perhaps even nuclear war. Flashpoints like Berlin, Cuba and Vietnam all demanded his time and tested his leadership. In the greater scheme of things, Australia and the south-west Pacific were rarely on his radar, with officials briefing Kennedy there were 'no important problems in ... bilateral relations with Australia'. Menzies was judged a 'strong friend of the US' and in time developed a good personal rapport with the new president. There was even talk of a 'New Pacific Community' to head off communist influence in the region, in which both America and Australia would play leading roles.

Perhaps not surprisingly, President Kennedy's most significant encounter with Australia once again came about through boats.

All his life, Jack Kennedy loved sailing and the sea. He rigged and raced yachts from boyhood and loved competing in the sea-washed summer sunlight of Cape Cod. Time spent aboard his sailboat the *Victura*, a fifteenth-birthday gift from his parents, was among the happiest of his life. Later, when he got the chance, his preferred choice of service was inevitably the US Navy.

And so, with the famous 'America's Cup' 12-metre yacht competition to be held off Newport, Rhode Island, it was only natural that Kennedy wanted to attend. He had not missed a series since 1934. So keen was the busy president that he made time to watch not only the first of five races on 15 September but also the second one on 18 September and the fourth one on 22 September 1962.

That year, for the first time, an Australian yacht challenged the New York Yacht Club for the Cup. Sir Frank Packer, the media magnate, headed a syndicate whose yacht *Gretel* (named after Packer's late wife) led the Royal Sydney Yacht Squadron's bid. While ultimately losing the contest to America's *Weatherly*, *Gretel* was surprisingly competitive, winning the second race and only narrowly losing the fourth one by twenty-six seconds. In any case, the Australian newcomers gave the Americans a good run for their money.

On the eve of the first race, Australia's ambassador to the United States and his wife, Sir Howard and Lady Beale, gave a dinner for the America's Cup crews at 'The Breakers', the grand former estate of the railroad and shipping magnate Cornelius Vanderbilt in Newport, Rhode Island. The guests of honour were the president and Mrs Kennedy, causing a stampede for the limited invitations to the dinner. Full of Australian politicians and 'men with urgent business in America', not to mention star-struck locals, the great ground-floor reception room was bursting. 'More than 600 journalists, radio, newsreel and TV men covered the Cup and more than 70 were accredited to the dinner,' recalled Stewart Cockburn, the Australian Embassy's press attaché.

Qantas flew in choice Australian produce for the banquet. Guests enjoyed Western Australian crayfish tails thermidor, roast Riverina lamb, Murwillumbah crystallised pineapple, and ice cream with Hawkesbury Valley passionfruit. The meal was washed down with Lindeman's and Penfolds wine, while an eight-piece orchestra struck up 'Waltzing Matilda', 'Botany Bay', 'Click go the shears' and 'Tie me kangaroo down, sport', among other timeless classics.

The president, according to Beale, was at 'the top of his form'. Kennedy spoke with great charm about the challengers, 'our friends from Australia, this extraordinary group of men and women numbering some 10 million' who are 'bound by an ocean' to the United States. 'We value very much the fact', he added, 'that on the other side of the Pacific the Australians inhabit a very key and crucial area, and that the United States is most intimately associated with them. So beyond this race, beyond the result, rests this happy relationship between two great people.'

'He liked Australians', Beale recalled, 'and he remembered with gratitude that he had been rescued in the Pacific through the efforts of an Australian coastwatcher, Lieutenant AR Evans. He also admired our record in war and our sporting prowess.' The dinner was a triumph, and in the ambassador's estimation 'it made many friends for Australia'. A week later Beale received a warm letter from Jacqueline Kennedy thanking him for a 'magnificent and stirring evening'.

The beginning of the first race the next day was a superb sight. 'This astonishing mass of more than 2,000 ships ...

churning along like an invasion fleet in the sparkling Rhode Island sunshine', wrote Cockburn, 'will always remain one of the most marvellous spectacles I have ever witnessed.' It must have presented quite a scene, as Cockburn gleefully adopted an Englishman's description of the flotilla as 'A sort of gay Dunkirk'.

Rather poignantly, the location of the America's Cup was only a few kilometres from the former site of the Motor Torpedo Boat Squadron Training Center at Melville, Rhode Island, through which Kennedy passed in 1942 and where he first met his PT-109 second-in-command, Lennie Thom. Alas, twenty years on, the shadow of another global conflict loomed large. With the Cuban Missile Crisis worsening, the crew of the freighter *Port Wyndham*, which was carrying *Gretel* back to Australia through the Caribbean after the America's Cup, was 'buzzed repeatedly … by U.S. military aircraft' which mistook it for a potential blockade runner.

The president and first lady watched the Cup aboard the destroyer USS *Joseph P Kennedy Jr*, named after his late older brother. Just a month later, the destroyer was deployed to the Caribbean to participate in the naval blockade of Cuba. On 26 October, the USS *Joseph P Kennedy Jr* accompanied by another destroyer, USS *John R Pierce*, stopped and boarded the Soviet-chartered freighter, *Marucla*. It was the only ship the US Navy stopped and boarded throughout the Cuban Missile Crisis. Ensign Paul Sanger of the USS *Joseph P Kennedy Jr* later recalled that the destroyer's crew 'knew they were either going to have a relatively uneventful day or they would be essentially starting the third world war'.

*

While the great and the beautiful were enjoying the America's Cup spectacle off Rhode Island, one of the unsung heroes of the PT-109 rescue finally got to have his day in the sun.

It was thanks to an unlikely intervention by Jack Paar. Intrigued by the PT-109 story he'd first explored with Evans on his show in May 1961, Paar went back to Solomon Islands in April 1962 to retrace the protagonists' movements and gather material for a special television event exclusively devoted to the mission. It would be the first episode of his new star vehicle, *The Jack Paar Program*, to debut in prime-time later that year.

Paar flew via Sydney, picking up Evans to take the coast watcher to film the locations where the PT boat was lost and where the survivors swam to. Reg spent nearly two weeks with Paar in the making of this light documentary and acted as an informal guide and adviser. Evans had a couple of nights on Kolombangara and even made the two-hour climb back to his old coast watcher camp. 'It's like coming home', he said. Ever the sceptic, Evans had taken 'with a grain of salt' Robert Donovan's claim in his bestseller that the people of Kolombangara sang songs about PT-109, only to discover that it was true. 'Not a bad song either', he commented. It was not the only song relating to Evans either; earlier that year an American country and western singer, Jimmy Dean, had a top 10 hit with 'PT-109'. The song became popular in Australia too.

Evans was also reunited with some of his scouts, for the first time since the war, and they fell back into an easy friendship. He introduced Paar to Benjamin Kevu, his trusted offsider. Kevu had been educated at a Methodist mission school and while he spoke and wrote English well, he did not talk much, and when he did, he spoke softly. Paar was quite taken with this quiet Islander. 'His slight frame, bare legs, and silver-rimmed spectacles', recalled Paar, 'gave him an appearance not unlike that of Mahatma Gandhi.' But when Paar and his crew left Evans and Kevu in the shadow of Evans' mountain hideout on Kolombangara, he never expected to see either man again.

However, as the date of the television special approached, Paar thought it would be exciting to bring Evans and Kevu across to New York to reunite with the crew of PT-109 and, perhaps, appear with him on broadcast night from the Rockefeller Center. It was easy enough to get Reg Evans back to the United States, but Kevu was another story. Paar organised for Kevu to travel by canoe from Vonavona Lagoon to Munda, where he caught the weekly flight to Port Moresby and then Australia. In Australia, Kevu joined Reg Evans and they flew together to New York to be welcomed on touchdown by Paar.

After the war, Kevu worked in the post office on the island of Gizo – he would later refer to himself as a 'retired civil servant' – making him locally something of a man of the world. But he had never been outside the western Solomons and knew little of Western society, except, ironically, the war, so his arrival in New York had Paar slightly concerned. Today we might call it culture shock. But Paar needn't have worried. Kevu was fascinated by early 1960s New York and pronounced skyscrapers, cathedrals and zoos as 'Number One'. 'I think that Washington City has more natives than New York,' Kevu told Barney Ross, commenting on the large African-American population of the capital. He was as cheerful as ever and took the novelty of it all in his stride.

The night before the show went to air, Paar held a party at 'Trader Vic's', 'a gilded Polynesian establishment with air-conditioned trade winds'. All the surviving PT boat crew were there, except of course for the president. 'The evening was a merry one, full of boozy reminisces, raucous stories, and ribald speeches,' Paar recalled. Although he had not originally invited Kevu to speak at the dinner, at one point in the evening Paar found himself being tugged at the elbow by the 'Mahatma Gandhi of the Solomons', who asked him, 'Aren't you going having me make speech?' At which point Kevu rose to his feet and made a brief and charming speech. In fact, he spoke so well that Paar asked if he would like to repeat it on the show itself.

The following night, 21 September 1962, Kevu made his TV debut alongside Evans, by now a comparative media veteran. It was a big night for Jack Paar too, being the first of his TV specials on NBC after finishing with the *Tonight Show*. He left nothing to chance in preparing for the program, even engaging in extended correspondence about it with Pierre Salinger. Now, introducing his television special, Paar did not hold back. He described the rescue of Kennedy and his crew by Reg Evans and the Islander scouts as 'the most exciting story of World War Two' and Evans as 'a great war hero'.

For the first fifteen minutes of the one-hour program, Paar outlined the history behind the rescue. Background to his voice-over was provided by the film he took in April 1962 as he journeyed to the Solomons and sailed the waters of Blackett Strait. There were many shots of Evans, shirtless, happy and rolling a cigarette, with a hot and sweaty Jack

Paar and a grinning Ben Kevu, including wonderful footage of Kevu, Evans and Paar walking on the very beach at Olasana nearly twenty years after Kennedy and his crew swam ashore. The action followed Paar and Evans as they docked at Kolombangara, the coast watcher returning to his hill-top lair. 'I've thought about that mountain for twenty years,' he mused. They then went back to tiny Gomu Island and the beach where Evans first met a bedraggled young US Navy Lieutenant, John F Kennedy.

Paar also screened an interview he conducted in Tokyo with Akira Nakijima, who was a lieutenant and medical officer onboard the *Amagiri*, and was on the bridge the night the destroyer hit PT-109. Speaking halting English, Nakijima told Paar that he only learned Kennedy's identity when the young Congressman visited Japan in 1951. To his 'great regret' he did not get to meet Kennedy.

Inconspicuously present among the audience were the crew of PT-109. In the latter part of the program, Paar asked them to stand up. They looked uncomfortable as Paar read out their names, though some smiled nervously, welcoming the moment they could slip back into obscurity.

But the real highlight of the show was left for the last six minutes, as Paar introduced his main guests. Reg Evans was called out first. A 'helluva guy', exclaimed Paar. The two laughed with the audience about Kennedy not returning the Japanese rifle that Reg lent him. Paar, a Republican, albeit one friendly to the Kennedys, quipped, 'The moral of all this is never give a gun to a Democrat.' Paar also told the audience that the Solomon Islanders who Evans worked with 'loved him'.

Then, a star was born. Before introducing Ben Kevu,

Paar said Kevu had come all the way from his village in Solomon Islands, had never seen a television let alone appeared on it, and 'I doubt if he's had anything on other than sandals before this trip.' As Kevu entered the stage, the crew of PT-109 rose from their chairs again and the audience applauded.

Kevu was shorter even than the diminutive Evans but possessed an endearing diffidence, warm-heartedness and grace. As Paar invited Kevu to speak, the studio audience fell silent. Still concerned about capturing Kevu's quiet voice, Paar moved the overhead microphone to just above his head. 'Well, ladies and gentlemen, and all members of PT-109,' said Kevu, 'I am very very pleased and very very happy indeed to be here in America. And, after all, I very much appreciate reaching the United States of America. My purpose to come here was being invited by Jack Paar to do with Mr Kennedy in Solomon Islands during World War Two. Wishing you all a very good night, and once again I say, thank you very much.'

It was the longest and loudest applause of the night. Kevu was a 'smashing presence', Paar later wrote. 'Benny showed no concern about appearing before a national audience of an estimated 30 million people, live and, as NBC says, in living color.' He was a natural. Paar called it 'very dramatic and touching' television and the *New York Times* described it as 'an absorbing hour'.

There was another surprise in store. President Kennedy was among the 30 million watching the show – he must have been a fan of Paar's – and learning that Kevu was in the United States, he phoned the former scout and invited him to the White House.

The day Kevu met with President Kennedy in the Oval Office was like no other in the Kennedy administration. With the fifth and final race of the America's Cup run the day before, for Ken O'Donnell, the president's appointment secretary, 25 September 1962 'must have been the longest and busiest working day of any President of the United States in modern times'. On that autumn Tuesday, the president had eleven appointments before lunch and then another four in the afternoon, before a night at the theatre for the premiere performance of the musical *Mr President* and supper at the British Embassy.

By mid-morning Kennedy was meeting with the South Vietnamese secretary of state for security, and was due to meet at 11 am with Australia's prime minister, Robert Menzies, back for a return visit. But then O'Donnell received word from Attorney-General Robert Kennedy's office that Barney Ross, PT-109's 'thirteenth man', was bringing over Ben Kevu, and that they would be arriving in minutes. So Menzies was bumped and 'kept … waiting in the Cabinet Room', O'Donnell recalled, 'while we brought to the president this other celebrated visitor from the same part of the world'.

There is a special bond between a rescuer and the rescued, and Kennedy now embraced his saviour. They had not seen each other since 1943 in a PT boat bound for Rendova, yet now they were sitting in an office at the apex of world power. Like Evans the year before, Kevu thought the president had not changed much. There were no awkward silences, just an easy intimacy born of men who survived when they easily might not have.

In this whirlwind day, the official schedule ballooning by the minute, the president, Kevu and Ross recounted their incredible story of survival and bravery. At one point, Kennedy jumped up from his favourite rocking chair and plucked from his desk the famous coconut with its scratched SOS message. He passed the coconut to Kevu and asked, 'Do you remember this, Ben?' Kevu looked closely at the coconut and nodded, 'Rendova.' The president then showed Kevu the framed message from Reg Evans that Kevu had carried to Kennedy, Ross and the rest of the crew on Olasana Island. Discovering that Kevu had six children, the president gave him gold PT boat tie clips to take back. 'And give some of them to those other fellows who were with you in the canoe that day', said Kennedy.

Kevu never would have said so himself, but the president turned to his assistant and confidant Dave Powers and said: 'Just think of it, Dave, if it wasn't for Ben Kevu, you wouldn't be here in the White House today.' 'You mean you wouldn't be here', replied Powers.

After photographs were taken, the president asked Powers to bring in Robert Menzies, who was waiting patiently in the Cabinet Room, and introduced the prime minister to Kevu. After that, the president watched as Kevu and Ross entered the West Lobby of the White House and were surrounded by reporters and photographers. Kevu took it all in his stride; he was, Paar later commented, 'quite a social lion during his Washington stay'.

Back in the Oval Office, the president met with Robert Menzies for nearly an hour. There were several more meetings waiting before lunch including an 'urgent off-the-record meeting about the growing Cuban crisis'. Later that crowded day, Kennedy told O'Donnell and Powers, 'Seeing Ben Kevu for the first time in nineteen years was enough of a surprise for one day ... What will you think of next?' But they couldn't top it.

*

Three years before his victory in the presidential election, Kennedy's wartime exploits first entered America's living rooms as part of the *Navy Log* television series. Screened first by CBS and then ABC between 1955 and 1958, it was based on 'real adventures of the United States Navy'. The 'PT-109' episode, the first of the show's third season, aired on 23 October 1957, with a re-run in March 1958. Kennedy, then a US senator for Massachusetts, made time to visit the set during filming and chat with actor John Baer, who portrayed him in the episode.

It was another six years before the story of the collision and the rescue hit the silver screen. The *PT-109* movie was based on Robert Donovan's bestselling book. As chief publicist for his son's wartime heroism, Joe Kennedy Sr now channelled all his Hollywood contacts and experience into assisting with the movie of these exploits, dabbling in all aspects of the production.

The president had wanted a young Warren Beatty to play him, but Beatty refused, not happy with the proposed executive producer of the film nor, perhaps, the script. In the end, the White House settled on Cliff Robertson to play the young Jack. Australian actor and Pacific war veteran Michael Pate was cast as Reg Evans. He was given only one line in the entire movie: 'Being a coast watcher is a lonely life.' True enough, but hardly an appropriate reflection of Evans' crucial role in the story. George Takei, later to gain fame as the helmsman on the starship *Enterprise*, got an uncredited appearance – one of his first – as the helmsman on the *Amagiri*. Some locals misinterpreted the filming of the movie around Little Palm Island in the Florida Keys as preparation for another attempted invasion of Cuba.

Like the Bay of Pigs two years before, the *PT-109* movie was not a success. As President Kennedy's press secretary later acknowledged, 'The White House, unfortunately, is not set up by experience or temperament to be a part of motion picture production.' Salinger 'liked' the final cut, but reported that 'the critics didn't, the public didn't, and it turned out to be one of the greatest bombs ever produced by Warner Brothers'.

A month before the movie was released in Australia, on 24 June 1963, Reg's wife Trudy Evans passed away. Her death notice in the *Sydney Morning Herald* described her as 'Beloved wife of Reg, loved sister of Cynthia ... and Kay Slaney Poole'. Reg would remarry a few years later.

*

Kennedy never made it back to Solomon Islands to revisit the places that held so many memories for him. He did have plans, however, to visit Australia, as part of a broader East Asia tour.

Jack Kennedy had already made a visit to south and east Asia in the fall of 1951. Accompanied by his brother Robert and sister Pat, Jack met with leaders in Pakistan, India, Thailand, Indonesia, Singapore, Malaya, Korea and French Indochina; a sound grounding in foreign policy for the ambitious young congressman. A highlight, however, was Japan, still under occupation following the war, but soon an important strategic ally in the Cold War.

But there was also a personal reason for the trip. Kennedy wanted to meet the skipper of the *Amagiri*, the destroyer that had sunk his boat, killed two of his crew and nearly killed him. He had no idea who the skipper was or where he lived, if he indeed survived the war. But through Japanese contacts his identity and location were discovered: Kohei Hanami was now forty-two years old and living as a farmer in a remote village in Fukushima Prefecture, more than 300 kilometres northeast of Tokyo.

Before contact with Hanami could be made, however, Jack fell gravely ill from a flare-up of his recurring Addison's disease. He was flown to an American military hospital in Okinawa where his temperature soared over 41 degrees and doctors believed he would not make it. He was given the last rites of the Catholic Church. But after a few days he pulled through and flew back home to make much of his new foreign policy credentials in preparing for the Senate race the following year. In the meantime, Hanami was tracked down. He remembered the night of the collision in Blackett Strait well but could hardly believe that anyone in the PT boat had survived it, with the explosion scorching the destroyer's paint work.

Hanami was very surprised to learn that Jack Kennedy, the commander of the PT boat, was a member of the United States House of Representatives and was now running for the United States Senate for Massachusetts. He penned a letter of friendship to Kennedy and endorsed his Senate run. The letter quickly made its way to Boston and was released during the campaign which Jack Kennedy won in November 1952. It was an unusual endorsement coming from a former enemy officer, but Kennedy took the time to thank Hanami, writing to him as a newly elected US senator. Kennedy remained in contact with Hanami for the rest of his life.

In 1962, Robert Kennedy, now attorney-general, visited Japan again as a prelude to what both he and the president hoped would be a first ever presidential visit to Japan. During his preparatory visit, Robert Kennedy did get to meet Hanami, unclipping his own PT-109 tie clip and presenting it to the former skipper of the *Amagiri*. The president hoped that his forthcoming visit to Japan would culminate in an emotional reunion between him and his surviving crew and those that had sunk PT-109, the officers and crew of *Amagiri*. It would have been a moment for the ages, a great symbol of reconciliation, reflecting the changing realities of Cold War politics that had brought the two former enemies together.

Had the visit to Australia taken place, no doubt it would have been a cross between a royal tour and Beatlemania. It wasn't just that no sitting American president had ever visited Australia before; no president before Kennedy had the same star quality. Not only the holder of the most important office in the world and Australia's most important ally, Kennedy's youth, good looks, charisma and glamour personified the United States at the height of its post-war cultural influence. America was Kennedy and Kennedy was America, and Australians, like much of the world, were enchanted.

Kennedy first told Ambassador Beale in April 1963 that he would 'very much like to go' to Australia in October as part of a Far Eastern tour. The president did say, however, that if the Soviet Union resumed atomic testing the United States would do the same, and the trip would have to be delayed. The president also asked Beale whether he needed to go to New Zealand. Beale replied that the New Zealanders 'were a bit sensitive on such things' and 'might be a little put out if he went to Australia and did not call on them', to which Kennedy replied that 'in these circumstances, he would pay them a very brief visit'.

As October approached, however, a December visit became more likely, though now also subject to progress of the president's legislative program in Congress. And by late October, delays in the passage of tax and civil rights bills had meant that he could not leave the United States that year at all. A trip to the Far East, including Australia, was now considered a 'lively possibility' for the Northern spring of 1964.

At least one person in Australia was not happy about the proposed new timing. Mr. JH Scholtens, the chief ceremonial officer of the Prime Minister's Department in Canberra, complained in a note to the secretary of the department that with the impending visits to Australia of the Japanese prime minister, Hayato Ikeda; the queen mother; and the maharaja of Mysore, 'my section would not be able to handle' a visit by President Kennedy.

Be that as it may, with public enthusiasm growing, planning for the visit went ahead. Everyone wanted their piece of the president and the first lady. Excited members of the Canberra Day 1964 Citizens Celebration Committee put in their bid for President Kennedy to officially open Lake Burley Griffin. No mention was made of whether a replica of PT-109 would be provided for the president to perform the honours from. As late as 22 November 1963, the secretary of the prime minister's department, John (later, Sir John) Bunting, was fielding applications from individuals and institutions hoping for their events to be included in the president's Australian program.

Later that same day President Kennedy was assassinated in Dallas. As a consequence of previous injuries, including those aboard PT-109, the back brace he wore made it impossible to slump after the first bullet. And so he remained upright in the back seat of an open-top presidential Lincoln Continental limousine when the second, fatal shot struck him.

CHAPTER 16

THE LEGACY

Twenty-second November 1963. Friday in America, it was Saturday morning, the 23rd, when Australians first learned the news from Dallas.

Stewart Cockburn, now back from Washington and working at the Adelaide *Advertiser*, wrote later, 'I have never known such public and private anguish in this country, certainly not after the death of an English monarch.' Cockburn reflected that for Australians, 'paradoxically, the shock and grief ... may well have been greater than in the US'. While Americans would no doubt dispute this – after Kennedy's death, nearly two-thirds told the pollsters they had voted for him (the real figure was just under fifty per cent) – Cockburn was not totally wrong in suggesting that Australians saw only Kennedy's 'ideal image', untrammelled by the partisan bickering and squabbles that bedevil every politician at home. Like all elected leaders, President Kennedy worked hard to keep his domestic audience happy. That struggle and its compromises lie at the very core of politics. But in Australia, unaffected one way or another by most of Kennedy's policies and oblivious of the everyday vagaries of his government, we had far fewer reasons to be critical.

A thread that runs through many of the condolence messages Australians sent to Jacqueline Kennedy is the belief that President Kennedy was 'our president too'. 'If only you lived near here, I could help you,' one woman wrote forlornly to Mrs Kennedy, 'perhaps looking after the kiddies or doing something practical.' This was a loss that went beyond political ties, close though they were. 'Most Australians experienced a great sadness and a sense of almost personal loss and bereavement,' wrote the Lord Mayor of Melbourne to the US ambassador to Australia, William C Battle, a friend of the late president's, who served in the same naval squadron in Solomon Islands. Kennedy was not just a political leader, but 'was mourned as if he had been a family member or a close personal friend', concluded Australian historian Jennifer Clark. His youth and charisma, attractive and photogenic family, war record, and, most of all, his portrayal on the relatively new medium of television made Australians assume an intimacy with the slain president perhaps never equalled by any other foreign leader.

A week from what would be his last federal election on 30 November, Menzies sent the president of the Senate, Sir Alister McMullin, to represent Australia at the funeral. He was criticised for not going to the United States himself, but, in any case, his government was returned with an increased majority.

When parliament resumed in early 1964, eulogies were limited to the prime minister and the leader of the opposition. In his speech, Menzies recalled the circumstances that first brought Jack Kennedy and Australia together: 'During the war he served with very great courage and distinction in the United States Navy and ... he had an association with our own country through the activities of an Australian coast watcher, activities which he never ceased to refer to with marked gratitude.'

'He was of great significance to us in Australia', Menzies went on, 'because in a simple, unaffected and inquiring way he had a feeling of friendship for Australia and a feeling of interest in this country which I am bound to say I have never known quite equalled by any of his predecessors.'

'He was a friend of ours', was the prime minister's verdict.

Labor Party Leader Arthur Calwell, who also had met Kennedy in the White House, was equally eloquent, drawing a parallel between Lincoln's struggles during the US Civil War and the 'bitter animosities' stirred up by President Kennedy's efforts to 'break down the barriers of racial discrimination'. 'May his memory remain ever-green', Calwell concluded his speech, 'and may the sum total of his achievements shine as a beacon light for those who seek the path to peace and a better life for all mankind.'

In Sydney, Reg Evans felt grief made deeper by shared history. 'It was like losing an old friend,' he recalled. From his village of Raramana, on the western tip of Vonavona Island (formerly Wana Wana), Benjamin Kevu wrote to Jack Paar: 'The message came through the air local news that the great friend J. F. Kennedy at the White House has get shot. It was a sad news … I feel deeply sorrow for this death.' Eroni Kumana, who along with Biuku Gasa first sighted Kennedy and his crew, mourned for a week upon learning of his 'friend's death'. Even in a small Japanese village, Kohei Hanami, the former skipper of the *Amagiri*, was devastated by the news. Kennedy escaped death by a few inches at the hands of the enemy at war, only to be killed by his own countryman in peacetime. Hanami travelled to the American Embassy in Tokyo to pay his respects.

In Washington, the president's body lay in repose in the East Room of the White House. A little after 12.30 pm on Sunday 24 November, before being taken to the US Capitol to lie in state, Jackie and Robert Kennedy asked for a final private viewing to say goodbye to Jack. They both placed in his coffin objects meaningful to them and the late president. For Jackie it was three letters, one from each of their two children, John Jr and Caroline, and one from her, as well as inlaid gold cufflinks she had bought Jack early in their marriage and a whalebone engraving of the presidential seal he kept in the right-hand corner of his Oval Office desk.

In his turn, wrote William Manchester, 'Bob Kennedy took off his PT tie pin. He said, "He should have this, shouldn't he?" "Yes," [Jackie] whispered. Then he drew from his pocket an engraved silver rosary Ethel had given him at their wedding. Bob placed this with the letters.' Lieutenant Kennedy was now ready for his last journey. The coffin was closed a final time and just after 1 pm the gun carriage carrying the president's body left the White House for the Capitol.

*

With his story finally out as the coast watcher who helped rescue Kennedy and his crew, Reg Evans would spend the next few decades enduring an occasional moment in the spotlight. He did not seek it but could hardly avoid it. There were television appearances and mentions in newspapers, magazines and books. Inevitably, Evans was sought out by authors writing about Kennedy, PT-109 or the coast watchers. Robert Donovan spent many hours with Evans in Sydney in 1961 and Reg was still assisting American historian Walter Lord in the mid-1970s for a history of coast watchers in the Solomons. He was even asked to comment when Solomon Islands achieved independence in July 1978.

For a while, the excitement of the PT-109 story generated renewed Australian interest in our coast watchers. There were proposals for home-grown movies and television series. In June 1960, two half-hour pilots for a planned series entitled *The Coastwatchers* was shot in New Guinea by Pacific Films. One of the two episodes was entitled 'Operation Plum Pudding', though unrelated to the small island the Europeans called Plum Pudding, the locals Kasolo, and which is now known as Kennedy Island. In early December 1960, both episodes were shown to members of Federal Parliament in Canberra as worthy examples of Australian television drama. Plans for the twenty-six-episode series were never realised, but the two pilots were consolidated as a film for television, entitled *The Coastwatchers*, and first screened on Anzac Day in 1962. Evans was shown a preview and enthusiastically endorsed the authenticity with which the lonely and dangerous life as the 'eyes and ears in the Pacific' was portrayed on the screen.

In March 1963, Waratah Films had written to Pierre Salinger requesting that they be 'given permission to portray Lt Kennedy as he was in August 1943'. On 1 April 1963, Salinger wrote in the affirmative, the president himself having looked over and approved Waratah's proposal. The ten-episode series entitled *Adventure Unlimited* aired on Australian television two years later, covering adventurous

Australian themes. Episode 4, 'The Coast Watcher', told the story of Reg Evans and the Islander scouts and their role in saving the lives of Kennedy and his crew.

Even Walter Brooksbank, senior civilian in the Naval Intelligence Division and sometime playwright, wrote a thirty-page script for a mooted television series called *The Australian Coastwatchers*. Episode 1 was 'The Evans Story'. The script is perhaps a touch romantic but brings to life the tension and perils of life behind enemy lines in the Pacific. In the closing scenes, Evans and Kennedy finally meet and chat in the jungle shack at Gomu. Evans' last words to Kennedy are, 'Well, here's to better days, John! And let's hope that perhaps one day we can meet again!' The episode ends with the narrator's voiceover reminding the viewers that they did indeed meet again, this time under 'far more auspicious circumstances'.

Reg Evans died on 31 January 1989 at the age of eighty-three. By then he had returned to perhaps welcome obscurity. There were no news stories upon his death and no glowing obituaries, just a small death notice in the classifieds section of the *Sydney Morning Herald*. It did not recall his wartime service nor his bravery decoration, the Distinguished Service Cross. Instead, it simply said, 'A passing of a true Australian'.

After his death, Evans continued to be remembered in works about coast watchers or PT-109. Australian authors Patrick Lindsay and Michael Veitch, as well as podcaster and author Michael Adams, have all been accurate if not generous in their acknowledgment of Evans and his role, as have American writers like Robert Ballard and William Doyle.

Yet, strangely, more general works on the life of John F Kennedy have not always been accurate. Bob Curran, who as editor of *Cavalier* magazine was instrumental in rescuing Reg Evans from suburban obscurity and transporting him into the glare of American media, was scathing of Evans' treatment in the television documentary *JFK: Reckless Youth*. Based on British historian Nigel Hamilton's bestselling biography, Evans had been 'removed from the story again'. It was particularly careless and galling as Hamilton himself had portrayed Evans as central to the rescue of Kennedy and his crew. A decade later, in 2003, Evans was written out of the PT-109 rescue by the distinguished American presidential historian Robert Dallek and again, in 2012, by popular author and television commentator Bill O'Reilly. Dallek refers to, but does not name, the 'New Zealand infantry lieutenant' responsible. But O'Reilly does. He identifies him as 'Lieutenant Wincote', repeating John Hersey's original misidentification from 1944, nearly seventy years prior.

*

Jack Kennedy might have misremembered Reg Evans' name and mistaken his nationality, but there was never any risk he would forget the Islanders who saved him and his crew. By the time they reached the safety of Rendova at daybreak on Sunday 8 August 1943, a powerful bond had grown between the young American lieutenant and the Solomon scouts. Kennedy presented Gasa with a gold coin that had been given to him as a good luck charm by Clare Boothe Luce. And before they returned to their home islands, Kennedy pulled aside Gasa, Kumana and Kari and repeatedly and earnestly thanked them, along with Ben

Kevu and his friends, for saving his life and those of his crew. He told them that he would never forget.

'After the rescue Kennedy promised us he would meet us again', recalled Kumana almost sixty years later. 'When he became president, he invited us to meet with him. But when we got to the airport we were met by a clerk who said we couldn't go. Biuki [Gasa] and I spoke no English. My feelings went for bad. Sometime later we hear Kennedy died. I sat down with his picture and cried. Knowing he was dead my sadness was great. I would never meet him ... I still think of Kennedy.'

Gasa and Kennedy corresponded briefly after the election, and Kevu, of course, did end up seeing Kennedy again in the White House. But if Gasa and Kumana never got to the United States, Jack Kennedy's extended family certainly had not forgotten them and their often unsung role in saving Lieutenant Kennedy. Members of the Kennedy clan kept faith with Jack's promise. They would visit Gasa and Kumana over the years – one could almost see it as a pilgrimage to sites sacred to family history and memory – and with other benefactors raised money to build better homes for the two Islander heroes. In 2002, during the filming of a TV documentary about PT-109, Maxwell (Max) Kennedy, son of Robert Kennedy, presented Gasa and Eroni with a bust of his uncle. Moved by the occasion, Eroni cried, laughed and then tickled Max.

Both scouts enjoyed long lives, becoming pillars of their local communities and respected elders of their extended clans. Gasa passed away on 23 November 2005 aged eighty-two. For countries like Solomon Islands that lie west of the international dateline it was the 42nd anniversary of

Kennedy's assassination. Kumana, who on occasions wore a hat and a T-shirt that read 'I rescued JFK', created a shrine with an obelisk to Jack Kennedy. In 2008 he asked that 'shell money', traditional Islander currency made from giant clam shells, be placed as tribute on the grave of the man he regarded as his chief, President John F Kennedy. His wish was carried out in a private ceremony at Arlington National Cemetery. Kumana died aged ninety-six, on 2 August 2014, exactly seventy-one years to the day after the search began for the crew of PT-109.

*

The fascination with PT-109 itself also continued over the years.

In 2002, a *National Geographic* expedition found what it believed were the remains of PT-109 on the ocean floor in Blackett Strait. Led by maritime archaeologist, Robert Ballard, the famed discoverer of the wrecks of the *Titanic* and *Bismarck*, the expedition's findings were later examined by US Navy experts. Taking into account the fact that no other PT boat was known to have sunk in this general location, they concluded that the wreck located and filmed by Ballard was indeed most likely that of PT-109.

The story of Jack Kennedy's PT boats does not quite end there, however. His final command, Gunboat No 1 or the former PT-59, was sold as surplus after the war and then renovated for use as a charter fishing boat in Manhattan until the 1970s. There it caught fire one night and sunk into the muddy Harlem River, where it lay under 'six feet of water and eight feet of mud'. Parts of the boat were eventually recovered in 2020, if only by accident, during construction work by New York City authorities on a new seawall.

A popular highlight of the John F Kennedy Presidential Library and Museum in Boston is President Kennedy's desk. It is an exact replica of the one he used in the Oval Office. On it lies the famous coconut, though the carved message is now somewhat obscured by the scratched and clouded plastic that encases the shell. And a few centimetres away, right next to the presidential seal, a PT boat etched on glass sails on forever through the waves.

AFTERWORD

By the time Reg Evans shook Jack Kennedy's hand and bid him goodbye and good luck on the beach at Gomu Island in August 1943, Australia had changed. So had America. Australia, because it encountered America; America, because it encountered the world. Neither Australia nor America – nor the world – would be the same again. The changes were fast, far-reaching and irrevocable.

In 1939, the overwhelming majority of Australians were of Anglo-Celtic stock, a state of affairs the White Australia Policy deliberately cultivated. By and large we considered ourselves British; to our bootstraps, as some would say. When Britain declared war upon Germany in September 1939, we inevitably followed: 'Australia is also at war', proclaimed Prime Minister Menzies. Like in the Great War, Australia sent soldiers first to north Africa, to prepare to fight Germany. We kept a wary eye on Japan, but they seemed locked in endless combat in China. Pearl Harbor changed everything. As Menzies's successor, John Curtin, said, 'The protection of this country is no longer that of a contribution to a world at war but the resistance to an enemy threatening to invade our own shore.' In the Great War, Australia had been a sharp arrow in the Allied quiver. Just over two years into the Second World War, we had become a target.

By late 1941, Australians believed their homeland was in peril. With Britain fighting for its own survival, we found ourselves alone and desperate for help. When the first US soldiers disembarked down the gang planks of the USS *Pensacola* and USS *Republic* in Brisbane on 22 December 1941, Australia caught its breath. Maybe we would be saved, after all. Hope renewed, it seemed a Christmas miracle.

Japan's lightning attacks through the western Pacific and south-east Asia finally brought Australia and the United States together. In an instant, years of indifference, misunderstanding and frustration were put aside. We didn't until then know much about Americans, and we didn't necessarily think much of them, but we were very grateful when they turned up. The negative stereotypes and unwholesome Hollywood caricatures were discarded, at first replaced by a vision of American GIs more worthy of saints that came marching in, and later, one more realistically befitting young men away from home for the first time, many only teenagers, both saviours and sinners.

Only a few days after the arrival of the *Pensacola* convoy, on 27 December, Prime Minister Curtin announced that already 'Australia looks to America' as a partner in 'the Pacific struggle', our main theatre of war. 'Australia can go and Britain can still hold on', said the prime minister. Without America, we couldn't. 'Australia is now inside the firing lines', Curtin warned the 'somewhat lackadaisical Australian' listener; 'if we were to save ourselves', an 'all-in-effort' was the only way. The message was a shock to the system.

Perhaps more striking was Curtin's direct appeal to the people of the United States on 14 March 1942. For Curtin, the timing was critical. A few days before he had a huge row with Churchill about deployment of Australia's 7th and 9th Divisions. The speech was also made during MacArthur's dramatic escape from the Philippines and three days before his arrival in Australia.

Curtin appealed to our common values and to our common threat. Both shared principles and shared interests bound the new alliance. The principles were clear:

> We fight for the same free institutions that you enjoy.
> We fight so that, in the words of Lincoln, 'government
> of the people, for the people, by the people, shall
> not perish from the earth'. Our legislature is elected
> the same as is yours; and we will fight for it, and for
> the right to have it, just as you will fight to keep the
> Capitol at Washington the meeting place of freely-
> elected men and women representative of a free
> people.

Just as clear was the threat.

> I give you this warning: Australia is the last bastion
> between the West Coast of America and the Japanese.
> If Australia goes, the Americas are wide open. It is
> said that the Japanese will by-pass Australia and that
> they can be met and routed in India. I say to you that
> the saving of Australia is the saving of America's west
> coast. If you believe anything to the contrary then you
> delude yourselves.

And, long before Hitler and Goebbels declared 'Total War' and fully mobilised all of Germany's resources to fight, Curtin assured the American people that Australia was 'fighting mad' and 'committed, heart and soul, to total warfare'. A pacifist and campaigner against conscription in the Great War, Curtin knew if Australia was to survive we could not do it alone. We needed the United States.

Writing just after the war, the American historian Dixon Wecter put it well: the 'American invasion' of Australia was a 'matter for awe, curiosity and delight – with combined aspects of the crusades, the circus and the gold rush'. More apt still was his conclusion, 'It also meant salvation to a brave but wholly unprepared people.'

It might have been a shotgun wedding between Australia and America, but it soon blossomed into much more. If there was sometimes tension between Australian and American servicemen, it was less than some wish to paint and meant little at the sharp end. For all the slights about pay, uniforms, food and fraternisation, when and where it mattered, in Papua and New Guinea and in the islands of the Pacific, in the jungle foxholes, in the rain, the heat and the fighting, Australians and Americans learned each other's mettle. There, a common language, common values, common commitment, and a common understanding made for mateship and ultimately victory. The closer to the front, the closer the troops were to each other. It was there that friendships were forged and an alliance cemented.

As it was around kitchen tables, pub counters and dance floors. Relations between the GIs and Australian civilians were almost always good and often excellent. Though the honeymoon waned somewhat with overfamiliarity and inflation born of the US servicemen's high salaries, civilians like my grandparents remained forever grateful to the Yanks for 'saving Australia'. No hindsight and no post-war revisionism can change these facts.

*

The United States was founded as an experiment in government. The experiment was both unprecedented and vulnerable. The American people first fought and won a war of independence from Britain and then excused themselves from alliances that might bind them to European states and drag them into European wars. The United States would be, in the vision of its founders, the shining 'City upon a hill', protected from all the troubles and corruption of the outside world by a moat of the two great oceans. It worked like that for a long while. Even the First World War could not change the American isolationist mindset. Only the Second World War did.

By war's end the United States wore the mantle of leadership, of superpower status. It had been transformed politically, economically, militarily, and even spiritually. It was no longer a virtuous amateur. Atomic weapons, Hiroshima and Nagasaki – never mind the conventional carnage – had seen to that. America was no longer largely content with the travails of its own backyard. It couldn't be. It was now a world power, with global responsibilities. It saw itself differently and so did every other nation. But more than that, America had also become a prism through which others saw themselves. It did not matter whether you loved or loathed what you saw. Forever compared, often aspired to, never ignored, the United States would be the lodestar and the ultimate reference point for the post-war world.

It was no different in Australia. The Americans made us think about ourselves and our future. A large majority still thought us 'British', and a proud part of the British empire, if no longer subservient to it. But in some ways we were ripe for the picking. 'Man for man, the GI probably had greater personal impact in Australia than anywhere else in the world between 1941 and 1945,' wrote Australian historian John H Moore. 'In England, France, Italy, North Africa, India, and China he encountered well-entrenched, even ancient, cultures not receptive to innovation by crass outsiders. Australia was different.'

The Yanks were similar enough not to scare us. We spoke the same language, had institutions we understood if did not always share, and were grateful that the Americans had come to our aid while Britain could not. And now they offered us a glimpse of a different way. Here was a decidedly multicultural nation – freedom-loving, bold and rich – and they were now the most powerful country on earth. Australians wondered what we might learn from them. We looked anew at ourselves. 'World War Two as experienced in the South-West Pacific by Americans and Australians – a mix of panic, frustration, excitement, fear, exhilaration, and disappointment – was a turning point in the life of both the continent and its people,' wrote Moore. Unknowingly and unwittingly, but perhaps inevitably, a million GIs and the American success they represented was a watershed in developing an Australian national consciousness and a new national identity. Australians became both more distinctive and at the same time more varied. 'World War II and the

American invader wrested Australia from isolation both geographical and social and set it forth on a new path.' By the end of the war, the place of women in Australian society had also changed dramatically. They had worked the jobs left vacant by men and gained new skills and independence. Progress was not easy, but there would be no turning back.

When Reg Evans said to Jack Kennedy on the Gomu beach in August 1943, 'I'm bloody glad to see you', he could have been speaking for seven million Australians. Evans knew that his homeland had by then been saved from the threat of Japanese invasion by the fellow countrymen of the skinny, sunburned and unshaven young officer whose hand he now grasped. Bedraggled perhaps, but also confident, energetic and optimistic, Jack Kennedy was America, a great and dynamic new power finally arisen from slumber and about to assume global responsibilities.

Older, more conservative and more reserved, Reg Evans, in turn, personified a nation whose venerable certainties had been shaken and which now faced an uncertain path ahead. Reg and Jack might have met in what was formally the British Protectorate of Solomon Islands, but it was not Britain that had come to protect these islands. The United States was now doing the heavy lifting; Jack Kennedy was at the pointy end of America's rising industry and military. In the Solomons, Kennedy and his crew were doing the fighting; Reg's role was one of support. This too was a portent for the future.

That day, their reach exceeded their grasp. The handshake on the Gomu beach, replicated on countless occasions in the years before and after by the two peoples, stands in as the avatar of the fateful encounter between America and

Australia and the beginning of the trans-Pacific friendship. No longer strangers to each other, Reg Evans and Jack Kennedy did not yet know it, but Australia and the United States would soon become the closest of allies, beyond the war with Japan, and into a new world unlike the old age of isolation and inertia. In this new era, ideas that bound them together would matter more than the distance that separated them.

*

Of course, the birth of the friendship is not the full story. There have been ups and downs and disagreements, if not discord, over the subsequent eighty years. It's not the purpose of this book to offer a detailed history or a comprehensive assessment of the relationship between the United States and Australia, or of the military-political alliance more specifically. This is merely a look at how it had first come about through the wartime meeting of millions of Australians and Americans, from Curtin and MacArthur, generals and leaders at the apex, down to countless ordinary soldiers and civilians in the streets of our towns and the jungles of the Pacific.

This encounter, born of John Curtin's momentous decision, in the words of Senator Penny Wong, now Australia's Foreign Minister, 'laid the ground for the post-war ANZUS treaty' and allowed Australians and Americans to forge an alliance. That this 'immensely valuable' relationship has continued is in no small part due to the fact that, as Wong wrote, 'Australia and the US have shared histories, mutual interests and common values ... [which] include our commitment to democratic political systems, open economies and free and just societies'. We first appreciated these things about each other only eighty years ago, in the storm of war, and this shared understanding has served as the basis of friendship ever since, through wars and peace, in good times and in bad.

Born in the struggle against Imperial Japan, strengthened throughout the decades of confronting communism, and now transforming to meet ever-new challenges, the alliance remains as central to Australia's security today as it was in Curtin's time. 'It acts as a deterrent to potential aggressors, provides our defence forces with leading edge technologies and opportunities for cooperation, training, and intelligence sharing, and gives Australia an ability to influence the world's leading power,' Wong has said. 'For the US, Australia is a trusted partner with a sophisticated and professional defence force capable of taking part in joint operations, a source of independent advice and counsel, and an important country in a region which is critical for world affairs.'

'If you look at what the US has done in the last two years', observed the White House's Indo-Pacific Co-ordinator, Kurt Campbell, 'virtually everything significant has included Australia. That's AUKUS, the NATO Asia gathering, the Quad, and the Partnership of the Blue Pacific … Australia has been the crucial partner in all we are doing.' It bears noting that the Quad, our diplomatic partnership with the United States, India and Japan, was first proposed by the United States in the Kennedy administration. In a 'Secret' memorandum to Prime Minister Menzies informing him of American proposals, the US State Department envisaged 'private diplomatic consultations from time to time between Australia, United States, Japan and India to make appreciations in common of the situation in particular countries of South East Asia and to examine in common how best Chinese Communist influence in those countries might be countered'.

Our relationship with the United States, of course, was never limited to formal alliances and security collaboration. Where distance once worked as a foil to contact and understanding, today no such barrier exists. Technology and cheap, fast travel have allowed person-to-person contacts on a scale similar to the Second World War but in ways undreamed of by the GIs, Diggers and civilians of yore.

For over eight decades now, many aspects of our lives, from our strategic interests through to our popular culture, have been influenced, if not decisively shaped by our Pacific ally. From fighting controversial wars and supporting ugly dictators abroad through to consuming KFC and Macca's, not to mention movies, music, games and fashion, some in Australia have criticised this closeness, if not dependence, and many more are wary. Complaints of 'Americanisation' and the corruption of our values have run hot since the war.

Such complaints as there are tend to rise and fall roughly in accord with Australia's sense of vulnerability. Anti-Americanism in Australia increases the more secure we feel. We think we need them less. With the United States the sole global hegemon throughout the 1990s and 2000s, there were grumbles aplenty in Australia (and elsewhere) of US ubiquity, of America as the world's policeman. It is the luxury of a country made secure by American arms. With a changing strategic environment over the last decade or so, such concerns, especially in the Pacific, have become more muted. Maybe, after all, the American sheriff is better than some other sheriff, or no sheriff at all.

Way back in 1946, Dixon Wecter wrote presciently, 'Australia knows clearly that she has more to fear from American isolation than from American intervention. Her worry is not our aggression, but our indifference, the reputation of our foreign policy for irresponsibility.' We applauded Obama's 'pivot to Asia' and were worried by Trump's early reluctance to engage with the region, but at the same time remembered Vietnam with trepidation. Like others, we want America's help, her gold and guns, but on our terms. If only things were so easy and simple.

Today, Australians overwhelmingly support the US alliance. While understanding the importance of trade with China, Australians now have a sharpened sense of the military and strategic implications of China's rise. The trade honeymoon has given way to a strategic headache. Despite the hardships for our exporters that tensions with China have caused over the past few years, Australia emerged unbroken and less dependent, if not richer. All things considered, the US remains our closest economic partner. If we are to survive and prosper as a liberal democracy in our region, we will need the support of the United States, and better still, other likeminded local democracies too. As we hope and pray that no global conflict blights Asia and the Pacific ever again, we also sleep more soundly knowing that we are not alone, exposed and defenceless in a turbulent world, for the USS *Pensacola* remains docked to our shore.

REFERENCES

Introduction

'Orphans of the storm': C Hartley Grattan, *The United States and the Southwest Pacific*, Harvard University Press, Cambridge, Mass., 1961, p. 182.

Announcement over PA system: Barry Ralph, *They Passed This Way: The United States of America, The States of Australia and World War II*, Kangaroo Press, Sydney, 2000, p. 30.

Kennedy and Evans meet at Gomu: Reg Evans, 'Found! The Unsung Hero Who Saved President Kennedy's Life', *Cavalier*, vol. 11, no. 96, June 1961, pp. 8–13, 82–3, at p. 9.

Kennedy – 'responsible in a way': as cited in Russell Baker, 'Kennedy, After 17 Years, Solves Mystery of His Pacific Rescuer', *New York Times*, 26 February 1961, pp. 1, 44, at p. 44.

Chapter 1 – 'Sea-minded, ship-crazy'

The main sources I have drawn upon for Reg Evans' life are his *Cavalier* article (Reg Evans, 'Found! The Unsung Hero Who Saved President Kennedy's Life', *Cavalier*, vol. 11, no. 96, June 1961, pp. 8–13, 82–3), as well as the recent podcast by Michael Adams (Michael Adams, 'The Aussie Who Saved John F Kennedy – Part One', *Forgotten Australia*, Season 5, Episode 10, 23 July 2022, <shows.acast.com/forgotten-australia/episodes/the-aussie-who-saved-john-f-kennedy-part-one>, and Michael Adams, 'The Aussie Who Saved John F Kennedy – Part Two', *Forgotten Australia*, Season 5, Episode 10, 23 July 2022, <shows.acast.com/forgotten-australia/episodes/the-aussie-who-saved-john-f-kennedy-part-two>. In addition, Evans' life can be traced through papers in the National Archives of Australia, the Australian War Memorial, and contemporary newspapers.

Not surprisingly, there are plenty more sources about John F Kennedy's life. The ones I have found most helpful were Nigel Hamilton, *JFK: Reckless Youth*, Random House, New York, 1992; Robert Dallek, *An Unfinished Life: John F Kennedy, 1917–1963*, Little, Brown, New York, 2003; and Fredrik Logevall, *JFK – Volume 1: 1917–1956*, Viking, London, 2020.

'Sea-minded, ship-crazy': Evans, 'Found! The Unsung Hero Who Saved President Kennedy's Life', p. 9.

Banjo Paterson on James Burns: Nicholas Halter, *Australian Travellers in the South Seas*, ANU Press, Canberra, 2021, p. 198.

Burns, Philp & Co and 'blackbirding': Edward W Docker, *The Blackbirders: The Recruiting of South Seas Labour for Queensland, 1863–1907*, Angus and Robertson, Sydney, 1970, p. 193.

'became shippers …': Clive Moore, *Tulagi: Pacific Outpost of British Empire*, ANU Press, Canberra, 2019, p. 84.

William C Groves – 'What a wonderful life …': as cited in Halter, *Australian Travellers in the South Seas*, p. 199.

The 1927 commission of inquiry in New Hebrides: as cited in Richard D Bedford and Ralph Shlomowitz, 'The internal labor trade in the New Hebrides and Solomon Islands: 1900–1941', *Journal de la Societe des oceanistes*, vol. 86, 1988, pp. 61–85, at p. 63.

Pacific Islands Monthly quotes: H Chaperlin, 'Asiatic Menace in Pacific', *Pacific Islands Monthly*, vol. 1, no. 5, December 1930, p. 1.

Arthur Mahaffy in Solomon Islands: Moore, *Tulagi*, p. 87.

Evans – 'got to know the islands like an old friend': Evans, 'Found! The Unsung Hero Who Saved President Kennedy's Life', p. 9.

Joseph Kennedy Sr. – 'before the shooting starts': as cited in Logevall, *JFK*, p. 139.

Kennedy's impressions of European countries in 1937: Hamilton, *JFK: Reckless Youth*, pp. 178–95.

Chapter 2 – Perfect strangers

A number of studies were useful on the history of contacts between Australia and the United States up to the outbreak of the Second World War, among them Roger J Bell, *Unequal Allies: Australian–American relations and the Pacific war*, Melbourne University Press, Melbourne, 1977; Peter G Edwards, *Australia Through American Eyes – 1935–1945: Observations by American Diplomats*, University of Queensland Press, Brisbane, 1979; Raymond A Esthus, *From Enmity to Alliance: U.S. – Australian Relations, 1931–1941*, Melbourne University Press, Melbourne, 1965; C Hartley Grattan, *The United States and the Southwest Pacific*, Harvard University Press, Cambridge, Mass., 1961; and Norman Harper, *A Great and Powerful Friend: A Study of Australian American Relations between 1900 and 1975*, University of Queensland Press, Brisbane, 1987.

'Sydney Ducks': Nicole Dahlberg, 'The Sydney Ducks and the San Francisco 49ers', MuSeaUm, 02 May 2018, <www.sea.museum/2018/05/02/the-sydney-ducks-and-the-san-francisco-49ers/>.

'flew above stores and saloons ...': Henrietta Drake-Brockman, 'The Americans Came', *American Quarterly*, vol. 1, no. 1, Spring 1949, pp. 44–57, at p. 45.

Australia's fear of Asia: see, for example, David Walker, *Anxious Nation: Australia and the Rise of Asia, 1850–1939*, University of Queensland Press, Brisbane, 1999; and Bill Hornadge, *The Yellow Peril: A Squint at Some Australian Attitudes Towards Orientals*, Review Publications, Dubbo, 1971.

The Russian scares: Clem Lack, 'Russian Ambitions in the Pacific: Australian War Scares of the Nineteenth Century', *Journal of the Royal Historical Society of Queensland*, vol. 8, no. 3, 1968, pp. 432–59.

Allan McLean – 'The stupendous struggle in the East ...': *Herald*, 13 June 1905, as cited in Neville Meaney, *The Search for Security in the Pacific 1901–1914: A History of Australian Defence and Foreign Policy*, Sydney University Press, Sydney, 2009, p. 130.

Henry Gole – 'war with Japan was a concern ...': as cited in Peter J Dean, *MacArthur's Coalition: US and Australian Military Operations in the Southwest Pacific Area, 1942–1945*, University Press of Kansas, Lawrence, Ka., 2018, p. 19.

'The Great White Fleet': see, for example, Ruth Megaw, 'Australia and the Great White Fleet 1908', *Journal of the Royal Australian Historical Society*, vol. 56, no. 2, April 1970, pp. 121–33.

'the gunboat variety': Russell Parkin, *Great White Fleet to Coral Sea: Naval Strategy and the Development of Australia-United States Relations, 1900–1945*, Department of Foreign Affairs and Trade, Canberra, 2008, p. 4.

'producing an orgy of pro-American and anti-Japanese sentiment': John Hammond Moore, *Over-sexed, Over-paid, and Over-here: Americans in Australia, 1941–1945*, University of Queensland Press, Brisbane, 1981, p. 1.

'become a lake': President Barack Obama quoting David Malouf in 'Remarks by President Obama at the University of Queensland', 15 November 2014, <obamawhitehouse.archives.gov/the-press-office/2014/11/15/remarks-president-obama-university-queensland>.

General John Monash – 'acquitted themselves most gallantly ...': as cited in Parkin, *Great White Fleet to Coral Sea*, p. 30.

'America really existed as the gangland ...': Rosemary Campbell, *Heroes and Lovers: A Question of National Identity*, Allen & Unwin, Sydney, 1989, p. 36.

C Hartley Grattan – all quotes: C Hartley Grattan, *Introducing Australia*, John Day, New York, 1944, p. 240.

Americans in Australia between the wars, all quotes: Moore, *Over-sexed, Over-paid, and Over-here*, pp. 2–3.

'the American public was so disinterested ...': Esthus, *From Enmity to Alliance: U.S. – Australian Relations, 1931–1941*, p. 138.

Mark Twain – 'old ties of heredity': as cited in Parkin, *Great White Fleet to Coral Sea*, p. xi.

Robert Hughes – 'largest forced exile of citizens ...': Robert Hughes, *The Fatal Shore: A History of the Transportation of Convicts to Australia, 1787–1868*, Vintage, London, 2003, p. 2.

Don Watson – 'was soldered together not in a fiery furnace ...': Don Watson, 'Rabbit Syndrome: Australia and America', *Quarterly Essays*, no. 4, 2001, pp. 1–59, at p. 33.

'Empire preference' and 'unadulterated evil': Esthus, *From Enmity to Alliance: U.S. – Australian Relations, 1931–1941*, p. 137.

Sir George Pearce's opinion on Australia–US relations: Esthus, *From Enmity to Alliance: U.S. – Australian Relations, 1931–1941*, p. 6.

Nicholas Roosevelt – 'As the bonds of Empire weaken ...' and 'We four are of the new world ...': Nicholas Roosevelt, *The Restless Pacific*, Scribner's, New York, 1928, p. 280.

Keith Hancock, all quotes: WK Hancock, *Australia*, Ernest Benn, London, 1930, pp. 254–55, 256, at p. 254.

Chapter 3 – Answering the call

On Australia in the Second World War, in political, military, economic and social aspects, I have found the following sources particularly useful: Peter Dennis et al (ed.), *Oxford Companion to Australian Military History*, Oxford University Press, Melbourne, 2008; John Robertson, *Australia at War 1939–1945*, William Heinemann, Melbourne, 1981; Michael McKernan, *All In! Australia During the Second World War*, Thomas Nelson, Melbourne, 1983; Joan Beaumont (ed.), *Australia's War 1939–45*, Allen & Unwin, Sydney, 1996; Department of Veterans' Affairs, *Australians in the Pacific War: Australia's Home Defence 1939–1945*, Department of Veterans' Affairs, Canberra, 2006; Roland Perry, *Pacific 360°: Australia's Battle for Survival in World War II*, Hachette, Sydney, 2012; Peter Stanley, *Invading Australia: Japan and the Battle for Australia, 1942*, Penguin, Melbourne, 2008; and Bob Wurth, *The Battle for Australia: A Nation and Its Leader Under Siege*, Pan Macmillan, Sydney, 2013.

The best source on the history of the 2/9th Field Regiment, Royal Australian Artillery is EW Glover (compiler), *Official Souvenir History of 2/9 Australian Field Regiment RAA AIF, 1940–1945*, 2/9 Australian Field Regiment, 1945. The quotes about the formation of the regiment come from p. 5.

Thomas Slaney Poole: 'Mr. Justice Poole Dead', *Adelaide News*, 3 May 1927, pp. 1, 7.

'These Islands': Patricia Hackett, *These Little Things*, Hunkin Ellis & King, Adelaide, 1938, pages not numbered.

Kennedy watching the House of Commons debate: Hamilton, *JFK: Reckless Youth*, pp. 280–82.

Menzies – 'What Great Britain calls the Far East …': as cited in Russell Parkin, *Great White Fleet to Coral Sea: Naval Strategy and the Development of Australia-United States Relations, 1900–1945*, Department of Foreign Affairs and Trade, Canberra, 2008, p. 131.

The Japanese foreign minister's announcement on 28 June 1940: John Hammond Moore, *Over-sexed, Over-paid, and Over-here: Americans in Australia, 1941–1945*, University of Queensland Press, Brisbane, 1981, pp. 6–7.

Lieutenant Ronald Shea – 'The situation in Iraq had deteriorated …': as cited in Peter Thompson and Robert Macklin, *The Battle of Brisbane: Australians and the Yanks at War*, ABC Books, Sydney, 2000, p. 47.

Damian Parer in the Middle East: Neil McDonald, *War Cameraman: The Story of Damien Parer*, Thomas C Lothian, Melbourne, 1994, chapter 10.

The 2/9th Field Regiment occupies Aleppo: Glover, *Official Souvenir History of 2/9 Australian Field Regiment RAA AIF, 1940–1945*, p. 13.

Billy Hughes – 'I can recall many historic demonstrations …': as cited in Moore, *Over-sexed, Over-paid, and Over-here*, p. 9.

Rear Admiral John H Newton – 'We just dropped in …': as cited in Myles Sinnamon, 'Brisbane rejoices as the UN Navy comes to town (March 1941)', State Library of Queensland Blog, 30 July 2013, <www.slq.qld.gov.au/blog/brisbane-rejoices-us-navy-comes-town-march-1941>.

Barry Ralph – 'proportionately, the greatest public display …': Barry Ralph, *They Passed This Way: The United States of America, The States of Australia and World War II*, Kangaroo Press, Sydney, 2000, p. 21.

'war … a probability': as cited in John Edwards, *John Curtin's War, Vol 1*, Viking, Melbourne, 2017, p. 307.

Admiral Isoroku Yamamoto – 'awaking the sleeping giant …': Crosby Day, 'Yamamoto's "Sleeping Giant" Quote Awakens a Gigantic Argument', *South Florida Sun-Sentinel*, 28 October 2001, <www.sun-sentinel.com/news/fl-xpm-2001-10-28-0110260564-story.html>.

Chapter 4 – 'Australia looks to America'

'Pacific Ablaze': *The Sun*, 8 December 1941, p. 1.

Curtin's address to the nation: as cited in Michael McKernan, *All In! Australia During the Second World War*, Thomas Nelson, Melbourne, 1983, p. 97.

Curtin's New Year address: John Curtin, 'The Task Ahead', *Herald*, 27 December 1941, p. 10.

C Hartley Grattan – 'the end of Australia's unswerving allegiance …': C Hartley Grattan, *The United States and the Southwest Pacific*, Harvard University Press, Cambridge, Mass., 1961, p. 181.

John Edwards – 'Japan's rapid, bold and extraordinary success …': John Edwards, *John Curtin's War, Vol. 1*, Viking, Melbourne, 2017, p. 312.

Curtin – '[t]he fall of Dunkirk initiated the battle for Britain …': as cited in 'Curtin's Call to Nation', *Herald*, 16 February 1942, p. 1.

Gunner Bruce Eglington – 'It was an awful place …': as cited in Peter Thompson and Robert Macklin, *The Battle of Brisbane: Australians and the Yanks at War*, ABC Books, Sydney, 2000, p. 52.

Italian leaflets dropped at Tobruk: Australian Military Forces, *Khaki and Green: With the Australian Army at Home and Overseas*, Australian War Memorial, Canberra, 1943, p. 48.

The story of the *Pensacola* convoy is well told in Barry Ralph, *They Passed This Way: The United States of America, The States of Australia and World War II*, Kangaroo Press, Sydney, 2000, chapter 4; and Thompson and Macklin, *The Battle of Brisbane*, chapter 2.

Captain Howard L Steffy: Ralph, *They Passed This Way*, p. 30.

Second-Lieutenant Mark Muller – both quotes: as cited in Ralph, *They Passed This Way*, p. 32.

'You grow rice here?': as cited in Thompson and Macklin, *The Battle of Brisbane*, p. 34.

Seaman 2nd class John Leeman – 'We knew nothing of this place …': as cited in Ralph, *They Passed This Way*, p. 34.

Elizabeth Harland – 'I remember looking at those ships …': as cited in Thompson and Macklin, *The Battle of Brisbane*, p. 33.

Chapter 5 – 'Our darkest hour'
'Scorched earth' plans for invasion: Sue Rosen, *Scorched Earth: Australia's Secret Plan for Total War Under Japanese Invasion in World War II*, Allen & Unwin, Sydney, 2017.

'There was more than a touch of panic in the Sydney air': as cited in Michael McKernan, *All In! Australia During the Second World War*, Thomas Nelson Australia, Melbourne, 1983, p. 104.

Curtin's radio broadcast on 14 March 1942: as cited in Department of Veterans' Affairs, 'All in – The Australian homefront 1939–1945', DVA Anzac Portal, <anzacportal.dva.gov.au/wars-and-missions/world-war-ii-1939-1945/resources/all-australian-homefront-1939-1945>.

Deputy Prime Minister Frank Forde – 'dark and evil days': as cited in McKernan, *All In!*, pp. 98–9.

First Minister Clarence E Gauss – 'It can truthfully be said that Australia …': as cited in Bob Wurth, *The Battle for Australia: A Nation and Its Leader Under Siege*, Pan Macmillan, Sydney, 2013, p. 58.

'Grim-faced, war-scarred veterans …': as cited in Glover, *Official Souvenir History of 2/9 Australian Field Regiment RAA AIF, 1940–1945*, p. 16.

'Victors, yes …': as cited in Australian Military Forces, *Khaki and Green: With the Australian Army at Home and Overseas*, Australian War Memorial, Canberra, 1943, p. 75.

General Douglas MacArthur – 'As the train pulled into Melbourne …': Douglas MacArthur, *Reminiscences*, McGraw-Hill, New York, 1964, p. 151.

MacArthur compared to Alexander the Great: William Manchester, *American Caesar: Douglas MacArthur 1880–1964*, Arrow Books, London, 1979, p. 17.

MacArthur – 'I put my arm about his strong shoulder …': MacArthur, *Reminiscences*, p. 151.

Kennedy's 'memorandum to self': as cited in Hamilton, *JFK: Reckless Youth*, pp. 465–69.

MacArthur – 'it will be followed by mopping up operations …': as cited in Roland Perry, *Pacific 360°: Australia's Battle for Survival in World War II*, Hachette, Sydney, 2012, p. 201.

MacArthur to Curtin – 'The security of Australia has now been assured': as cited in Perry, *Pacific 360°*, p. 205.

'No less than fifty-eight men who joined the Unit …': Glover, *Official Souvenir History of 2/9 Australian Field Regiment RAA AIF, 1940–1945*, p. 21.

'most conspicuous and sustained gallantry …': Second Supplement to the *London Gazette* of Tuesday, 25 November 1941, no. 35360, p. 6825, <www.thegazette.co.uk/London/issue/35360/supplement/6825>.

Chapter 6 – Coast Watchers

For the background information on the Coast Watch Organisation, I have drawn from the following sources: AB Feuer (ed.), *Coast Watching in the Solomon Islands: The Bougainville Reports, December 1941 – July 1943*, Praeger, New York, 1992; Eric Feldt, *The Coast Watchers*, Currey O'Neil, Melbourne, 1981 (originally published by Oxford University Press in 1946); Patrick Lindsay, *The Coast Watchers: The Men Behind Enemy Lines Who Saved the Pacific*, William Heinemann, Sydney, 2011; Betty Lee, *Right Man, Right Place, Worst Time: Commander Eric Feldt – His Life and His Coastwatchers*, Boolarong Press, Brisbane, 2019; Walter Lord, *Lonely Vigil: Coastwatchers of the Solomons*, Viking Press, New York, 1977; and Michael Veitch, *Australia's Secret Army: The Story of the Coastwatchers*, *the Unsung Heroes of Australia's Armed Forces during World War II*, Hachette, Sydney, 2022. There are also a number of good first-hand recollections from the coast watchers themselves, including Reg Evans, 'Found! The Unsung Hero Who Saved President Kennedy's Life', *Cavalier*, vol. 11, no. 96, June 1961, pp. 8–13, 82–3; Martin Clemens, *Alone on Guadalcanal: A Coast Watcher's Story*, Naval Institute Press, Annapolis, MD, 2004; Dick C Horton, *Fire over the Islands: The Coast Watchers of the Solomons*, Reed, Sydney, 1970; Frederick A Rhoades, *Diary of a Coastwatcher in the Solomons*, The Admiral Nimitz Foundation, Fredericksburg, Texas, 1982; as well as an interview I conducted with 'the last coast watcher' Jim Burrowes OAM on 16 December 2022.

John Fahey – 'dislocated "chancers" living in remote places': John Fahey, *Australia's First Spies: The Remarkable Story of Australia's Intelligence Operations, 1901–45*, Allen & Unwin, Sydney, 2018, p. 84.

Eric Feldt – 'It is easier to teach a man how to operate a teleradio …': Eric Feldt, 'The Coastwatchers' (excerpts from Feldt's 1946 monograph *As You Were!: A Cavalcade of Events with the Australian Services from 1788 to 1946), The Battle for Australia 1942–43*, <www.battleforaustralia.org/Theyalsoserved/Coastwatchers/Feldt_Coastwatchers.html>.

'Are there any special benefits that go with this duty?': Walter Lord, 'Foreword', in Feuer, *Coast Watching in the Solomon Islands*, p. xiii.

'Never for a minute …' and 'just excitement and fun …': interview with Jim Burrowes OAM conducted on 16 December 2022 by the author.

Dick Horton – 'All this hazardous and highly-skilled work …': Horton, *Fire over the Islands*, p. 150.

Eric Feldt – 'it would be impossible to conduct such operations …': Feldt, 'The Coastwatchers'.

On the Islander perspectives on the Second World War and the Islander role in coast watching, see particularly Anna Annie Kwai, *Solomon Islanders in World War II: An Indigenous Perspective*, ANU Press, Canberra, 2017; Alan C Elliott and Anna A Kwai, *Rescuing JFK: How Solomon Islanders Rescued John F Kennedy and the Crew of PT-109*, Alan Elliott, August 2022; David Riley, *Pasifika Coastwatchers*, Reading Warrior, Auckland, 2020; and Hugh Laracy and Geoffrey White (eds), 'Taem Blong Faet: World War Two in Melanesia', *A Journal of Solomon Islands Studies*, no. 4, Special Issue, 1988; pp. 85–104.

'the Big Death': Geoffrey M White, David W Gegeo, David Akin and Karen Watson-Gegeo (eds), *The Big Death: Solomon Islanders Remember World War II [Bikfala Faet: Olketa Solomon Aelanda Rimembarem Wol Wo Tu]*, Institute of Pacific Studies, Solomon

Islands College of Higher Education and the University of the South Pacific, Suva, 1988.

Prime Minister Sir Peter Kenilorea – 'The Second World War was not our war': as cited in Kwai, *Solomon Islanders in World War II*, p. 100.

Walter Lord – 'had no conception of nationality ...': Lord, *Lonely Vigil*, p. 56.

Ruby Olive Boye: Alan Powell, 'Ruby Olive Boye-Jones (1891–1990)', *Australian Dictionary of Biography*, Vol. 17, Australian National University, Canberra, 2007; see also Ruby Boye-Jones, 'Oral history interview', National Museum of the Pacific War, Digital Archive, <digitalarchive.pacificwarmuseum.org/digital/collection/p16769coll1/id/1743/>.

Martin Clemens – 'She always sounded so cheerful and imperturbable ...': Clemens, *Alone on Guadalcanal*, p. 43.

Boye – 'with fond memories ...': Boye-Jones, 'Oral history interview'.

Martin Clemens – 'My God, I was afraid ...': Clemens, *Alone on Guadalcanal*, p. 152.

Evans – 'They weren't so fussy this time' and 'teaching rough Army types ...': Evans, 'Found! The Unsung Hero Who Saved President Kennedy's Life', pp. 9, 11.

Commander Rupert 'Cocky' Long, 'the intrigue master': Barbara Winter, *The Intrigue Master: Commander Long and Naval Intelligence in Australia, 1913–1945*, Boolarong Press, Brisbane, 1995.

Evans' and Admiral Halsey's quotes on Long: Evans, 'Found! The Unsung Hero Who Saved President Kennedy's Life', p. 11.

'the eyes and ears of the Pacific': Evans, 'Found! The Unsung Hero Who Saved President Kennedy's Life', p. 11.

'sixty-day wonders': Hamilton, *JFK: Reckless Youth*, p. 497.

Kennedy to Billings – 'this job on these boats ...': as cited in Dallek, *An Unfinished Life*, p. 88.

Clemens on Guadalcanal, all quotes: Clemens, *Alone on Guadalcanal*, p. 187.

Paul Mason – 'Twenty-four bombers headed yours': as cited in James Griffin, 'Paul Edward Mason (1901–1972)', *Australian Dictionary of Biography*, Vol. 15, Australian National University, Canberra, 2000.

Lieutenant Akogina – 'I killed some ants and ate them ...': as cited in Kwai, *Solomon Islanders in World War II*, p. 26.

'the fork in the road': as cited in 'The Solomon Islands Campaign: Guadalcanal', The National WWII Museum, <www.nationalww2museum.org/war/articles/solomon-islands-campaign-guadalcanal>.

Herbert Merillat – 'a test of national will and an index of prestige': Herbert C Merillat, *Guadalcanal Remembered*, Avon Books, New York, 1990, p. 2.

Robert Leckie's quotes: Robert Leckie, *Helmet for My Pillow*, Ebury, London, 2011, pp. 139, 141, 143.

Lieutenant-Commander George Gill – 'Had they been able to deliver their many attacks ...': Lieutenant-Commander George Gill, 'Foreword', in Eric Feldt, *The Coast Watchers*, Currey O'Neil, Melbourne, 1981, p. xviii.

Halsey – 'I could get down on my knees every night ...': 'Admiral's thanks to Aust coastwatchers', *The Courier Mail*, 28 April 1954, p. 3.

Halsey – 'If it had not been for the Australian Coastwatchers ...': quoted in Osmar White, 'The Man in the Panama who Mothered the Coastwatchers', *Pacific Islands Monthly*, vol. 28, no. 4, November 1957, pp. 50–41, at p. 50.

Halsey – 'saved Guadalcanal ...': as cited in Feldt, *The Coast Watchers*, p. 285.

Chapter 7 – Solomons-bound

Evans – 'learned the ropes': Reg Evans, 'Found! The Unsung Hero Who Saved President Kennedy's Life', *Cavalier*, vol. 11, no. 96, June 1961, pp. 8–13, 82–3, at p. 12.

On the friendship between Mackenzie, Feldt and Long: see also Peter Jones, *Australia's Argonauts: The Remarkable Story of the First Class to Enter the Royal Australian Naval College*, Echo Books, Canberra, 2016; and Betty Lee, *Right Man, Right Place, Worst Time: Commander Eric Feldt – His Life and His Coastwatchers*, Boolarong Press, Brisbane, 2019, chapter 2.

Mackenzie 'knew no fear, and no organization either': Walter Lord, *Lonely Vigil: Coastwatchers of the Solomons*, Viking Press, New York, 1977, p. 56.

Donald Kennedy: see, for example, Mike Butcher, '... *when the long trick's over': Donald Kennedy in the Pacific*, Holland House, Melbourne, 2012; Anna Annie Kwai, *Solomon Islanders in World War II*, ANU Press, Canberra, 2017, pp. 60–63; and Lord, *Lonely Vigil*, chapter 11.

Evans comes to Kolombangara: all quotes from Evans, 'Found! The Unsung Hero Who Saved President Kennedy's Life', pp. 12–13.

Feldt – 'From his position ...': Eric Feldt, *The Coast Watchers*, Currey O'Neil, Melbourne, 1981 (originally published by Oxford University Press in 1946), p. 250.

'bastard of a place': Peter Brune, *A Bastard of a Place: The Australians in Papua*, Allen & Unwin, Sydney, 2004.

Samuel Eliot Morison – 'The Aussies were fighting mad ...': Samuel Eliot Morison, *History of United States Naval Operations in World War II, Vol. VI: Breaking the Bismarcks Barrier – 22 July 1942 – 1 May 1944*, Castle Books, Edison, NJ, 2001 (originally published in 1950), p. 38.

Sergeant Arthur Traill – 'From then on the only good Jap was a dead one':

as cited in Michael Veitch, *Turning Point: The Battle for Milne Bay 1942 – Japan's first defeat in World War II*, Hachette, Sydney, 2019, p. 120.

Field Marshal Sir William Slim – 'Some of us may forget that of all the Allies …': William Slim, *Defeat into Victory*, Cassell, London, 1956, p. 188.

Kennedy sailing to the Solomons, all quotes from Nigel Hamilton, *JFK: Reckless Youth*, Random House, New York, 1992, p. 531.

Lord – 'Most of the fliers …': Lord, *Lonely Vigil*, p. 176.

Eric Bergerud – 'In this period …': Eric Bergerud, *Touched With Fire: The Land War in the South Pacific*, Penguin, New York, 1997, p. 235.

Henrietta Drake-Brockman – 'there was comparatively little fraternization …': Henrietta Drake-Brockman, 'The Americans Came', *American Quarterly*, vol. 1, no. 1, Spring 1949, pp. 44–57 at p. 55.

Bergerud – 'It is one of the curiosities of war …': Bergerud, *Touched With Fire*, p. 236.

Donald Fall – 'I think we were the best …': as cited in Bergerud, *Touched With Fire*, p. 243.

Bergerud – 'The Japanese constructed …': Bergerud, *Touched With Fire*, p. 215.

Conditions at Buna-Gona likened to tropical trench warfare: Dudley McCarthy, *Australia in the War of 1939-1945, Series 1 - Army: Volume V - South-West Pacific Area - First Year: Kokoda to Wau*, Series 1, Army, v. 5; Australian War Memorial, Canberra, 1959, p. 434.

General Michael Eichelberger – 'nightmare' and 'I want you to take Buna …': Michael Eichelberger, *Our Jungle Road to Tokyo*, Battery Press, Nashville, Tenn., 1989 (originally published in 1950), pp. 17, 21.

Eichelberger had earned the Order of the Rising Sun: Antony Beevor, *Russia: Revolution and Civil War 1917–1921*, Viking, London, 2022, p. 325.

'was doom for the Japanese': Bergerud, *Touched With Fire*, p. 222.

'orient the 32nd Division …': Bergerud, *Touched With Fire*, p. 225.

Ernest Gerber – 'Australian soldiers were kind and good people …': as cited in Bergerud, *Touched With Fire*, p. 243.

Eichelberger – 'It was a spectacular and dramatic assault …': Eichelberger, *Our Jungle Road to Tokyo*, p. 44.

Bergerud – 'No American Division in the South Pacific …': Bergerud, *Touched With Fire*, p. 225.

Chapter 8 – Cartwheel
PT boats' guns nicknamed '50-calibers-at-50 paces': Nigel Hamilton, *JFK: Reckless Youth*, Random House, New York, 1992, p. 546.

William Doyle, all quotes about PT boats and torpedoes: William Doyle, *PT 109: An American Epic of War, Survival, and the Destiny of John F Kennedy*, William Morrow, New York, 2015, p. 55.

Leonard Nikolovic – 'The only thing they were really effective at …': as cited in Doyle, *PT 109*, p. 57.

James Michener – 'I have become damned sick and tired …': as cited in Robert J Donovan, *PT-109: John F Kennedy in WWII*, MJF Books, New York, 2001 (40th anniversary edition, originally published 1961); p. 36.

Lt John Bulkeley – 'Those of you who want to come back …': as cited in Hamilton, *JFK: Reckless Youth*, p. 505.

Kennedy – 'filled an important need in World War II …': John F Kennedy, 'Foreword', in Robert J Bulkley, *At Close Quarters: PT Boats in the United States Navy*, Naval History Division, Washington, 1962, p. vii.

Johnny Isles – 'It was written all over the sky …': as cited in Hamilton, *JFK: Reckless Youth*, p. 543.

On Kennedy, 'liked him' and the other quotes in the paragraph: Donovan, *PT-109*, pp. 32, 34.

Kennedy as 'Shafty': Donovan, *PT-109*, pp. 33–34.

Kennedy taking side of Australian plantation owners: Donovan, *PT-109*, p. 31.

Kennedy to Arvard – 'I asked for it honey and I'm getting it': as cited in Robert Dallek, *An Unfinished Life: John F Kennedy, 1917–1963*, Little, Brown, New York, 2003, p. 92.

Evans – 'stared in delighted amazement …': Samuel Eliot Morison, *History of United States Naval Operations in World War II, Vol. VI, Breaking the Bismarcks Barrier, 22 July 1942 – 1 May 1944*, Castle Books, Edison, NJ., 2001, p. 115.

Evans – 'When it was all over …': Reg Evans, 'Found! The Unsung Hero Who Saved President Kennedy's Life', *Cavalier*, vol. 11, no. 96, June 1961, pp. 8–13, 82–3, at p. 13.

Frank Nash – 'This was not my idea of the war': as cited in Walter Lord, *Lonely Vigil: Coastwatchers of the Solomons*, Viking Press, New York, 1977, p. 264.

Nash – 'sort of deserted': as cited in Lord, *Lonely Vigil*, p. 264.

Ron Soodalter – Evans and Nash 'hit it off immediately …': Ron Soodalter, 'The Yank Coastwatcher who risked all in the Pacific', HistoryNet, 15 December 2020, <www.historynet.com/the-yank-coastwatcher-not-in-colorado-anymore/>.

Evans – 'glad to have him …': Evans, 'Found! The Unsung Hero Who Saved President Kennedy's Life', p. 13.

Evans – '[t]oo much movement …' and 'there was some strife around Gizo': Evans, 'Found! The Unsung Hero Who Saved President Kennedy's Life', p. 82.

Lieutenant Dick Keresey – 'a screwed-up action': as cited in Hamilton,
  JFK: Reckless Youth, p. 563.
'the most confused and least effective action the PT's had been in': as cited
  in Dallek, *An Unfinished Life*, p. 95.

Chapter 9 – Adrift

In addition to Evans' *Cavalier* article and Kennedy biographies mentioned
  before, the main sources on the sinking of PT-109 and the rescue
  of Kennedy and his crew are Reg Evans' coast watcher log book
  ('Evans, Arthur "Reg" (Coastwatcher)', Accession No. PR90/011,
  Wallet 1, Australian War Memorial); Byron White's official report,
  'Action Report of the Loss of the USS PT-109 on August 1–2, 1943',
  MTBRONS SOPAC 13 January 1944, Records of the Office of
  the Chief of Naval Operations, <catalog.archives.gov/id/305237>;
  John Hersey, 'Survival', *The New Yorker*, 17 June 1944, <www.
  newyorker.com/magazine/1944/06/17/survival>; William Doyle,
  *PT 109: An American Epic of War, Survival, and the Destiny of John
  F Kennedy*, William Morrow, New York, 2015; Robert J Donovan,
  PT-109: John F Kennedy in WWII, MJF Books, New York, 2001
  (40th anniversary edition, originally published 1961); and Walter
  Lord, *Lonely Vigil: Coastwatchers of the Solomons*, Viking Press, New
  York, 1977, chapter 13. On the scouts' perspective: Hugh Laracy
  and Geoffrey White (eds), 'Taem Blong Faet: World War Two in
  Melanesia', *A Journal of Solomon Islands Studies*, no. 4, Special Issue,
  1988, pp. 85–104; Alan C Elliott and Anna A Kwai, *Rescuing JFK:
  How Solomon Islanders Rescued John F. Kennedy and the Crew of PT-
  109*, Alan Elliott, August 2022; and, more generally, David Riley,
  Pasifika Coastwatchers, Reading Warrior, Auckland, 2020. It bears
  noting that, infuriatingly, these sources disagree about many of the
  details, including the timing of various events. I have tried, to the best
  of my ability and judgment, to reconcile various versions and arrive at
  a timeline of events that makes most sense.
Kennedy – 'Some men are killed in a war …': President John F Kennedy,
  News Conference, 21 March 1962, </www.jfklibrary.org/
  archives/other-resources/john-f-kennedy-press-conferences/news-
  conference-28>.
Planned memorial service for PT-109 crew: Fredrik Logevall, *JFK –
  Volume 1: 1917–1956*, Viking, London, 2020, p. 343.
Lieutenant-Commander George Warfield requested the Air Force bomb
  any remains of PT-109: Nigel Hamilton, *JFK: Reckless Youth*, Random
  House, New York, 1992, p. 595.
Evans – 'No survivors so far …': Reg Evans, 'Found! The Unsung Hero
  Who Saved President Kennedy's Life', *Cavalier*, vol. 11, no. 96, June
  1961, pp. 8–13, 82–3, at p. 82.

'Barracuda will come up under a swimming man and eat his testicles':
Doyle, *PT 109*, p. 134.
'thinking [they] were Japanese': Elliott and Kwai, *Rescuing JFK*, p. 32.
'Biuku Gasa - No mata yu waet skin, yu Japani': as cited in Elliott and
Kwai, *Rescuing JFK*, p. 34.

Chapter 10 – The rescue
Kennedy's message on the coconut: Nigel Hamilton, *JFK: Reckless Youth*,
Random House, New York, 1992, p. 591.
Evans – 'heard the snap of a twig …': Reg Evans, 'Found! The Unsung
Hero Who Saved President Kennedy's Life', *Cavalier*, vol. 11,
no. 96, June 1961, pp. 8–13, 82–3, at p. 82.
Evans: 'Eleven survivors …': Evans, 'Found! The Unsung Hero Who
Saved President Kennedy's Life', p. 83.
Colonel George Hill – 'started swinging his machete …': as cited in
Hamilton, *JFK*, p. 596.
'Bot wea? Man ya hemi siki!': as cited in Alan C Elliott and Anna A
Kwai, *Rescuing JFK: How Solomon Islanders Rescued John F. Kennedy
and the Crew of PT-109*, Alan Elliott, August 2022, p. 53; Elliott
and Kwai name Gasa as the scout waving the machete at Colonel
Hill.
Bejamin Kevu – 'I have a letter for you, Sir': as cited in Hamilton, *JFK*,
p. 594.
Kennedy – 'You've got to hand it to the British': as cited in Robert J
Donovan, *PT-109: John F Kennedy in WWII*, MJF Books, New York,
2001 (40th anniversary edition, originally published 1961), p. 158.
'great news' that PT-109 crew are still alive: Evans, 'Found! The Unsung
Hero Who Saved President Kennedy's Life', p. 83.
Evans – 'Could only man one canoe …': Evans, 'Found! The Unsung Hero
Who Saved President Kennedy's Life', p. 83.
Rendova to Evans – 'Three PT boats proceed tonight …': Evans, 'Found!
The Unsung Hero Who Saved President Kennedy's Life', p. 83.
Ben Kevu was 'wreathed in smiles': Jack Paar, *P.S. Jack Paar*, Doubleday,
New York, 1983, p. 286.
Kennedy to Evans – 'Man, am I glad to see you!': Evans, 'Found! The
Unsung Hero Who Saved President Kennedy's Life', p. 9.
Evans – 'He was relieved …': Evans, 'Found! The Unsung Hero Who
Saved President Kennedy's Life', p. 83.
Evans – 'recall[ed] the day very, very clearly …': as cited in Doyle, *PT 109*,
p. 159.
Evans to Rendova – 'Lieut Kennedy considers it advisable …': Evans,
'Found! The Unsung Hero Who Saved President Kennedy's Life',
p. 83.

Evans – 'no glory-and-haloes stunt ...': Evans, 'Found! The Unsung Hero Who Saved President Kennedy's Life', p. 9.

Evans gave Kennedy a pair of his 'coveralls': Jack Paar, *3 on a Toothbrush: Adventures and Encounters Around the Globe*, Doubleday, New York, 1965, p. 59.

'The rifle disappeared': Donovan, *PT-109*, p. 163.

Kennedy – 'Where the hell have you been?' and 'Thanks, I've just had a coconut': as cited in Doyle, *PT 109*, p. 167.

'It's OK. If they die, we die, too': as cited in Elliott and Kwai, *Rescuing JFK*, p. 57.

'all admired, and in some cases revered, Kennedy ...': Donovan, *PT-109*, p. xv.

'Yes, Jesus Loves Me!': Samuel Eliot Morison, *History of United States Naval Operations in World War II, Vol. VI, Breaking the Bismarcks Barrier, 22 July 1942 – 1 May 1944*, Castle Books, Edison, NJ., 2001 (originally published in 1950), p. 212.

Chapter 11 – Aussies and Yanks

There are many sources, including scores of memoirs and reminiscences, that describe the 'first encounter' between American servicemen and Australian soldiers and civilians. I have found the following of most interest: Darryl McIntyre, *Paragons of Glamour: A Study of the United States Military Forces in Australia 1942–45*, PhD thesis, University of Queensland, Brisbane, 1989; John Hammond Moore, *Oversexed, Over-paid, and Over-here: Americans in Australia, 1941–1945*, University of Queensland Press, Brisbane, 1981; E Daniel Potts and Annette Potts, *Yanks Down Under 1941–45: The American Impact on Australia*, Oxford University Press, Melbourne, 1985; Barry Ralph, *They Passed This Way: The United States of America, The States of Australia and World War II*, Kangaroo Press, Sydney, 2000; and Peter Thompson and Robert Macklin, *The Battle of Brisbane: Australians and the Yanks at War*, ABC Books, Sydney, 2000.

Instructions for American Servicemen in Australia – 1942 is available both in reprints and online: <www.army.gov.au/sites/default/files/2019-11/instructions_for_american_servicemen_in_australia_1942_0.pdf>.

Dean Andersen – 'The people here aren't as ambitious as Americans ...': Dean W Andersen, *Praise the Lord and Pass the Penicillin: Memoir of a Combat Medic in the Pacific in World War II*, McFarland, Jefferson, NC, 2003, p. 41.

Nelson T Johnson – 'the average Australian desires a high standard of living ...': as cited in Peter G Edwards, *Australia through American Eyes 1935–1945: Observations by American Diplomats*, University of Queensland Press, Brisbane, 1979, p. 12.

American outraged by wartime strikes in Australia: Hal G P Colebatch, *Australia's Secret War*, Quadrant Books, Sydney, 2013, pp. 11–12.

Charles Schroeder – 'kindred ideas …': as cited in Potts, *Yanks Down Under*, p. xxii.

Henrietta Drake-Brockman – 'Those first United States troops …': Henrietta Drake-Brockman, 'The Americans Came', *American Quarterly*, vol. 1, no. 1, Spring 1949, pp. 44–57, at p. 50.

'Yes, we were jealous …': Jim Burrowes OAM, interviewed on 16 December 2022 by the author.

The 'Battle of Brisbane' is subject of an excellent book by Peter A Thompson and Robert Macklin, *The Battle of Brisbane: Australia and the Yanks at War*, ABC Books, Sydney, 2000.

Donald Friend – 'the American village …': Donald Friend, *The Diaries of Donald Friend, Vol. 1*, National Library of Australia, Canberra, 2001, p. 444.

Major Bill Thomas – 'The Australians … had very solid reasons to be aggrieved …': as cited in Thompson and Macklin, *The Battle of Brisbane*, p. 236.

John Curtin – 'the better for everyone concerned': as cited in Thompson and Macklin, *The Battle of Brisbane*, p. 236.

Lyndon B Johnson – 'El Paso desert country' and 'the best damn folks in the world …': as cited in Robert A Caro, *The Years of Lyndon Johnson: Means of Ascent*, Alfred A Knopf, New York, 1990, p. 44.

Very little has been written so far about 'the Townsville mutiny', as the story only recently emerged from the United States archives. Ironically, the most comprehensive reconstruction of events is in Judy Nunn's bestselling historical romance novel, *Khaki Town*, William Heinemann, Sydney, 2019. But see also Josh Bavas, 'Secret documents lift lid on WWII mutiny by US troops in north Queensland', *ABC News*, 10 February 2012, <www.abc.net.au/news/2012-02-10/historian-reveals-details-on-townsville-mutiny/3821906>.

David Malouf – 'When Brisbane became a garrison town in 1942 …': David Malouf, *12 Edmondstone Street*, Penguin, Melbourne, 1986, p. 8.

Graham Smith's two-year-old brother: Graham Smith, *Shadows of War: On the Brisbane Line*, Boolarong Press, Brisbane, 2011, p. 149.

Reg Saunders – 'Australian soldiers I met in the Army …': as cited in 'The History of Indigenous Australian Service men and woman [sic]', LaTrobe University, 6–13 July 2014, p. 16, <www.latrobe.edu.au/__data/assets/pdf_file/0009/585594/NAIDOC-2014-Servicing-Country-.pdf>.

'the main point is they like us, and we like them': *Instructions for American Servicemen in Australia – 1942*, p. vi.

'I had five prices for a melon ...': James A Michener, *Return to Paradise*, Random House, New York, 1951, p. 352.

Marjorie Robertson – 'My brother was away with the Royal Australian Air Force ...': as cited in Thompson and Macklin, *The Battle of Brisbane*, p. 156.

Andersen – 'I like this country ...': Andersen, *Praise the Lord and Pass the Penicillin*, p. 33.

'The experience of having so many Americans ...': Potts and Potts, *Yanks Down Under 1941–45*, p. xvii.

'The Australians need our help in winning this war ...': *Instructions for American Servicemen in Australia – 1942*, p. 4.

'There's no finer soldier in the world': *Instructions for American Servicemen in Australia – 1942*, p. 35.

Chapter 12 – To the end

Eric Feldt – 'The difficulty of finding hidden [Japanese] barges ...': Eric Feldt, *The Coast Watchers*, Currey O'Neil, Melbourne, 1981 (originally published by Oxford University Press in 1946), p. 292.

Evans – 'seemed to be jinxed': as cited in Jack Paar, *3 on a Toothbrush: Adventures and encounters around the globe*, Doubleday, New York, 1965, p. 57.

Evans – 'Because Kolombangara was a Japanese-held island ...': as cited in Paar, *3 on a Toothbrush*, p. 57.

'Evans – no longer call on [their] co-operation': Feldt, *The Coast Watchers*, p. 293.

Field Marshal Erwin Rommel – 'Give me two Australian divisions ...': said, perhaps apocryphally, during the siege of Tobruk in 1941.

Eric Bergerud – 'kill ratio...' Eric Bergerud, *Touched With Fire: The Land War in the South Pacific*, Penguin, New York, 1997, p. 507.

John Robertson – 'More than any of his western allies ...': John Robertson, *Australia at War: 1939–1945*, William Heinemann, Melbourne, 1981, p. 3.

Bergerud – 'In July 1942 the Japanese Army was invincible ...': Bergerud, *Touched With Fire*, p. xii.

Joan Beaumont – '"Allied" troops when Australian troops were doing the fighting ...': Joan Beaumont, 'Australia's war: Asia and the Pacific', in Joan Beaumont (ed.), *Australia's War, 1939–45*, Allen & Unwin, Sydney, 1996, pp. 26–53, at p. 40.

General Robert Eichelberger – ' Our Air [Force] made it possible ...': Robert Eichelberger, *Our Jungle Road to Tokyo*, Battery Classics, Nashville, Tenn., 1989 (originally published in 1950), pp. 91–2.

Bergerud – 'When brought up to strength ...': Bergerud, *Touched With Fire*, p. 268.

Kennedy – 'I am alive …': Fredrik Logevall, *JFK – Volume 1: 1917–1956*, Viking, London, 2020, p. 350.

'so many muzzles, [they] bristled like a porcupine': Nigel Hamilton, *JFK: Reckless Youth*, Random House, New York, 1992, p. 610.

Prime Minister John Curtin – 'balanced war effort': as cited in Paul Hasluck, *Australia in the War of 1939–1945, Series 4 – Civil: Volume II: The Government and the People, 1942–1945*, Australian War Memorial, Canberra, 1970, p. 370.

Max Hastings – 'Australia seemed almost to vanish …': Max Hastings, *Nemesis: The Battle for Japan, 1944–45*, HarperCollins, London, 2007, p. xxi.

Bergerud – 'Australia was, when all was said and done …': Bergerud, *Touched With Fire*, p. 249.

Hastings – 'The evident futility of these embittered many men …': Hastings, *Nemesis*, p. 363.

Chapter 13 – Sailing to the White House

The look of Kennedy's office as that of a 'navy man': William Manchester, *Bright Shining Moment: Remembering Kennedy*, Little, Brown, Boston, 1983, p. 140.

'talismans from the event that paved his path to power': William Doyle, *PT 109: An American Epic of War, Survival, and the Destiny of John F Kennedy*, William Morrow, New York, 2015, p. 237.

The claims that Kennedy behaved recklessly, allowing his nimble craft to be rammed by a Japanese destroyer: see, for example, Mark White, 'Apparent Perfection: The Image of John F Kennedy', *History*, vol. 98, no. 2, 2013, pp. 226–46, at p. 244; Joan Blair and Clay Blair, *The Search for JFK*, Berkley Publishing, New York, 1976, chapter 18 and pp. 586–87.

'the seeds of his presidency were sown': Robert J Donovan, *PT-109: John F Kennedy in WWII*, MJF Books, New York, 2001 (originally published 1961), p. xx.

Hersey's article: John Hersey, 'Survival', *New Yorker*, 17 June 1944, <www.newyorker.com/magazine/1944/06/17/survival>.

'I am in command of a New Zealand infantry patrol …': Hersey, 'Survival'.

Hersey – 'The wording and signature of this message …': John Hersey, *Of Men and War*, Scholastic, New York, 1963, p. 24, footnote 1.

Evans – 'I've kept my trap shut …': Reg Evans, 'Found! The Unsung Hero Who Saved President Kennedy's Life', *Cavalier*, vol. 11, no. 96, June 1961, pp. 8–13, 82–3, at p. 9.

Richard Donohue – 'was the entire basis of his political life': as cited in Doyle, *PT 109*, p. xvi.

Theodore White – 'In the newspapers Kennedy advertisements ...':
Theodore White, *The Making of the President 1960*, Atheneum
Publishers, New York, 1961, p. 108.

Nixon did not try to embellish his war record: Richard Nixon, *RN: The
Memoirs of Richard Nixon*, MacMillan, Melbourne, 1978, p. 29.

Nixon's duties described as 'Ground Aviation Officer': Duane Hove,
*American Warriors: Five Presidents in the Pacific Theatre of World
War II*, Burd Street Press, Shippensburg, Penn., 2003, p. 106.

William Doyle – 'Joseph Kennedy's dream had finally come true ...':
Doyle, *PT 109*, p. 235.

Dave Powers – 'Without PT 109 ...': as cited in Doyle, *PT 109*,
p. 235.

Evans – 'interesting change': 'US's 35th President – by Courtesy of
"Ferdinand"', *Pacific Islands Monthly*, vol. 31, no. 6, January 1961,
pp. 49–51, at p. 50.

Trudy's letter reproduced in the *Advertiser*: 'Life on Gold Coast Has Its
Excitements', *Advertiser*, 9 April 1948, p. 7.

'There has been speculation in New Zealand ...': 'Who was the Kiwi who
gave wartime aid to Kennedy?', *Pacific Islands Monthly*, vol. 31, no. 3,
October 1960, pp. 45–7, at p. 47.

Eric Feldt – 'had no record of that particular rescue ...': 'Who was that
who Helped President-elect Kennedy?', in the 'Editors' Mailbag',
Pacific Islands Monthly, vol. 31, no. 4, November 1960, p. 28.

Evans – 'began hearing again of Kennedy ...': 'US's 35th President – by
Courtesy of "Ferdinand"', p. 50.

Evans – 'October issue about Kennedy and the Lieutenant Wincote ...':
'US's 35th President – by Courtesy of "Ferdinand"', p. 51.

Evans – 'to give ... his version of the story ...': 'Evans: No Kiwi Helped
Kennedy, He Says', *Pacific Islands Monthly*, vol. 31, no. 5, December
1960, p. 25.

The 'Niddites' dinner: Alan Nicholls, 'Niddites', *The Age*, 29 November
1960, p. 2.

Evans – 'impressed' and 'even more interested ...': 'US's 35th President –
by Courtesy of "Ferdinand"', p. 49.

Ray Castle – 'As far as I know, this is the first time ...': Ray Castle,
'Aussie who saved US President', *Daily Telegraph*, 21 December
1960, p. 4.

Chapter 14 – Reunited

Pat McMahon – 'Kennedy stood up, grinned ...': Sharon Whitley Larsen,
'Remembering JFK and PT-109 heroism', *San Diego Union-Tribune*,
21 November 2014, <www.sandiegouniontribune.com/opinion/
commentary/sdut-remembering-jfk-and-pt-109-heroism-2013nov21-
story.html>.

Gasa and Kennedy correspondence: as cited in William Doyle, *PT 109:*
An American Epic of War, Survival, and the Destiny of John F Kennedy,
William Morrow, New York, 2015, p. 241.

Salinger confirmed Evans' identity: Russell Baker, 'Kennedy, After
17 Years, Solves Mystery of his Pacific Rescuer', *New York Times*,
26 February 1961, pp. 1, 44.

Evans – 'next time he writes any note …': as cited in 'President Kennedy
Makes it Official', *Pacific Islands Monthly*, vol. 31, no. 8, March 1961,
p. 26.

Menzies' thoughts about Kennedy: Robert G Menzies, *Afternoon Light:*
Some Memories of Men and Events, Cassel, Melbourne, 1967,
pp. 143–4.

Graham Parsons – 'completely informal, completely relaxed …': as cited in
AW Martin, *Robert Menzies: A Life, vol. 2, 1944–1978*, Melbourne
University Press, Melbourne, 1999, p. 425.

Kennedy – 'that he had just learned that Australia was responsible …':
Baker, 'Kennedy, After 17 Years, Solves Mystery of his Pacific
Rescuer', p. 44.

Menzies – 'I have no doubt that President Kennedy …': Menzies,
Afternoon Light, p. 143.

'weeks before the *Daily Telegraph* …': 'The Coastwatcher Mixture as
Before', *Pacific Islands Monthly*, vol. 31, no. 7, February 1961,
pp. 26–7, at p. 27.

'squeeze just a bit more out of the story' and 'browned off …': as cited in
'President Kennedy Makes it Official', p. 26.

Bob Curran – 'When I talk to prospective journalists …': Bob Curran,
'JFK's Forgotten Rescuer', *Buffalo News*, 30 November 1993,
<buffalonews.com/news/jfks-forgotten-rescuer/article_2c9b8e82-
f0a6-5acc-98d0-87837c08b94c.html>.

'charming letter': 'Word from the White House', *Pacific Islands Monthly*,
vol. 31, no. 9, April 1961, p. 27.

Kennedy – 'drop by the White House on May 1st, at 11:30am …': as cited
in Sue Boswell, 'The man who saved a President', *Daily Telegraph*,
8 July 1978, p. 15.

'"Here he comes!" …': Francis Sugrue, 'Kennedy's War Rescuer Flies In',
New York Herald-Tribune, 28 April 1961, p. 8.

'New Yorkers today turned on a hero's welcome …': 'Hero's welcome for
Reg Evans', *Daily Telegraph*, 29 April 1961, p. 3.

Evans – 'As far as I was concerned …': as cited in 'Kennedy's War Rescuer
Flies In', p. 8.

Evans and Kennedy meet in the Oval Office: Reg Evans, 'My Half Hour
with the President', *Daily Telegraph*, 3 May 1961, p. 3.

'happy ending' and the following quotes: 'The President Meets Reg
Evans', *Pacific Islands Monthly*, vol. 31, no. 10, May 1961, p. 141.

The *Cavalier* article: Reg Evans, 'Found! The Unsung Hero Who Saved President Kennedy's Life', *Cavalier*, vol. 11, no. 96, June 1961, pp. 8–13, 82–3.

Chapter 15 – Mr Kevu goes to Washington

'no important problems in …' and 'strong friend of the US': James Curran, *The Prime Ministers in America*, Lowy Institute, Sydney September 2013, p. 4, <interactives.lowyinstitute.org/archive/the-prime-ministers-in-america/assets/The-Prime-Ministers-in-America-2019.pdf>.

Beale – 'men with urgent business in America': Howard Beale, *This Inch of Time: Memoirs of Politics and Diplomacy*, Melbourne University Press, Melbourne, 1977, p. 130.

'Stewart Cockburn – More than 600 journalists …': as cited in Jennifer Cockburn, *Writing for His Life: Stewart Cockburn, Crusading Journalist*, Australian Scholarly Publishing, Melbourne, 2022, p. 210.

Dinner menu and entertainment: Bridget Griffen-Foley, 'Playing with Princes and Presidents: Sir Frank Packer and the 1962 Challenge for the America's Cup', *Australian Journal of Politics and History*, vol. 46, no. 1, 2000, pp. 51–66, at pp. 61–2.

Beale – 'the top of his form': Beale, *This Inch of Time*, p. 130.

Kennedy's speech at the America's Cup dinner: President John F Kennedy, 'Remarks at the America's Cup Dinner Given by the Australian Ambassador, September 14, 1962', John F Kennedy Presidential Library and Museum, <www.jfklibrary.org/archives/other-resources/john-f-kennedy-speeches/americas-cup-dinner-19620914>.

Beale – 'He liked Australians …': Beale, *This Inch of Time*, p. 178.

Beale – 'it made many friends for Australia' and 'magnificent and stirring evening': Beale, *This Inch of Time*, p. 130.

Cockburn – 'This astonishing mass …' and 'A sort of gay Dunkirk': as cited in Cockburn, *Writing for His Life*, p. 211.

'buzzed repeatedly … by U.S. military aircraft': Associated Press, 'Yacht Carrier Buzzed Off Cuba', *Washington Post*, 12 December 1962.

Ensign Paul Sanger – 'knew they were either going to have a relatively uneventful day …': Larry Chapman, 'One Minute To Midnight: The Real Story Of The Cuban Missile Crisis – Part 5 Of 8', NBC, 23 October 1992, <www.gettyimages.co.nz/detail/video/production-unit-specials-media-type-aired-show-media-news-footage/1276160984>.

Evans – 'It's like coming home', 'with a grain of salt' and 'Not a bad song either': as cited in 'Coastwatcher Evans Goes Back', *Pacific Islands Monthly*, vol. 32, no. 11, June 1962, pp. 15–16.

Jack Paar – 'His slight frame …': Jack Paar, *P.S. Jack Paar*, Doubleday, New York, 1983, p. 287.

'retired civil servant': Jack Paar, *3 on a Toothbrush: Adventures and Encounters Around the Globe*, Doubleday, New York, 1965, p. 63.

Benjamin Kevu – 'Number One': as cited in Paar, *3 on a Toothbrush*, p. 68.

Kevu – 'I think that Washington City has more natives …': as cited in Paar, *3 on a Toothbrush*, p. 73.

Dinner at 'Trader Vic's': Paar, *P.S. Jack Paar*, p. 288.

Jack Paar Show, all quotes: Jack Paar Show, 'PT 109 Story', NBC, 21 September 1962, Accession no. F03487, Australian War Memorial.

Paar – 'smashing presence', 'Benny showed no concern …', 'very dramatic and touching' and 'an absorbing hour': Paar, *P.S. Jack Paar*, pp. 287–89.

Ken O'Donnell – 'must have been the longest and busiest working day …': Kenneth P O'Donnell and David F Powers, *'Johnny, We Hardly Knew Ye': Memories of John Fitzgerald Kennedy*, Little, Brown, Boston, 1972, p. 257.

Kevu and Kennedy meeting, all quotes: O'Donnell and Powers, *'Johnny, We Hardly Knew Ye'*, pp. 259–60.

Paar – 'quite a social lion during his Washington stay': Paar, *3 on a Toothbrush*, p. 74.

'urgent off-the-record meeting …': O'Donnell and Powers, *'Johnny, We Hardly Knew Ye'*, p. 261.

Kennedy – 'Seeing Ben Kevu …': as cited in O'Donnell and Powers, *'Johnny, We Hardly Knew Ye'*, p. 263.

'*Navy Log*: PT-109': 'Navy Log: PT-109 (TV)', *The Paley Centre for Media*, <www.paleycenter.org/collection/item/?q=peter+…9&p=187&item=120468>.

Salinger – 'The White House, unfortunately, is not set up …', 'liked' and 'the critics didn't …': Pierre Salinger, *With Kennedy*, Jonathan Cape, London, 1967, pp. 103, 105.

Trudy Evans' death notice: *Sydney Morning Herald*, 25 June 1963, p. 26.

Kennedy and Beale conversation about visit to Australia: Howard Beale, 'For Menzies from Beale', Department of External Affairs Inward Cablegram I.10775, 26 April 1963, in File No. 63/6277, Prime Minister's Department, National Archives of Australia.

'lively possibility': Australian Embassy, Washington, 'President's Proposed Tour', Department of External Affairs Inward Savingram I.29450, 26 October 1963, in 'President JF Kennedy of USA, Visit to Australia, General Reps', File No. 62/4749, Prime Minister's Department, National Archives of Australia.

JH Scholtens – 'my section would not be able to handle': JH Scholtens, 'Mr Kennedy's Visit', Letter to the Secretary, Prime Minister's

Department, 12 September 1963, in 'President JF Kennedy of USA, Visit to Australia, General Reps' File No. 62/4749, Prime Minister's Department, National Archives of Australia.

Kennedy invited to open Lake Burley Griffin: GF Wynn, 'Lake Burley Griffin, Your reference 62/4749 of 27th June, 1963', Letter to the Secretary, Prime Minister's Department, 6 August 1963, in 'President J F Kennedy of USA, Visit to Australia, General Reps', File No. 62/4749, Prime Minister's Department, National Archives of Australia.

John Bunting fielding applications: EJ Bunting, Letter to JG Frost, Assistant to the Warden, The University of New South Wales, 22 November 1963, in 'President J F Kennedy of USA, Visit to Australia, General Reps', File No. 62/4749, Prime Minister's Department, National Archives of Australia.

Chapter 16 – The legacy

Cockburn – 'I have never known ...', 'paradoxically, the shock and grief ...' and 'ideal image': as cited in Jennifer Cockburn, *Writing for His Life: Stewart Cockburn, Crusading Journalist*, Australian Scholarly Publishing, Melbourne, 2022, p. 223.

'our president too': Jennifer Clark, '"Our president too": Australians and the death of John Kennedy', *Australian Historical Studies*, vol. 29, 1998, pp. 127–48.

'If only you lived near here, I could help you ...': as cited in Clark, '"Our president too"', p. 137, footnote 59.

'Most Australians experienced a great sadness ...': as cited in Clark, '"Our president too"', p. 135.

Jennifer Clark – 'was mourned as if he had been a family member ...': Clark, '"Our president too"', p. 137.

Menzies' eulogy: House of Representatives, *Hansard*, 25 February 1964, pp. 14–15.

Calwell's eulogy: House of Representatives, *Hansard*, 25 February 1964, pp. 15–16.

Evans – 'It was like losing an old friend': as cited in Sue Boswell, 'The man who saved a President', *Daily Telegraph*, 8 July 1978, p. 15.

Benjamin Kevu – 'The message came through the air local news ...': as cited in Jack Paar, *3 on a Toothbrush: Adventures and encounters around the globe*, Doubleday, New York, 1965, p. 75.

'friend's death': William Doyle, *PT 109: An American Epic of War, Survival, and the Destiny of John F Kennedy*, William Morrow, New York, 2015, p. 268.

'Bob Kennedy took off his PT tie pin ...': William Manchester, *The Death of a President: November 20–November 25, 1963*, Harper & Row, New York, 1967, p. 517.

Proposed *The Coastwatchers* TV series: Stephen Vagg, 'Forgotten Australian TV Plays: *The Coastwatchers*', *FilmInk*, .

Adventure Unlimited TV series: 'Historic Rescue', *Sydney Morning Herald*, 15 November 1965, p. 18.

Proposed *The Australian Coastwatchers* TV series: 'Evans, Arthur "Reg" (Coastwatcher)', Accession No. PR90/011, Wallet 1, Australian War Memorial.

Evans' death notice: 'Death Notices', *Sydney Morning Herald*, 2 February 1989, p. 31.

Works regarding or including Evans published after his death: Patrick Lindsay, *The Coast Watchers: The Men Behind Enemy Lines Who Saved the Pacific*, William Heinemann, North Sydney, 2011; Michael Veitch, *Australia's Secret Army: The Story of the Coastwatchers, the Unsung Heroes of Australia's Armed Forces during World War II*, Hachette, Sydney, 2022; Michael Adams, 'The Aussie Who Saved John F. Kennedy – Part One', *Forgotten Australia*, Season 5, Episode 10, 23 July 2022, <shows.acast.com/forgotten-australia/episodes/the-aussie-who-saved-john-f-kennedy-part-one>, and Michael Adams, 'The Aussie Who Saved John F. Kennedy – Part Two', *Forgotten Australia*, Season 5, Episode 10, 23 July 2022, <shows.acast.com/forgotten-australia/episodes/the-aussie-who-saved-john-f-kennedy-part-two>; William Doyle, *PT 109*; Robert D Ballard, *Collision with History: The Search for John F Kennedy's PT-109*, National Geographic, Washington, D.C., 2002.

Bob Curran – 'removed from the story again': Bob Curran, 'JFK's Forgotten Rescuer', *Buffalo News*, 30 November 1993, <buffalonews. com/news/jfks-forgotten-rescuer/article_2c9b8e82-f0a6-5acc-98d0-87837c08b94c.html>.

Evans written out of the PT-109 rescue by Robert Dallek: Robert Dallek, *An Unfinished Life: John F Kennedy, 1917–1963*, Little, Brown, New York, 2003, p. 97.

Bill O'Reilly misidentifies Evans: Bill O'Reilly, *Killing Kennedy: The End of Camelot*, Macmillan, London, 2012, pp. 30–31.

Kumana's reminiscences about Kennedy: as cited in 'The Search for Kennedy's PT-109' (TV documentary), *National Geographic*, 2003, at 42.10 mins, <www.youtube.com/watch?v=ehXGm_y6NF4>.

Gasa and Kumana in later life: Rob Brown, 'The Solomon Islanders who saved JFK', *BBC News*, 6 August 2014, <www.bbc.com/news/magazine-28644830>.

The wreck of PT-109 located: Ballard, *Collision with History*; and *The Search for Kennedy's PT-109* (TV documentary), *National Geographic*, 2003.

The wreck of Gunboat No 1/PT-59 found: 'John F Kennedy's WWII-era patrol boat is raised from Harlem River', ABC7NY, 16 June 2020, <abc7ny.com/wwii-world-war-two-ii-pt-59/6248927/>.

Afterword

John Curtin – 'The protection of this country ...': as cited in 'Mr Curtin's Call to Nation', *Border Watch*, 17 February 1942, p. 1.

Curtin – 'Australia looks to America ...': John Curtin, 'The Task Ahead', *Herald*, 27 December 1941, p. 10.

Curtin – 'We fight for the same free institutions that you enjoy ...': John Curtin, 'Speech to America', 14 March 1942, <john.curtin.edu.au/audio/00434.html>.

Dixon Wecter – 'American invasion ...': Dixon Wecter, 'The Aussie and the Yank', *Atlantic Monthly*, vol. 177, no. 5, May 1946, pp. 52–56, at p. 54.

John H Moore – 'Man for man ...' and 'World War Two as experienced in the South-West Pacific ...': John Hammond Moore, *Oversexed, Over-paid, and Over-here: Americans in Australia, 1941–1945*, University of Queensland Press, Brisbane, 1981, p. 282.

Penny Wong, all quotes from: Penny Wong, 'John Curtin's turn to America, 75 years on', *Penny Wong*, 1 October 2016, </www.pennywong.com.au/media-hub/opinion-pieces/john-curtin-s-turn-to-america-75-years-on/>.

Kurt Campbell – 'If you look at what the US has done in the last two years ...': as cited in Peter Hartcher, 'Australia reaps reward for standing ground on China', *Sydney Morning Herald*, 19 November 2022, <www.smh.com.au/politics/federal/australia-reaps-reward-for-standing-ground-on-china-20221118-p5bzhg.html>.

'private diplomatic consultations ...': Memorandum from JF Nimmo (Deputy Secretary, Prime Minister's Department), 2 July 1963, Personal Papers of Prime Minister Menzies, Overseas visits, 1963, p. 247, M2576, 20, National Archives of Australia.

Wecter – 'Australia knows clearly ...': Wecter, 'The Aussie and the Yank', p. 56.

FURTHER READING

Adams, Michael, 'The Aussie Who Saved John F Kennedy – Part One', *Forgotten Australia*, Season 5, Episode 10, 23 July 2022, <shows. acast.com/forgotten-australia/episodes/the-aussie-who-saved-john-f-kennedy-part-one>.

Adams, Michael, 'The Aussie Who Saved John F Kennedy – Part Two', *Forgotten Australia*, Season 5, Episode 10, 23 July 2022, <shows. acast.com/forgotten-australia/episodes/the-aussie-who-saved-john-f-kennedy-part-two>.

Ballard, Robert D, *Collision with History: The Search for John F Kennedy's PT-109*, National Geographic, Washington, D.C., 2002.

Beaumont, Joan (ed.), *Australia's War 1939–45*, Allen & Unwin, Sydney, 1996.

Bell, Roger J, *Unequal Allies: Australian–American relations and the Pacific war*, Melbourne University Press, Melbourne, 1977.

Bergerud, Eric, *Touched With Fire: The Land War in the South Pacific*, Penguin, New York, 1997.

Blair, Joan and Clay Blair, *The Search for JFK*, Berkley Publishing, New York, 1976.

Borneman, Walter R, *MacArthur at War: World War II in the Pacific*, Back Bay Books, New York, 2016.

Brune, Peter, *A Bastard of a Place: The Australians in Papua – Kokoda, Milne Bay, Gona, Buna, Sanananda*, Allen & Unwin, Sydney, 2003.

Clemens, Martin, *Alone on Guadalcanal: A Coast Watcher's Story*, Naval Institute Press, Annapolis, MD, 2004.

Collie, Craig, *On Our Doorstep: When Australia Faced the Threat of Invasion by the Japanese*, Allen & Unwin, Sydney, 2020.

Dallek, Robert, *An Unfinished Life: John F Kennedy, 1917–1963*, Little, Brown, New York, 2003.

Dean, Peter J, *MacArthur's Coalition: US and Australian Military Operations in the Southwest Pacific Area, 1942–1945*, University Press of Kansas, Lawrence, Ka., 2018.

Dennis, Peter et al (ed.), *Oxford Companion to Australian Military History*, Oxford University Press, Melbourne, 2008.

Department of Veterans' Affairs, *Australians in the Pacific War: Australia's Home Defence 1939–1945*, Department of Veterans' Affairs, Canberra, 2006.

Donovan, Robert J, *PT-109: John F Kennedy in WWII*, MJF Books, New York, 2001 (40th anniversary edition, originally published 1961).

Doyle, William, *PT 109: An American Epic of War, Survival, and the Destiny of John F Kennedy*, William Morrow, New York, 2015.

Drake-Brockman, Henrietta, 'The Americans Came', *American Quarterly*, vol. 1, no. 1, Spring 1949, pp. 44–57.

Edwards, Peter G, *Australia Through American Eyes – 1935–1945: Observations by American Diplomats*, University of Queensland Press, Brisbane, 1979.

Elliott, Alan C and Anna A Kwai, *Rescuing JFK: How Solomon Islanders Rescued John F. Kennedy and the Crew of PT-109*, Alan Elliott, August 2022.

Esthus, Raymond A, *From Enmity to Alliance: U.S. – Australian Relations, 1931–1941*, Melbourne University Press, Melbourne, 1965.

Evans, Reg, 'Found! The Unsung Hero Who Saved President Kennedy's Life', *Cavalier*, vol. 11, no. 96, June 1961, pp. 8–13, 82–3.

Feldt, Eric, *The Coast Watchers*, Currey O'Neil, Melbourne, 1981 (originally published by Oxford University Press in 1946).

Feuer, AB (ed.), *Coast Watching in the Solomon Islands: The Bougainville Reports, December 1941 – July 1943*, Praeger, New York, 1992.

Glover, EW (compiler), *Official Souvenir History of 2/9 Australian Field Regiment RAA AIF, 1940–1945*, 2/9 Australian Field Regiment, 1945.

Grattan, C Hartley, *Introducing Australia*, John Day, New York, 1944.

Grattan, C Hartley, *The United States and the Southwest Pacific*, Harvard University Press, Cambridge, Mass., 1961.

Hamilton, Nigel, *JFK: Reckless Youth*, Random House, New York, 1992.

Harper, Norman, *A Great and Powerful Friend: A Study of Australian American Relations between 1900 and 1975*, University of Queensland Press, Brisbane, 1987.

Hersey, John, 'Survival', *The New Yorker*, 17 June 1944, <www.newyorker.com/magazine/1944/06/17/survival>.

Horton, Dick C, *Fire over the Islands: The Coast Watchers of the Solomons*, Reed, Sydney, 1970.

Hoskins, Ian, *Australia & the Pacific: A history*, NewSouth Publishing, Sydney, 2021.

Kwai, Anna A, *Solomon Islanders in World War II: An Indigenous Perspective*, ANU Press, Canberra, 2017.

Laracy, Hugh and Geoffrey White (eds), 'Taem Blong Faet: World War Two in Melanesia', *A Journal of Solomon Islands Studies*, no. 4, Special Issue, 1988.

Lee, Betty, *Right Man, Right Place, Worst Time: Commander Eric Feldt – His Life and His Coastwatchers*, Boolarong Press, Brisbane, 2019.

Lindsay, Patrick, *The Coast Watchers: The Men Behind Enemy Lines Who Saved the Pacific*, William Heinemann, Sydney, 2011.

Logevall, Fredrik, *JFK – Volume 1: 1917–1956*, Viking, London, 2020.

Lord, Walter, *Lonely Vigil: Coastwatchers of the Solomons*, Viking Press, New York, 1977.

McIntyre, Darryl, *Paragons of Glamour: A Study of the United States Military Forces in Australia 1942–45*, PhD thesis, University of Queensland, Brisbane, 1989.

McKernan, Michael, *All In! Australia During the Second World War*, Thomas Nelson, Melbourne, 1983.

Moore, John Hammond, *Over-sexed, Over-paid, and Over-here: Americans in Australia, 1941–1945*, University of Queensland Press, Brisbane, 1981.

Morison, Samuel Eliot, *History of United States Naval Operations in World War II, Vol. VI: Breaking the Bismarcks Barrier – 22 July 1942 – 1 May 1944*, Castle Books, Edison, NJ, 2001 (originally published in 1950).

Paar, Jack, *3 on a Toothbrush: Adventures and Encounters Around the Globe*, Doubleday, New York, 1965.

Paar, Jack, *P. S. Jack Paar*, Doubleday, New York, 1983.

Parkin, Russell, *Great White Fleet to Coral Sea: Naval Strategy and the Development of Australia–United States Relations, 1900–1945*, Department of Foreign Affairs and Trade, Canberra, 2008.

Perry, Roland, *Pacific 360°: Australia's Battle for Survival in World War II*, Hachette, Sydney, 2012.

Potts, E Daniel and Annette Potts, *Yanks Down Under 1941–45: The American Impact on Australia*, Oxford University Press, Melbourne, 1985.

Ralph, Barry, *They Passed This Way: The United States of America, The States of Australia and World War II*, Kangaroo Press, Sydney, 2000.

Rhoades, Frederick A, *Diary of a Coastwatcher in the Solomons*, The Admiral Nimitz Foundation, Fredericksburg, Texas, 1982.

Riley, David, *Pasifika Coastwatchers*, Reading Warrior, Auckland, 2020.

Robertson, John, *Australia at War 1939–1945*, William Heinemann, Melbourne, 1981.

Rosen, Sue, *Scorched Earth: Australia's Secret Plan for Total War Under Japanese Invasion in World War II*, Allen & Unwin, Sydney, 2017.

Soodalter, Ron, 'The Yank Coastwatcher who risked all in the Pacific', HistoryNet website, 15 December 2020, <www.historynet.com/the-yank-coastwatcher-not-in-colorado-anymore/>.

Stanley, Peter, *Invading Australia: Japan and the Battle for Australia, 1942*, Penguin, Melbourne, 2008.

Thompson Peter and Robert Macklin, *The Battle of Brisbane: Australians and the Yanks at War*, ABC Books, Sydney, 2000.

Veitch, Michael, *Australia's Secret Army: The Story of the Coastwatchers, the Unsung Heroes of Australia's Armed Forces during World War II*, Hachette, Sydney, 2022.

Wurth, Bob, *The Battle for Australia: A Nation and Its Leader Under Siege*, Pan Macmillan, Sydney, 2013.

ACKNOWLEDGMENTS

It all started with a look out my window. These days, Brisbane River's foreshore welcomes joggers, cyclists and strollers, and the river's peace is only occasionally broken by a CityCat ferry. But eighty years ago, Capricorn Wharf, in what is now the suburb of Teneriffe and was then New Farm, was a base for dozens of US submarines and some 800 American service personnel. Ships of the *Pensacola* convoy docked just a few hundred metres further downstream. Even today, Brisbane, like many other towns and cities around Australia, is full of reminders of those often dark days of the Second World War. We are surrounded by stories waiting to be told.

At the same time, Australia's world is changing again, perhaps coming full circle. All say we are underprepared; some say we have less than three years. While I hope they are wrong – on all accounts – our geography ever makes us vulnerable, and our values and way of life continue to put us at odds with autocratic powers seeking hegemony in the Asia-Pacific. We can't do anything about the former, and we definitely shouldn't change anything about the latter, but one thing we can control are our friendships and alliances.

This book was conceived during the delivery of another one, *Wizards of Oz: How Oliphant and Florey helped win the war and shape the modern world.* It was but the blink of an eye from first conversations with Elspeth Menzies, Executive Publisher at NewSouth Publishing, and formal proposal, to commencement of writing. It had to be, as with anniversaries looming time was of the essence. It is eighty years ago this August, 2023, that Lieutenant Reg Evans met Lieutenant Jack Kennedy on a beach on Gomu Island in Solomon Islands. And on a sad note, it is sixty years since President Kennedy's death in November 1963. Only Elspeth could have managed these two books in two years. My special thanks to you and your team.

My heartfelt gratitude to Arthur Chrenkoff for his vital assistance throughout this project. His friendship soothed the tough times, and his intellect drove the good times.

I first met Robin Prior playing cricket with ANU in the late 1980s. He was then the club's most formidable wicketkeeper/historian. Now as an eminent professor and authority on both world wars, he kindly agreed to read the manuscript. My sincere thanks to him for ensuring that even as conclusions are contestable the facts are not. Needless to say, all mistakes that remain are mine.

I am grateful to the last coast watcher, Jim Burrowes OAM, for recounting his wartime stories. Now 100, I could still hear the excitement in Jim's voice.

The John F Kennedy Presidential Library and Museum in Boston is the go-to place for the hungry researcher on all aspects of President Kennedy's life. Stacey Chandler and James B Hill filled my plate high, as is America's wont. Jennifer J Quan from the John F Kennedy Library Foundation helped when I most needed it. I am grateful they took time out to assist an Australian author.

The Australian War Memorial, even amid a major building program, warmly welcomes researchers. Thanks to the Director (and incidentally, a former high commissioner to Solomon Islands) Matt Anderson PSM and Robyn Van Dyk, Head of the AWM's Research Centre, for all their assistance and support.

The National Archives of Australia were a revelation. I could easily have spent weeks in its musty yet delightful embrace. Thanks to Gina Grey, Director of Reference and Description Services, Renee Shuttleworth and William Edwards.

All hail the National Library of Australia. Its Director-General, Dr Marie-Louise Ayres FAHA, staff, and Library Council are active and passionate custodians of this country's documentary heritage and formidable advocates of unlocking those treasures for a national – and, indeed, an international – audience. It remains an honour to Chair that magnificent council. Trove, the Library's unparalleled digital collection, was again indispensable. Special thanks to Kathryn Favelle, Director of Reader Services, and Damian Cole for their assistance in tracking down materials.

The State Library of Queensland is the Sunshine State's great research resource and refuge. The State Librarian, Vicki McDonald AM FALIA, and her enthusiastic team are an author's best friends. I cannot thank them enough.

My gratitude also goes to Professor John Scott, Alison Imber and all my colleagues at the School of Justice at the Queensland University of Technology for continuing to host me. I could not undertake this research without them.

Anna Kwai of the School of Pacific Studies at the Australian National University reminds us all that without the Solomon Islanders, Lieutenant Kennedy would never have been found, let alone rescued. The stories of the Islander coast watchers during the Second World War are only starting to be told thanks to her work and others like David Riley of Reading Warrior in Auckland.

Thanks as well to the former Australian Ambassador to the United States, the Hon. Arthur Sinodinos AO, for his kind assistance.

As always, Jack Fisher lightened the load while Brenden Kocsis sometimes had to carry it. And to my old friend Marcel Healey who kept the secret, while Ming and the beagles kept me laughing. As with *Wizards of Oz*, Tom and his crew at Sippy Tom brewed the coffee that made everything more bearable.

This book benefitted from the deft editorial hand of expert wordsmith Jocelyn Hungerford. At NewSouth Publishing, Paul O'Beirne, Rosina Dimarzo, and the design and marketing teams were as creative and resourceful as ever. Thank you for helping to bring the story of Reg Evans and Jack Kennedy to new generations of readers.

And finally thanks to family - David Mason, Judith de Boer and John Provan - for reminding me of my great-uncle, Lieutenant Frank Barrett DCM, a coast watcher with 'M' Special Unit. He was killed in action in New Britain on 24 October 1943 and is remembered on the roll of the fallen at the Coast Watchers Memorial Lighthouse at Madang in Papua New Guinea.

PICTURE CREDITS

INDEX